D0768545

FIFTY KEY THINKERS ON RELIGION

Fifty Key Thinkers on Religion is an accessible guide to the most important and widely studied theorists on religion of the last 300 years. Arranged chronologically, this book explores the lives, works and ideas of key writers across a truly interdisciplinary range, from sociologists to psychologists.

Thinkers covered include:

- Friedrich Nietzsche
- James Frazer
- Sigmund Freud
- Emile Durkheim
- Ludwig Wittgenstein
- Mary Douglas
- Talal Asad
- Søren Kierkegaard.

Providing an indispensable one-volume map of our understanding of religion in the West, this book is fully cross-referenced throughout and includes authoritative guides to important primary and secondary texts providing signposts for those who wish to explore further.

Gary E. Kessler is Professor Emeritus of Philosophy and Religious Studies at California State University, USA. An experienced teacher of introductory courses in both Philosophy and Religion, he is also the author of *Studying Religion: An Introduction Through Cases* (2005) and *Voices of Wisdom: A Multicultural Philosophy Reader* (2008).

ALSO AVAILABLE FROM ROUTLEDGE

Religion: The Basics
Malory Nye
978-0-415-44948-9

Religious Studies: The Key Concepts
Carl Olson
978-0-415-48722-1

The Bible: The Basics
John Barton
978-0-415-41136-3

Buddhism: The Basics
Cathy Cantwell
978-0-415-40880-6

Islam: The Basics (Second Edition)
Colin Turner
978-0-415-58492-0

FIFTY KEY THINKERS ON RELIGION

Gary E. Kessler

LONDON AND NEW YORK

First published 2012
by Routledge
2 Park Square, Milton Park, Abingdon, Oxon OX14 4RN

Simultaneously published in the USA and Canada
by Routledge
711 Third Avenue, New York, NY 10017

Routledge is an imprint of the Taylor & Francis Group, an informa business

© 2012 Gary E. Kessler

The right of Gary E. Kessler to be identified as author of this work has been asserted by him in accordance with sections 77 and 78 of the Copyright, Designs and Patents Act 1988.

All rights reserved. No part of this book may be reprinted or reproduced or utilised in any form or by any electronic, mechanical, or other means, now known or hereafter invented, including photocopying and recording, or in any information storage or retrieval system, without permission in writing from the publishers.

Trademark notice: Product or corporate names may be trademarks or registered trademarks, and are used only for identification and explanation without intent to infringe.

British Library Cataloguing in Publication Data
A catalogue record for this book is available from the British Library

Library of Congress Cataloging in Publication Data
Kessler, Gary E.
  Fifty key thinkers on religion / Gary Kessler.
    p. cm. – (Routledge key guides)
  Includes index.
  1. Religion – Philosophy – History. I. Title.
  BL51.K45 2012
  200.92'2 – dc22
            2011003625

ISBN: 978-0-415-49260-7 (hbk)
ISBN: 978-0-415-49261-4 (pbk)
ISBN: 978-0-203-80747-7 (ebk)

Typeset in Bembo
by Taylor & Francis Books

MIX
Paper from
responsible sources
FSC® C004839
www.fsc.org

Printed and bound in Great Britain by
TJ International Ltd, Padstow, Cornwall

CONTENTS

CHRONOLOGICAL LIST OF
CONTENTS

ALPHABETICAL LIST OF CONTENTS

PREFACE

The academic study of religion is an incredibly diverse and inter-disciplinary field. Humanists, social scientists, and natural scientists engage in the study of religion. Philosophers, historians, psychologists, sociologists, anthropologists, evolutionary biologists, to name only a few, have all made important contributions to our understanding of religion. In spite of differences in method and theory, they share the goal of describing and explaining religion in the same manner that they would describe any other human activity on which their particular discipline might focus. I have tried to keep this diversity in mind when selecting my list of key figures, but it has not been my main concern. My main concern has been to select thinkers whose ideas have been influential in their historical context for advancing our understanding of religion and its study.

Starting and stopping points are always to some extent arbitrary. I start with **David Hume** in the eighteenth century because his book, *The Natural History of Religion*, was influential in spreading the idea that religion is a natural, not a supernatural phenomenon. I end in the first decade of the twenty-first century with **Pascal Boyer** because the rise of the cognitive scientific study of religion has given a new direction to the field. I selected the scholars between **Hume** and **Boyer** because their ideas are key, both in the sense of importance and in the sense of unlocking doors to new avenues of research. These are scholars most frequently cited in beginning textbooks dealing with religion and are useful for students to know something about in courses on methods and theories. They also represent various research orientations ranging from humanistic to social scientific.

I have, in each case, focused on a few central ideas for which the scholar in question is best known. I have opened each selection with a quotation that catches the reader's interest and states a core argument or position. I have also indicated some general lines of criticism but, given the limited space available, I have mostly concentrated on what the thinker had to say that influenced subsequent developments in the field. A selected list of major works and suggestions for further reading points students to sources they may wish to pursue. I have placed in bold the names of other thinkers included in this volume in order to facilitate cross-referencing, as well as technical terms that appear in the glossary. I decided to arrange my list of key thinkers in chronological order so instructors and students have the option of following the developments in religious studies as they have unfolded primarily in the European and North American context.

There is no doubt that the boundaries of a book like this are fuzzy, and informed readers are bound to think of others who might be included. My list of key figures is only one of many possibilities. Unfortunately not every one of importance can be discussed in a small volume but I believe those I have included are representative of central trends in scholarship on religion in the modern period.

Religious studies is now going global and my focus on the European and North American developments may seem too Eurocentric. Even though boundaries had to be drawn someplace, the reader should be aware that the academic study of religion is becoming a truly global undertaking (see Alles 2008).

I owe a debt of gratitude to the editors and staff at Routledge who supported this project and helped to guide it to completion, especially David Avital, Katherine Ong, Amanda Lucas, Andy Humphries, Cathy Hurren and Rebecca Shillabeer. I am grateful to colleagues who offered valuable criticisms and suggestions. No doubt I should have heeded more of their sage advice.

Further reading

Alles, Gregory D., ed. (2008) *Religious Studies: A Global View*, London: Routlege. Multiple contributors provide useful information on the practice of religious studies ranging from Western Europe to Latin America.

Hinnells, John R., ed. (2005) *The Routledge Companion to the Study of Religion*, New York: Routlege. In Part I various experts discuss key approaches to the study of religion and in Part 2 key issues are explained. The introduction includes an essay by Hinnells on the value of studying religion and a useful essay by Eric Sharpe provides a historical perspective.

Jones, Lindsay, ed. (2005) *Encyclopedia of Religion*, 2e., 15 vols., Farmington, Hills, MI: Thomson Gale. This useful encyclopedia includes entries on significant thinkers in the field of religious studies and key concepts along with bibliographies.

Kessler, Gary E. (2008) *Studying Religion: An Introduction Through Cases*, 3e., Boston, MA: McGraw-Hill. An introductory text designed to help students learn to apply theories and analyze cases drawn from the world religions.

Kunin, Seth D., ed., with Jonathan Miles-Watson. (2006) *Theories of Religion: A Reader*, New Brunswick, NJ.: Rutgers University Press. Kunin has assembled selections from influential writings of scholars in the field of religious studies.

Olson, Carl. (2003) *Theory and Method in the Study of Religion: A Selection of Critical Readings*, Belmont, CA: Wadsworth. A collection of source material with useful introductions selected from the writings of important theorists.

——(2011) *Religious Studies: The Key Concepts*, London: Routlege. Olson provides an opening essay on approaches to the study of religion along with a discussion of the different ways religion is defined. The terms discussed range from afterlife to worship.

Pals, Daniel L. (2006) *Eight Theories of Religion*, 2e., New York: Oxford University Press. The author provides excellent in-depth essays on figures such as Freud, Marx, and Geertz.

Segal, Robert A., ed. (2009) *The Blackwell Companion to the Study of Religion*, Chichester: Wiley-Blackwell. Contributions by leading scholars dealing with approaches (Part 1) to the study of religion (e.g. anthropology, psychology) and discussions of various topics (Part 2) such as myth, fundamentalism, and secularization.

Sharpe, Eric J. (1986) *Comparative Religion: A History*, 2e., London: Duckworth. A classic survey of major thinkers and developments in the field of religious studies.

Smith, Jonathan Z., ed. (1995) *The HarperCollins Dictionary of Religion*, New York: HarperCollins and The American Academy of Religion. The dictionary provides basic information on the world's religions, religious figures, important concepts, and beliefs.

Stausberg, Michael, ed. (2009) *Contemporary Theories of Religion: A Critical Companion*, London: Routledge. A critical exposition of recent theories about religion including the findings of cognitive science.

FIFTY KEY THINKERS ON RELIGION

DAVID HUME (1711–76)

The wise man, therefore, proportions his belief to the evidence.

(Hume 1955: 118)

This statement occurs in Section X "Of Miracles" in David Hume's *An Inquiry Concerning Human Understanding* (1748). It succinctly expresses a philosophical principle that has spawned much debate in the philosophy of religion about the relationship between faith and reason. It also expresses Hume's general skepticism about any claims to knowledge not based on sensations. As an advocate of **empiricism**, Hume regarded sensation as the primary source of whatever ideas we might enlist in forming and justifying beliefs. He combined skepticism about claims based entirely on human reason (**rationalism**), be they philosophical or religious, with an uncompromising empiricism that limits knowledge claims to what our senses tell us.

David Hume was born in Edinburgh, Scotland and grew up at the family estate, Ninewells. His father died when he was two and his mother raised and educated him until he entered the University of Edinburgh at the age of eleven (he was, as his mother remarked, very "acute") with the intention of preparing for a career in law. However, his interest in the law waned and he turned his attention to the study of history and philosophy. He never succeeded in gaining an academic appointment because of his skepticism in religious matters but he did become, after some initial disappointments, a celebrated writer, earning fame as both a philosopher and a historian. His six-volume *History of England* (1754–62) became the standard work for many years.

Hume, by all accounts a respected and even-tempered man, found religious beliefs not only intellectually restrictive but also lacking any convincing proof. Many theologians and philosophers of his day viewed Christianity as a reasonable and rational religion whose truth could be established by two basic arguments: the argument from miracles and prophecy and the argument from design. Hume included a discussion of both in two sections of *An Inquiry Concerning Human Understanding*.

He began his discussion of miracles and prophecy by establishing the principle that experience will be his guide in reasoning about these matters. Although he recognized that experience is not free of error, those who are wise will carefully weigh the evidence experience affords and proportion their beliefs accordingly, from the least certain to those with the highest degree of probability.

The argument from miracle and prophecy relies on the testimony of others and the degree of certainty we give to such testimony depends, Hume argued, on how closely what is reported coincides with our usual expectations. Reports of the deaths of others do not surprise us because human death is part of our common and ordinary experience of life. Reports that someone died and then came back to life do surprise us, indeed amaze us, because they do not agree with our usual experiences. If we mean by "a miracle" a violation of the laws of nature brought about by God or some other invisible agent, then just "as a firm and unalterable experience has established these laws, the proof against a miracle, from the very nature of the fact, is as entire as any argument from experience can possibly be imagined" (Hume 1955: 122). In other words, there must be a "uniform experience against every miraculous act, otherwise the event would not merit that appellation. And as a uniform experience amounts to a proof, there is here a direct and full *proof*, from the nature of the fact, against the existence of any miracle" (Hume 1955: 122–23).

It should be noted that Hume did not deny the possibility of miracles and if there is very strong testimony concerning highly unusual events that might count as miracles, it is reasonable to investigate. However, the investigation of alleged miracles is very difficult because there may well be natural causes of such events that cannot now be proved or, perhaps, even clearly imagined. Our knowledge of the natural world is, at any given time, always limited. A proof that some event is actually a miracle would require a complete knowledge of all possible causes of such an event so that every natural explanation could be eliminated. It is extremely unlikely we shall ever fully possess such knowledge and hence ever possess a clear proof that a violation of nature's laws has actually occurred. It would be best, Hume concluded, not to base an entire "system of religion" on testimony of alleged miracles and prophecy. If one does, it is better to openly acknowledge that this is a matter of faith, not of reason.

Hume understood that many religious believers would be quite content with this conclusion because they sincerely think that religious belief is a matter of faith. However, we must not forget that if, as Hume claimed, wise men proportion their beliefs to the evidence, then the appeal to faith leads to a rational dead end. The idea that there are good reasons based on experience that support religious belief would have to be abandoned along with the claim that religion can be rationally justified.

Hume titled Section XI of the *Inquiry* "Of a Providence and a Future State." Hume did not directly discuss the topics of the title, but indirectly criticized them by an examination of the argument from design on which these beliefs are based. He disguised his own views by writing this section as a report of a conversation with an **Epicurean** friend who "loves skeptical paradoxes."

The "friend" states that the central argument for the existence of God can be found in the very order of the universe. The beauty, order, and arrangement we observe in nature leads our minds quite naturally to a consideration of the cause of such effects, a cause that can be nothing less than an intelligent designer. Hume's skeptical friend notes that this type of argument proceeds by inferring a cause from effects. There are two important, logical consequences. The first is the requirement that we cannot ascribe to the cause anything more than the effects will allow because our only knowledge of that cause is based on the observation of the effects, namely, the order we find in nature. The second is that the inference "upward" from effect to cause does not allow us to infer "downward" from the cause to new effects. This downward inference is illogical because we know nothing of the cause (the alleged designer of the order we observe in nature) than what the effects tell us.

Order, of course, is not the same as design. There can be many causes for the order we experience. And we should not ignore the fact that the world exhibits disorder as well as order. However, even if the inference that the cause of the order is an intelligent designer is correct, we cannot reasonably infer all the sorts of things Christians wish to say about such intelligence. How could we claim that the designer is wise, or providential, or justly distributes future rewards and punishments? Indeed, such a designer, if there is one, may not be benevolent at all given the amount of evil, disorder, and suffering we see about us.

In *The Natural History of Religion* (1757) Hume turned his attention to the question of how religion began and developed. His answer focused on human nature. Early peoples, Hume argued, found nature fearsome. In an attempt to control nature, its elements (wind, water, fire, and so on) were personified as invisible powers then offered gifts through sacrifice and worship in the hope that they would be benevolent. Religion originated, if Hume is correct, not in divine revelations but in the human emotions of fear and adulation.

Hume chose to have his most concentrated and developed critique of theism published after his death even though he wrote it in the 1750s. It is titled *Dialogues Concerning Natural Religion* (1778) and "records" a discussion among three protagonists: Cleanthes, who offers a rational defense of Christianity, Demea, a Christian who argues that faith, not reason, is the only legitimate basis for religion, and Philo, a skeptic.

Cleanthes begins the discussion by setting forth a version of the design argument. According to Cleanthes, the argument centers on an analogy. The world or universe is like a finely tuned machine. We know that human intelligence is required to create machines. It follows that the hypothesis that the world is caused by a divine intelligence is a reasonable one because only a divine being would have the abilities to produce a universe.

Philo responds by developing several lines of criticism. For example, Philo argues that the analogy between the universe and a machine is a very weak and misleading analogy because other things, such as biological generation, can cause the order we experience. Maybe the universe is more like a plant that grows than a machine that is made. He also points out that arguments based on experience require observation of a constant conjunction of associated events before we can conclude that one event caused another. However, we have only experienced one universe and have no independent experience of the invisible agent who presumably caused it.

In Parts X and XI, Philo turns his attention to the **moral attributes** of God, such as his goodness and mercy, mounting what many consider to be his strongest objection. He paints a dark picture of the world and society in which we actually live, describing its evils, chaos, and untold suffering. Philo then points out that given our experience, one might just as well infer that the alleged intelligence that created this universe is evil, or defective, or greatly limited.

The final section of the *Dialogues* has surprised many readers. In it Philo appears to do an "about face" and concedes that it is obvious that some intelligence is behind the world and his main point is simply that the analogy used by the theists is weak. He then espouses a **fideist** position, stating that faith not reason is the foundation of religion. Exactly what this means for discovering Hume's own views is a matter that interpreters of Hume have been arguing about ever since.

Hume's arguments have been debated and supported or rejected by scores of philosophers. His definition of miracles has been attacked as inadequate, his concept of experience as too limited, and his criticisms of the design argument have been met either by reformulations of the argument (reformulations that are still going on today) or counter claims that seek to undermine his criticisms. Whatever we make of his arguments, Hume transformed the study of religion in ways that make its contemporary study possible. His views are still carefully discussed in courses on the philosophy of religion, and his writings widely anthologized. His location of the origin of religion in human nature and his emphasis on its evolution significantly shaped subsequent developments in the history of religion.

See also: **Boyer, Feuerbach, Kant, Schleiermacher, Wittgenstein**

Major works

(1874–75) *The Philosophical Works of David Hume*, ed. T. H. Green and T. H. Grose, 4 volumes, London: Longman, Green.

(1935) *Dialogues Concerning Natural Religion*, ed. Norman Kemp Smith, Oxford: Oxford University Press.

(1955) *An Enquiry Concerning Human Understanding*, ed. Charles W. Hendel, New York: The Liberal Arts Press.

(1967) *The Natural History of Religion*, ed. H. E. Root, Stanford, CA: Stanford University Press.

Further reading

O'Connor, D. (2001) *Routledge Philosophical Guidebook to Hume on Religion*, London: Routledge.

Passmore, John. (1952) *Hume's Intentions*, Cambridge: Cambridge University Press.

Smith, Norman Kemp. (1941) *The Philosophy of David Hume*, London: Macmillan.

Tweyman, Stanley. (1995) *David Hume: Critical Assessments*, 6 vols., London: Routledge.

http://www.utm.edu/research/iep/h/humereli.htm.

IMMANUEL KANT (1724–1804)

> I have found it necessary to deny knowledge, in order to make room for faith.
>
> (Kant 1929: 29)

With these enigmatic words, the German philosopher Immanuel Kant signaled that his philosophy, which was highly critical of conventional religion, was significant for discerning the relationship between knowledge and faith. To understand what he meant is to discover both how revolutionary Kant's thinking was and to see how critical analysis of religious ideas can illuminate why faith is so vitally important to many different religions.

Kant was born in Königsberg in East Prussia into a Protestant home deeply influenced by the Pietist movement that stressed the devotion of the heart in contrast to ritual observances and doctrinal purity. He obtained a masters degree from the University of Königsberg in 1755 and spent his entire professional career there teaching and writing.

Many regard Kant as the greatest philosopher of the **Enlightenment**, the thinker who not only celebrated the power of reason by endorsing the call to "think for yourself" but also showed that reason had its limits. **Hume**, Kant said, woke him from his "dogmatic slumber" by showing how the rationalists' claim to *a priori* knowledge of the way things really were apart from sensations could not withstand critical examination. Knowledge is, as empiricists like **Hume** claimed, derived from sensations (*a posteriori*). However, it did not follow, Kant argued, that the rationalists were entirely wrong. There was an essential role for reason in the production of knowledge.

We derive the objects of knowledge from the appearance of things to our senses, as **Hume** had said, but such data make no sense unless they are formed and shaped by human reason. The mind is not merely a passive receiver of sensations, but an active power organizing and categorizing what the senses reveal. Reason supplies the "glasses" through which we see the sensate or **phenomenal** world. For Kant, the thing-in-itself (*Ding an sich*), or the **noumenal** as Kant called it, is something we can never know by our senses but to understand what our senses tell us reason must posit its existence.

It takes only a moment's reflection to see that any claims to know things beyond our senses, such as God, the immortality of the soul, and human free will are bound to fail. Should we then discard such notions as unreasonable? Kant argued that while we could not have *knowledge* of such things, nevertheless, it was reasonable to posit their existence.

If we look closely at the traditional arguments for the existence of God, of which rationalists are so fond, we can see that all of them fail to provide the knowledge they claim. The design argument, already shredded by **Hume**, fails to tell us much if anything about a God who is religiously meaningful. From the fact that some intelligent designer might have caused all this we cannot conclude that such a designer is good, merciful, cares about us, or about what we do. Would such a God be worthy of worship?

In addition to the design argument, many rationalists were fond of the ontological argument, which claimed that the very existence of God follows logically from the definition of God as the greatest possible being of which humans can think. But existence is not a predicate or attribute such that by knowing the definition of something we can deduce its existence. I might define God as the greatest possible for thought but that definition still does not tell me if there is such a being as proponents of the ontological argument claimed. To know the definition of, let us say, a tree is not the same as knowing whether there are any.

Cosmological arguments that move from the existence of the world to the existence of God as its first cause improperly apply the concept of cause. Causation applies to the **phenomenal** world and we simply cannot know whether it also applies to the **noumenal** or supersensory world. If the traditional arguments for God's existence fail, is there any reason at all to believe that God might exist? Kant answers that there is. The foundation of religion is not to be sought in speculative reason or in sense experience but in morality.

All humans, Kant argued, recognize, however dimly, that they have an obligation to do their moral duty, whatever that may be. Careful philosophical analysis shows that rational laws or "maxims" govern morality; chief among them is the categorical imperative. This imperative or command is categorical, not instrumental. It does not tell us to do what is expedient but what is morally necessary. It can be formulated in various ways but one way is to think of it is as the imperative always to treat people as ends and never as means. Another way is to view it as the command to act in such a way that the rule or maxim supporting the act can be generalized as a universal requirement. If you think it is right to lie, then universalize that maxim so everyone is obligated to lie. If you do, you will immediately see why telling the truth is a moral duty.

Morality is a matter of what Kant called "practical reason." There are three major postulates of practical reason, which make it possible for humans to live the good life, a life in which virtue and happiness coincide. These postulates affirm the existence of God, freedom, and immortality.

It makes moral sense to postulate the existence of a God who makes possible the conjunction of virtue and happiness. If that postulate were not reasonable, then there is no hope that striving to do what is morally right will ever lead to a happy life. Why is that the case? It is the case because it is obvious that in this life bad things can happen to good people and good things can happen to bad people. Life cannot be happy unless this sort of injustice is somehow overcome. So immortality as well as God's existence makes sense because if there is no justice in this life, there can be justice in the next.

And freedom makes sense too. If we were not free to do good the whole of morality, and with it society, collapses because it would be pointless to ask people to be moral or pass laws that require it. Granted that in the **phenomenal** world the law of causality dominates. If it did not, our experiences would make no sense because we could never discover the causes of things and events would just appear out of nowhere without any antecedent causes. Events are determined by their causes and if human actions are events, they too are determined by their causes. There seems no room for freedom. Yet it is reasonable to postulate the existence of freedom, if not in the **phenomenal** realm then in the **noumenal**, in order to make sense of morality.

It is important to realize that Kant did not believe that he had proved that God, freedom, and immortality were objects of knowledge. Only appearances can be objects of knowledge. However, God, freedom, and immortality can be reasonable postulates that make it possible for humans to live a meaningful and virtuous life. The denial that knowledge of such things is possible is not irreligious or immoral, it is necessary in order to "make room for faith."

When we read Kant's *Religion within the Limits of Reason Alone* (1793), we can clearly see the influence of his pietistic background. He distinguishes between inner religion or faith and outer religion (rituals, dogmas, institutions). External religion centers on an anthropomorphic concept of the divine as a very powerful human-like being who demands under threat of eternal punishment our service, prayers, and praises much like some despotic king. In contrast there is a "natural religion" that the natural power of the human mind can comprehend without the aid of any alleged supernatural revelations that priests control and interpret.

What are we to make of the classic Christian doctrines like original sin, incarnation, and the kingdom of God? All of them can be reinterpreted to bring out their moral meaning. The myth of the Fall from goodness into sin is just that, a myth. The story about humans being created good and then sinning means that humans have the freedom and capacity to follow the moral law as well as the freedom to fail morally. The story of the incarnation of God in Jesus means that Jesus is an example of what we all should strive for, namely moral perfection. And the kingdom of God is a way of talking about an ideal ethical community that treats each of its members as ends-in-themselves rather than as means to satisfying their own selfish desires.

Kant asserted the unity of all religions because natural religion belongs to all people by virtue of practical reason. Particular religions show differences because of social and historical contingencies and because they have come to emphasize the externals of religion. Even so, they can still, however dimly, display the natural inner religion of faith and morality.

Kant's ideas were the objects of both criticism and adoption right from the start. Theologians objected that he had failed to take into account the need for grace and had reduced religion to little more than morality. Philosophers claimed he had bifurcated reality into two irreconcilable realms. The distinction between the **phenomenal** and **noumenal**, while helpful in some ways, now made it even more difficult to understand the world. Yet Kant's ideas played a key role in the reduction of the supernatural to the natural that gave rise to the modern world. The **transcendence** of the supernatural became for Kant functionally **immanent** in the natural world of morality. Subsequent philosophers, such as **Hegel**, furthered this process by making the supernatural God an **immanent** force in history, culture, and the development of human self-consciousness. The modern secular world would simply not have been possible without Kant and the echoes of his ideas are still found in those who distinguish the spiritual from institutional religion and elevate the former to a position of greater value than the latter.

See also: **Asad, Buber, Derrida, Feuerbach, Foucault, Hick, Kierkegaard, Otto, Schleiermacher, J. Z. Smith**

Major works

(1929) *Critique of Pure Reason*, trans. N. Kemp Smith, London: Macmillan.
(1949) *Critique of Practical Reason*, trans. L. Beck, Chicago, IL: University of Chicago Press.
(1950) *Prolegomena to Any Future Metaphysics*, trans. L. W. Beck, New York: Bobbs-Merrill.
(1952) *Critique of Judgement*, trans. J. C. Meredith, Oxford: Clarendon Press.
(1960) *Religion Within the Limits of Reason Alone*, trans. T. M. Greene and Hoyt H. Hudson, New York: Harper and Brothers.
(1964) *Groundwork of the Metaphysics of Morals*, trans. H. J. Paton, New York: Harper and Row.

Further reading

Beck, Lewis White. (1960) *A Commentary on Kant's Critique of Practical Reason*, Chicago, IL: University of Chicago Press.

Cassirer, Ernst. (1981) *Kant's Life and Thought*, trans. James Haden, New Haven, CT: Yale University Press.
Wood, Allen W. (1970) *Kant's Moral Religion*, Ithaca, NY: Cornell University Press.
http://plato.stanford.edu/entries/kant-religion.

FRIEDRICH SCHLEIERMACHER (1768–1834)

> Why do you not regard the religious life itself, [which is] the first of those pious exaltations of the mind in which all other known activities are set aside or almost suppressed and the whole soul is dissolved in the immediate feeling of the Infinite and Eternal?
>
> (Schleiermacher 1958: 15–16)

With these words the Protestant theologian Friedrich Schleiermacher challenged those he characterized as "cultured despisers" of religion who had found little useful in the traditional Christianity of their day. He also inaugurated a new era in both Christian theological thinking and reflection on the nature of religion. Religion was not, as **Hume** suggested, a matter of the intellect going astray, nor was it primarily a matter of morality as **Kant** argued. In keeping with the **Romantic** age in which he lived, Schleiermacher elevated feeling to center stage as an important category for understanding religion. Exactly what this "immediate feeling" was, Schleiermacher later specified as a feeling of absolute dependence.

> The common element in all howsoever diverse expressions of piety, by which these are conjointly distinguished from all other feelings, or, in other words, the self-identical essence of piety, is this: the consciousness of being absolutely dependent, or, which is the same thing, of being in relation with God.
>
> (Schleiermacher 1963: Vol. I, 12)

This emphasis on feeling is not too surprising given the fact that Schleiermacher's father was a Prussian army chaplain who sent his son to Moravian schools. There he encountered the teachings of German Pietism, which stressed the inner life of faith and the importance of personal spiritual conviction. In 1787 he entered the University of Halle, where the Pietist heritage ran deep. He went to Berlin in 1796 and came into contact with artists and intellectuals who were prime movers in the German **Romantic** Movement. In 1799 his *On Religion* appeared and became an immediate hit. In 1811 he accepted the chair of theology at the new University of Berlin and in 1821 and 1822 he published his theological masterpiece, *The Christian Faith*, which was to transform modern Protestant theology.

The cultured had come to see religion as irrelevant to their lives and had done so, Schleiermacher asserted, because they misunderstood what religion is. They had confused it with metaphysical arguments for the existence of God or with lists of moral dos and don'ts. They had, to use Schleiermacher's metaphor, confused the "husk with the kernel." What he wanted to do was to reveal the inner core of all genuine religions, the essence hidden from view by layers of dogma, rituals, rational arguments, and cultic practices. Religion, true religion, had nothing to do with all these outward trappings. If it did, then the more one knew about dogmas, or the better one was at theological argument, the more religious one would be. But this is manifestly not the case.

Psychology tells us that there are three fundamental elements of life: perception, feelings, and activity. Perception provides knowledge, and activity is essential to the conduct of the moral life, but if the essence of religion is not to be found in either of these two, it can only be found in the third element of life, feeling. One can never understand religion without also understanding the unique feeling on which it is based. This feeling, however, is not simply emotion, or subjective imagination, rather it is the result of the impact of something greater on our self-consciousness. This impact results in the sense that we are creatures who are finite and limited and that our lives are dependent on something unlimited. Not all feelings are religious, but only this unique feeling of *absolute* dependence. "The sum total of religion is to feel that, in its highest unity, all that moves us in feeling is one ... to feel, that is to say, that our being and living is a being and living in and through God" (Schleiermacher 1958: 49–50).

How can such a feeling be cultivated? Not by study or teachings. Piety cannot be taught because teachings speak only to the mind not the heart. Rather it must be discovered in personal, individual experience. This is not to deny that there is a social or communal element to religion. The deeper we penetrate into our personal life, Schleiermacher claimed, the clearer our connections to the common nature of all humanity appear. Personal religion must be cultivated in calm meditation, apart from the distractions of the world, but it need not cut us off from human relationships. Indeed intimate and close association with others who are also seeking to cultivate the religious feeling can be quite helpful.

If the heart of religion is to be found in feeling, why have religions developed creeds, dogmas, and doctrines? These are not the essence of religion but they are the natural products of thinking about what our feeling of absolute dependence might imply. These reflections naturally issue in different ideas. Some people develop anthropomorphic conceptions of God, as if he is a great big human being, while others develop more abstract **pantheistic** ideas. Different sacred writings appear with different stories. But these differences in ideas and literary products are not the kernel but the husk. What counts is the way in which we cultivate this profound feeling, not the imperfect way this feeling may be conveyed in ideas, like "God", or the "Absolute."

Schleiermacher, unlike others of his day, celebrated the plurality of religions. Religion always finds expression in some definite form. There is, he asserted, no such thing as "religion in general." We should beware of abstract and unhistorical concepts of religion, such as "the natural religion of mankind" celebrated by the **Deists**. This exists only in the human mind. In reality there are specific religions with different ideas, different scriptures, different practices, and institutions. The important thing is to develop the religious feeling at the heart of religion as best one can through whatever religion one belongs to or, if one does not belong, in one's own personal way apart from any affiliation.

Schleiermacher himself considered Christianity more spiritually sublime than the other religions. However, he did not see any reason why he should try to convert others to his faith, or to insist that Christianity was the only true religion while the others were false.

While Schleiermacher's *On Religion* had its greatest impact on the development of the academic study of religion, *The Christian Faith* deeply influenced and transformed Protestant theology, earning him the title of "the father of modern theology." In that work he sets forth his reinterpretations of the main dogmas of Christianity based on the idea that dogmatics is primarily the linguistic expression of prior Christian feelings that have developed in the Christian community of faith. Hence theology is both confessional and an exercise in communal self-analysis. Its task is not to defend the faith and convince others of its truth. Its task is to understand and bear witness to a faith shared by a specific religious community, the Christian church. This means that con-sciousness of the redemption that Jesus the Christ has accomplished must inform all theological teaching. Christian theology must be, he contended, Christocentric.

God as he is in himself cannot be known by the finite human mind. However, God can be known in relation to us. So all the tra-ditional attributes of God must be rethought in ways that articulate how they relate to human experience. Christians must also reinterpret the key stories of the faith in this way. For example, the story of the Fall into sin of the first Adam needs to be seen as a symbolic way of talking about the propensity to sin found in all humans. And the original goodness of humanity needs to be understood as the capacity all humans have to develop God-consciousness. Jesus, the second Adam, enters the story as someone who perfectly realized in this historical reality full and perfect God-consciousness. As such he is the exemplar of what is possible for humans. Schleiermacher does not mean by this what **Kant** meant when he called Jesus a moral example. Jesus is not merely a moral example (although he is that), but is much more. The Christ is the medium for the communication to humans of God's redemptive power. He is the way God has opened for humans to develop their latent God-consciousness.

Schleiermacher's influence extended beyond religious studies and Christian theology into philosophy and the social sciences through his work in **hermeneutics**, the art of interpretation. How do we know what a text means? Where is the meaning of a text to be found? Is it in the intentions of the author or in the reading of the many audiences? Schleiermacher thought that to understand human expression as a bearer of meaning one needed to focus on both the general cultural and historical context and the unique intention of any given author. The hermeneutical goal is to understand an author better than he or she understands himself or herself. This requires not only careful textual, philological, comparative, and historical research but a kind of intuitive leap into the mind of the author based on linguistic and other evidence.

Wilhelm Dilthey (1833–1911) was to develop these ideas into a contrast between *Verstehen* (understanding), which is the distinctive method and goal of the cultural sciences, and *Erklärung* (explanation), which is distinctive of the physical sciences. Schleiermacher's views helped spur biblical criticism to take the historical context of the Bible seriously. His arguments for a unique religious intuition influenced the development of **nonreductionistic** approaches to the study of religion.

Though others in religious studies, theology, philosophy, and the social sciences have used and developed Schleiermacher's ideas, he has not been without his critics. **Rudolph Otto** developed Schleiermacher's claims into the idea that at the heart of all religion is an experience of the Holy as a "wholly other" that can never be fully comprehended by human thought and at the same time echoed a widespread criticism that Schleiermacher's understanding of religion was far too subjective.

Whatever one may think of Schleiermacher's ideas, he, along with other **Romantics**, found a way of understanding the idea of divine **immanence** that rendered the **Deistic** emphasis on the radical **transcendence** of God increasingly irrelevant. **Hegel**, although critical of Schleiermacher, systematically developed a critical philosophy of history and human consciousness that once again placed the divine within a dynamic universe.

See also: **Burkert, Buber, Eliade, Hick, Jung, Kierkegaard, Lévi-Strauss, Radcliffe-Brown, Suzuki, J. Z. Smith, Tillich, Weber**

Major writings

(1958) *On Religion: Speeches to its Cultural Despisers*, trans. J. Oman, New York: Harper and Row.

(1963) *The Christian Faith*, ed. H.R. Mackintosh and J. S. Stewart, 2 vols., New York: Harper and Row.

(1998) *Lectures on Hermeneutics, Criticism and Other Writings*, trans. Andrew Bowie, Cambridge: Cambridge University Press.

Further reading

Gerrish, B. A. (1984) *A Prince of the Church: Schleiermacher and the Beginnings of Modern Theology*, London: SCM.

Niebuhr, Richard R. (1964) *Schleiermacher on Christ and Religion: A New Introduction*, New York: Charles Scribner's Sons.

Redeker, M. (1973) *Friedrich Schleiermacher*, Philadelphia, PA: Fortress Press.

http://plato.stanford.edu/entries/schleiermacher.

GEORG HEGEL (1770–1831)

> What is rational is actual and what is actual is rational.
>
> (Hegel 1942: 13)

This claim, from the Preface to Hegel's *Philosophy of Right* (1821) contains, commentators say, the key to the great German philosopher's thought. But what does it mean? Does it mean, as many have claimed, that Hegel is an Absolute Idealist in the sense that the whole of reality is mind? And if the rational is the real (actual) and the real is the rational what does this imply about religion? If religion is real, then it must be a rational practice for humans. Does that imply that all religions are true?

Georg Wilhelm Friedrich Hegel was born August 27, 1770. He decided on a clerical career and began theological studies at Tübingen University after graduating from the Gymnasium in 1788. He shared rooms with Friedrich Shelling (1775–1854) who became an influential idealist philosopher. Hegel became dissatisfied with theology and moved on to the study of philosophy. He became a lecturer at the University of Jena and eventually established a teaching career at the University of Berlin, having been offered the chair of philosophy in 1818.

The goal of philosophy, according to Hegel, is to think the whole of reality as a rational totality by thinking mind and world together. In short, it is to think the Absolute. Schelling had introduced the term the Absolute in order to designate the unconditional foundation of subject (mind) and object (world). This implied that subject and object were identical. But how could they be? Hegel thought that Schelling had failed to think deeply enough about how subject and object were related. He missed the fact that their relationship had to be dynamic in order to account for the obvious development that characterizes history, the world, human consciousness, and such human practices as religion.

If we are to understand how things develop we need to grasp how opposites are related. In philosophy, theology, and other disciplines, divisions abound. **Kant** had famously divided **phenomena** from **noumena**, and other philosophers had distinguished **empiricism** from **rationalism**, fact from value, science from religion, and mind from matter. Theologians had distinguished a **transcendent** God from sinful humans, good from evil, revealed religion from natural religion, and faith from knowledge. But if there is an Absolute truth that encompasses everything, if the rational is the real and the real is the rational, then these divisions must be capable of being overcome.

The goal of dialogue, of discussing the pros and cons of some issue, is to arrive at agreement. Perhaps the clue to how opposites are related is to be found in the deep logic of dialogue. That logic Hegel described by the word dialectic. He conceived of it as a critical examination of some idea, let us say being, until the inner contradiction of that idea was revealed. Being is indeterminate. It is an abstraction from all existing things. It is, in short, nothing in particular. But nothing is the opposite of being. How could critically examining the idea of being lead to thinking its opposite? The answer is to be found in the nature of thought itself. To think something is to think what it is and what it is not. For example, to think that something is round is also to imply that it is not square.

So thought about being has led us to think its opposite, nothing. How can being and nothing be connected? They are connected in the idea of becoming. Becoming encompasses both being and nothing because something cannot become unless it becomes something it was not. Hegel called this reconciliation of an idea and its opposite into a more encompassing idea *aufgehoben*. This German word names a complex concept involving the notions of movement to a higher, more encompassing, level of thought while preserving the opposing concepts.

If rationality is dialectical and if the rational and the real are one, then dialectic must also describe the structure of reality itself. Reality is constantly changing but that change has a structure. That structure, Hegel argued, is dialectical. Philosophic reason has shown us not only a way of thinking, but also the way of history, of religion, of politics, of art, of science, and of truth itself. What remains is to show in concrete detail the dialectical pattern in all aspects of reality.

We cannot here describe in detail Hegel's metaphysics (theory of reality), epistemology (theory of knowledge), and axiology (theory of value) but we can say something about his dialectical analysis of religion. Religion was a central concern of Hegel from the very beginning of his career, and there is evidence to indicate that it was his thinking about Christianity, in particular, that led him to understand the importance of dialectical thought. He rejected both **Kant**'s reduction of religion to morality and **Schleiermacher**'s reduction of religion to feeling. He was also critical of traditional Christian theology with its emphasis on correct dogma and claims to know the will of a **transcendent** God. But he thought he saw something in the history of religion that revealed—albeit dimly and in poetic "images and representations"—an important insight into human consciousness.

Hegel claimed that all history, including the history of religion, developed in stages. With respect to religion, the first stage was nature religion. The forces of nature—wind and storm, sun and moon—were projected as conscious and therefore treated in cultic practices as if they were persons (see **Boyer**). If, in the first stage of religion, nature were deified, what would constitute the second stage? The monotheistic religions of Judaism, Christianity, and Islam developed in the subsequent stages and what they all have in common is an emphasis on a deity that transcends nature. Nature is not divine but a **transcendent** creator of nature is divine. How might the opposition between nature religion and monotheism be overcome in a way that preserves the truth of each, yet advances to a higher level of reconciliation?

The story of the Garden of Eden tells us about what Hegel called a "dreaming innocence." It describes a situation of unreflective awareness and hence a time before any consciousness of good and evil. It is a state akin to that of other animals because it is a state in which humans are not yet self-conscious. The importance of Judaism as a "world historical religion" is its poetic rendering of the movement from the unreflective innocence of the human race to self-consciousness. This is described in the story of the Fall. The Fall marks the arrival of "unhappy consciousness." It is unhappy because with the arrival of self-consciousness comes self-alienation. The monotheistic religions describe the "fall" into self-consciousness as sin and evil. But it is a "necessary evil" because the self-estrangement it brings about is the necessary prelude to a higher good.

How can the opposition between a paradise of dreaming innocence and the sinful world of estranged consciousness be reconciled? We cannot go home again without giving up something necessary and precious, awareness of self. If we can't go back, then our only hope is to go forward and move to a "higher" level. Here Christianity, which Hegel describes as the "consummate religion," enters the story. The poetic story of the incarnation, resurrection, and ascension of the Christ points the way. The uniqueness of Christ does not consist in his moral teachings but in his person. The claim that in Christ the **transcendent** God became human, that is became **immanent** in the world, is a vital step on the road to reconciliation of the opposites of God and humanity.

If God is infinite, then the story of the incarnation signals that the infinite has become its opposite, the finite. This logically implies (necessitates, in Hegel's language) the death of Christ because death is the final manifestation of finitude. However, if the story stopped there, it would stop in the negativity of death. If we follow the dialectic, then the negation that is death must itself be negated. If the infinite is negated by the finite, then the finite itself must be negated and the poetic account of this is found in the stories of the resurrection and ascension of Christ. The death of God turns out to be, following the dialectical structure of reality, a transitional phase leading to the arrival of the spiritual community for which humans hope. This is the restoration of paradise at a higher level, a level at which a human community of love and peace overcomes self-alienation without sacrificing self-consciousness.

However, the consummate religion is not the last word because it is poetic and not conceptual. Its philosophic import must be made clear. We have seen above how Hegel reinterpreted the stories of the

Fall, incarnation, and resurrection in order to bring out their philosophic content. It remains to show how this dialectic is the dialectic of the Absolute itself. In order to be the totality of all reality the Absolute must realize itself as Absolute. It too must become self-conscious by objectifying itself in its opposite and then moving to a higher level that preserves yet overcomes the oppositions of subject and object in *Geist* (spirit or mind). In order for the Absolute to be more than a conceptual abstraction it must become actualized in a community of finite minds. In theological language we might say that God and the world require one another. God may be **transcendent** of the world but if consciousness is to evolve in the world, then God must also be **immanent** in it. The history of the world and all it contains (art, religion, politics, science, philosophy) is the self-manifestation of the Absolute dialectically becoming the Absolute, that is, completing itself.

Hegel's philosophy became immensely influential at the same time as it became immensely controversial. Most of his critics focused on what they saw as the inadequacies of his idea of the dialectic, claiming his philosophy was built on contradictions. Yet others found in his notion of dialectic a method for understanding everything from religion and economics to history and nature. His followers split into right-wing Hegelians that identified the Absolute with God and left-wing Hegelians like **Marx** and **Feuerbach** who turned Hegel's dialectical idealism into a dialectical materialism. To them humans were not the projection of a divine mind, as the right wing claimed, but a divine mind was a projection of humans. The ambiguities of Hegel's language almost insured that his followers and his critics would explain his philosophy in different ways – **pantheistic**, theistic, and even atheistic. Nevertheless, his conception of reality as an interdependent process and his historical orientation constitutes a lasting legacy. Henceforth the study of religion would have to take the comparative study of its history seriously.

See also: **Berger, Foucault, Kierkegaard, Lévi-Strauss, Müller, Radhakrishnan, Scholem, Tillich, Troeltsch**

Major works

(1942) *Philosophy of Right*, trans. T. M. Knox, London: Oxford University Press.

(1948) *Early Theological Writings*, trans. T. M. Knox, Chicago, IL: University of Chicago Press.

(1967) *Phenomenology of Spirit*, trans. A. V. Miller, New York: Harper and Row.

(1984–85) *Lectures on the Philosophy of Religion*, ed. P. C. Hodgson, Berkeley, CA: University of California Press.

(1993) *The Science of Logic*, trans. A. V. Miller, 3 vols., Atlantic Highlands, NJ: Humanities Press.

Further reading

Jaeschke, Walter (1990) *Reason in Religion: The Foundations of Hegel's Philosophy of Religion*, trans. J. Michael Stewart and Peter C. Hodgson, Berkeley, CA: University of California Press.

Singer, Peter (2001) *Hegel: A Very Short Introduction*, Oxford: Oxford University Press.

Taylor, Charles (1975) *Hegel*, Cambridge: Cambridge University Press.

http://plato.stanford.edu/entries/hegel.

LUDWIG FEUERBACH (1804–72)

> Religion is the dream of the human mind. But even in dreams we do not find ourselves in emptiness or in heaven, but on earth, in the realm of reality, we only see real things in the entrancing splendour of imagination and caprice, instead of in the simple daylight of reality and necessity. Hence I do nothing more to religion ... than open its eyes, or rather to turn its gaze from the internal towards the external, i.e., I change the object as it is in the imagination into the object as it is in reality.
>
> (Feuerbach 1957: xxxix)

This claim is from the Preface to Ludwig Feuerbach's most influential book *The Essence of Christianity* (1841) and, as we shall shortly see, it began a revolution that changed the way intellectuals thought about the nature of religion.

Feuerbach was born in Landshut, Bavaria. His father was a famous professor of jurisprudence. Ludwig, who as a child was deeply religious, became interested in theology, and while attending Gymnasium, his tutor introduced him to the speculative Christian theology inspired by **Hegel**.

In 1823 Feuerbach entered Heidelberg University to study theology. As he moved deeper into his study of **Hegel**, Feuerbach became troubled by his inability to reconcile belief in a personal God with **Hegel**'s notion of Absolute Spirit. One of his professors suggested that he go to Berlin to study with **Hegel** himself, which he did in 1824.

For financial reasons, he later transferred to Erlangen. There he began a study of botany, anatomy, and physiology while finishing his dissertation (*On the Infinitude, Unity, and Universality of Reason*) in which he supported and developed **Hegel**'s idea that reason is the ground of all individuals. However, he was eventually to shift from being a disciple of **Hegel** to becoming one of his most insightful critics.

In 1828 he accepted an appointment as a Privatdozent (an unpaid lecturer) at Erlangen. His teaching career was cut short, however, with the publication in 1830 of a book titled *Thoughts on Death and Immortality*. In that book he maintained that individual consciousness is part of an infinite consciousness and will become absorbed into that infinite mind after death. This logically implied that belief in a personal deity who granted individuals immortality amounted to little more than selfishness. He appended, unwisely as it turned out, some satiric epigrams making fun of popular Christian beliefs and the authorities confiscated the book. He was dismissed from his position, and was never again able to gain an academic appointment.

In 1837 he married Bertha Löw, who was a part owner of a porcelain factory, and retired to Bruckberg to take up the life of an independent scholar. In 1860 the porcelain factory went bankrupt and from then to the end of his life friends and admirers in both Europe and the United States supported him.

In *The Essence of Christianity* four interrelated ideas stand out: the concept of self-alienated humanity, the role of transformative criticism, the claim that thought about God (theology) is disguised and distorted thought about humanity (anthropology), and, consequently, a theory of religion as projection.

For Feuerbach, humans are divided beings. As consciousness develops into self-consciousness a division occurs between who we actually are and an idealized version of our self. This division results in self-alienated existence. The popular cartoon depiction of a person with a devil on one shoulder and an angel on the other is a humorous (and simplified) version of a more serious problem. Our idealized self (the angel) becomes, in religion, projected as a perfect being or God who exists apart from us and our world while its opposite (the devil) is appropriated as our sinful and far from perfect selves when measured by the divine perfection. In reality, humans are a mixture of moral and immoral impulses but in the dream that is religion humans are denigrated as evil and unworthy beings in need of salvation bestowed by the divine Other.

In **Hegel**'s philosophy, the Absolute comes to know itself as spirit or consciousness by projecting itself or objectifying itself in human consciousness and history. Feuerbach argued that the truth is the exact opposite of what **Hegel** proclaimed. God (the Absolute understood theistically) is in reality the human subject in its form of self-alienation. Grasping this truth requires what Feuerbach called "transformational criticism." This kind of criticism allows us to see that theology is really a disguised anthropology. Talk about God is, in fact, talk about human-ity. Thus the object of religion "as it is in imagination" is transformed into the object "as it is in reality."

Two examples drawn from Christianity will help us understand better what Feuerbach meant by "transformational criticism." What is "really" going on in the story (myth) about Christ's resurrection? Humans fear death and do not want to die. They wish for a life after death, a wish that forms the basis of the religious quest of humanity and accounts for the persistence of religion in the face of strong evi-dence to the contrary (a corpse). All so-called "proofs" of life after death fail to convince human reason beyond all doubt because certainty requires some concrete demonstration. What better demonstration than a story of someone rising from the dead with the added claim that, if we believe, we too can rise from the dead.

The paradoxical Christian doctrine of the Trinity—one God in three persons—can also be transformed into anthropology when we probe exactly what sort of truth about human relationships is masked in this theological language. Feuerbach argued that this is nothing less than the idealized projection of the experience of love and commu-nity between self and other, or I and Thou to use his terminology (see **Buber**). God the Father (I) loves God the Son (Thou) and the Holy Spirit symbolizes this beloved community (a human ideal).

The value of unmasking the truth concealed in Christian mythol-ogy and the inversion of **Hegel**'s philosophical interpretation of Christianity results in the overcoming of self-alienation, thereby freeing humans to love and unite in true social solidarity and mutual moral concern. Feuerbach called this "realized Christianity" and argued that it alone can bring about true community because community brought about by political means is always a forced unity based on power and frequently violence. The core of Christianity is best exemplified by Jesus' teachings about love but this core has been distorted and marginalized by supernaturalism (see **Kant**).

Feuerbach knew that by rejecting a supernatural interpretation of God he would be labeled an atheist. However, he claimed that to label his views atheistic was an oversimplification. To deny God is, for him, nothing more than the denial of the "negation of man." His motivation, he insisted, was religious and like the Protestant reformer Martin Luther (1483–1546), who gave birth to a new form of Christianity, he intended to give birth to a new religion of humanity.

When Feuerbach wrote *The Essence of Christianity* he was still partly under **Hegel**'s influence because like **Hegel** he viewed Christianity as the historical fulfillment of all religions. However, Feuerbach came to realize that this **Hegelian** view of Christianity was false and hence his theory of Christianity as a projection of human self-alienation had to be revised and generalized if it was to be applied to all religions, especially primal nature religions and nontheistic Asian religions.

After 1841, he attempted to work out a more general theory of religion in three books: *The Essence of Religion* (1845), *Lectures on the Essence of Religion* (1848) and *Theogonie* (1857). In these books Feuerbach revised his theory that religion is a projection of human self-alienation by paying more attention to human dependence on nature. He argued that in primal and archaic societies humans are more dependent on animals and plants than in the societies of his day. This dependence leads to feelings of fear, awe, and attraction, which in turn give rise to projecting the forces of nature as gods and goddesses in need of worship and sacrifice in order to be controlled. Even though this sort of nature religion is primarily selfish, it acknowledges the limits that nature places on human beings. Christianity rejects the limits of nature by imagining that humans can transcend death. Even his own version of "realized Christianity" rejected the limits of nature by imagining the perfectibility of the human species in a perfect community of love. With this insight he finally overcomes any lingering remnants of Hegelianism by rejecting the idea that Christianity is the most advanced form of religion. Compared to nature religions, Christianity, even when reinterpreted humanistically, amounts to an attempt on the part of humans to exceed their natural limits and a refusal to see themselves as a part of nature.

In *Theogonie*, Feuerbach made another shift in his thinking. He argued that the explanation of religion can be found in the human desire for happiness. The ground of religion is, he now argued, in the human desire for happiness and the human fear that death and nothingness will destroy any hope of lasting happiness. Religion is wishfulfillment in the sense that it assures humans that their wish for happiness will be eternally fulfilled.

Feuerbach's projection theory of religion along with his idea of wish fulfillment may have indirectly influenced **Freud**'s views on religion. Also **Nietzsche**'s critique of Christianity as a world-renouncing religion owes much to Feuerbach's views on how religious obsessions with a supernatural world and life after death sever humans from their connections with nature. **Karl Marx** is also deeply indebted to Feuerbach. His theory of how capitalism produces self-alienation and the role that religion plays as an "opiate" that makes humans content with pie in the sky by and by (thereby leaving the real "pie" for the capitalist to enjoy in this life) contains strong echoes of Feuerbach's ideas. More important than any specific influences is the way

Feuerbach reinforced **Hume**'s view of religion as something humans invent. The task of religious studies is not theological reflection on an alleged divine revelation. Rather its task is to understand this human invention – the reasons behind it, and why it has value for human life.

See also: **Berger, Boyer, Durkheim**

Major works

(1957) *The Essence of Christianity*, trans. George Eliot, New York: Harper and Row.

(1966) *Principles of the Philosophy of the Future*, trans. Manfred H. Vogel, Indianapolis, IN: Bobbs-Merrill.

(1967a) *Lectures on the Essence of Religion*, trans. Ralph Manheim, New York: Harper and Row.

(1967b) *The Essence of Faith According to Luther*, trans. Melvin Cherno, New York: Harper and Row.

(1980) *Thoughts on Death and Immortality from the Papers of a Thinker, along with an Appendix of Theological-Satirical Epigrams edited by One of His Friends*, trans. James A. Massey, Berkeley, CA: University of California Press.

(2004) *The Essence of Religion*, trans. Alexander Loos, Amherst, NY: Prometheus Books.

Further reading

Harvey, Van A. (1995) *Feuerbach and the Interpretation of Religion*, Cambridge: Cambridge University Press.

Wartofsky, Marx. (1977) *Feuerbach*, Cambridge: Cambridge University Press.

Wilson, Charles A. (1989) *Feuerbach and the Search for Otherness*, New York: Peter Lang.

http://plato.stanford.edu/entries/ludwig-feuerbach.

SØREN KIERKEGAARD (1813–55)

For an objective reflection the truth becomes an object, something objective, and thought must be pointed away from the subject. For subjective reflection the truth becomes a matter of appropriation, of inwardness, of subjectivity, and thought must probe more and more deeply into the subject and his subjectivity.

(Kierkegaard 1992: 117)

The Danish religious thinker Søren Kierkegaard made the phrase "truth is subjectivity" both famous and infamous. The above quotation from his *Concluding Unscientific Postscript* published in 1846 is both a not so veiled criticism of **Hegel**'s objective idealism, and the beginning of a line of thought that leads to a philosophical movement called **existentialism** that probed ever "more deeply into the subject and his subjectivity."

Kierkegaard was the son of a successful and deeply pious Copenhagen businessman who was haunted by guilt over an affair. The father–son relationship left Kierkegaard struggling with depression and a sense of inadequacy. In addition to his troubled relationship with his father, another decisive relationship for the young Kierkegaard was his brief engagement to Regine Olsen. The reasons he broke off the engagement are not entirely clear but part of the reason may have been the recognition that his own tormented and introspective personality was incompatible with Regine's. The gloomy, brooding part of his personality is revealed in his journals, but outwardly he was a *bon vivant* and known as something of a "man about town" in social circles.

At the University of Copenhagen Kierkegaard studied theology and philosophy. His study of **Hegel** convinced him that **Hegel**'s views on Christianity were wrong. Hegelian thought was much in vogue because it reinforced the idea that Christianity was a rational religion whose truth could be objectively demonstrated. For Kierkegaard the truth of Christianity, which he believed revealed authentic human existence, was not objective, but subjective in the sense that it had to be inwardly appropriated through faith. But how could this be communicated in a culture that presumed everyone was Christian by virtue of birth and baptism? How could he accomplish his goal of "the reintroduction of Christianity into Christendom"?

In order to solve the problem of communication, Kierkegaard developed a method of "indirect communication" involving pseudonymous authorship designed to probe from different viewpoints the structure of selfhood and the stages of existence. This method makes it difficult to interpret his writings and to discover what he actually thought. Some read him as someone whose intent is to subvert the positions of others without advancing a position of his own. Others read him straightforwardly as if everything he wrote represented his own views even though he attributed many of his writings to fictional authors. Still others opt for a "middle way" arguing that his goal was to subvert conventional Christianity and the rationalistic philosophy on which it was based while also showing what authentic faith was like.

Kierkegaard was an astute observer of human nature and was able to discern and describe recurrent patterns in the variety of lives people led. He arranged these patterns "dialectically" in "stages" but his use of a dialectical structure was not formalistic and logical in the Hegelian sense. The stages were "forms of life" and ever-present human options. There was nothing necessary or determined about a progression from lower to higher stages.

In *Either/Or* (1843) Kierkegaard explored two forms or "stages" of human existence, the aesthetic and the ethical. The three primary moods of the aesthetic are sensual immediacy symbolized by Don Juan, doubt symbolized by Faust, and despair symbolized by the Wandering Jew. The chief characteristics of these ways of living are detachment, experimentation, lack of involvement, and the inability to make a lasting commitment. Even though the aesthete lives a life in the pursuit of satisfaction, it is ultimately an "unhappy life." The person trapped in the pursuit of sensual pleasure lacks moral will and finds himself or herself the victim of the pleasurable moment. Such people ultimately despair of ever being free from seeking pleasure. The person trapped in doubt is constantly seeking the truth but despairs of ever finding it. The absence of hope is the chief characteristic of the despairing individual. This sort of despair can lead to either spiritual death or an awakening to higher possibilities.

The next "higher possibility" for living after the aesthetic is the ethical. The route to this higher way of existing is neither necessary nor inevitable. Since despair is a "sickness unto death" one either dies without hope or one awakens to the possibility of the ethical life. The movement from the aesthetic to the ethical mode of existence is more like a leap made in the depths of despair than a logical transition. It is summed up by the phrase "choose thyself."

For Kierkegaard, choosing oneself means choosing passionately and in an unconditional way. To accept the demand of the ethical on one's life requires an absolute commitment to transforming oneself into someone who is willing to submit to the universal demand of morality. The life of immediacy that characterizes aesthetic existence is replaced by a life of discipline and vocation. This choice gives a person a sense of inner coherence and a calling to a life larger than self-gratification. The character of Judge William symbolizes the ethical stage. He is devoted to an ethical vocation and to the practice of the civic virtues. Judge William or the ethical person seeks to realize universal values in the conduct of his life.

Kierkegaard was more interested in the nature of moral commitment than he was in the rules of some moral system or a theory of ethics that would produce guidance in making day-to-day moral decisions. Formal theories and moral rules, whatever they may be, are always inadequate because they fail to consider the individual and his or her unique situation. Kierkegaard takes **Kant**'s ethical theory to task for assuming that "ought" implies "can." His ethics of duty does not sufficiently recognize that humans are immersed in sin and guilt, so even if they recognize rationally what they ought to do, they are not always able to do it. It also fails to recognize that in some situations there may be demands that are higher than the universal. Kierkegaard, in *Fear and Trembling* (1843), sees the story of Abraham and Isaac as illustrative of what he called the "teleological suspension of the ethical." Abraham is commanded by God to sacrifice his son Isaac and intends to obey that command. Hence he is a "Knight of faith" and shows that there are individual exceptions to the **Kantian** claim that the ethical life must be guided by a universal moral imperative. There is a stage or mode of existence higher than the ethical. This is because absolute moral goodness is simply unattainable for humans and insofar as the moral life demands moral perfection it must end in failure.

The crisis of the ethical stage can make possible a third option for living beyond the aesthetic and the ethical—the religious. This stage offers two options, "Religiousness A" and "Religiousness B." The first form is the religion of **immanence** and is exemplified by Socrates. Kierkegaard selected Socrates as the figure to represent this religious option because he taught that truth is within every individual and the teacher (Socrates) provides the occasion for remembering the truth within. So Socrates teaches as a midwife would, he assists the birth of truth by his critical questioning of the values and ideas people take for granted.

Religiousness B is the religion of **transcendence** because the truth comes from without and is revealed by a savior, not a teacher. Jesus is the figure who best represents this type of religiousness because he is the Absurd, that is, the absolute paradox of a God-Man. This means that an historical event can be the occasion for eternal happiness because the eternal God has become a temporal man. The eyewitness to the life of Jesus has no advantage over those who come after because Jesus appeared no more divine than you or I. Hence the disciple believes, not based on any evidence either empirical or rational, but only because he has received the condition (grace) from God. Faith is as paradoxical as the claim that God became flesh in Jesus because it too is absurd. It is a leap into the unknown just as Abraham's belief that the voice that commanded him to kill his son was in fact a divine voice.

For Kierkegaard, the full actualization of authentic selfhood only becomes possible in the religious stage. Faith is a decision that must be made over and over again in the face of an irreducible paradox. By these decisions the individual takes full responsibility for his or her life by acknowledging that the foundation of a meaningful human life is nothing more or less than decisions made in the face of objective uncertainty. Religious truth thereby becomes subjective and the individual thereby becomes truthful.

Not surprisingly Keirkegaard's **fideism** (the insistence on complete reliance on faith) has been criticized for fostering a radical subjectivism and individualism. He has been accused of distorting the nature of religion by ignoring its communal dimension and the role that community plays in initiating and sustaining faith. The image of the lone individual standing before a divine being who demands complete obedience to a "truth" for which there is no objective evidence appears to reduce religion itself to an absurdity. If **Hegel** discovered the essence of religion in Reason, **Kant** found it in the Moral Will, and **Schleiermacher** located it in feeling then Kierkegaard, so the critique goes, has reduced its essence to irrationality.

However, in spite of these criticisms, Kierkegaard's analysis of the human condition has proved remarkably influential in theology, philosophy, psychology, and literature. The ideas of **Fredrich Nietzsche**, Martin Heidegger, Jean-Paul Sartre, and Albert Camus, to name a few, would be hard to imagine without Kierkegaard's insights into human existence. And while his analysis of religion would seem to undermine the modern attempt to develop an objective study of religion, it stands as a reminder that however useful the objective studies of the religious scholar are, for many people there appears to be something illusive about religion that defies reduction to scientific analysis.

See also: **Buber, Smart, W. C. Smith, Tillich, Wittgenstein**

Major writings

Princeton University Press published all of the following.

(1967) *Philosophical Fragments*, trans. Howard V. Hong.
(1980) *The Concept of Dread*, trans. Walter Lowrie.
(1983) *Fear and Trembling*, trans. Walter Lowrie.
(1985) *Sickness unto Death*, trans. Walter Lowrie.
(1987) *Either/Or*, Vols. I & II, Vol. 1 trans. David and Lillian Swenson, Vol. 2 trans. Walter Lowrie.
(1992) *Concluding Unscientific Postscript*, trans. David Swenson.

Further reading

Hannay, A. (1982) *Kierkegaard*, London: Routledge and Kegan Paul.

Rudd, A. (1993) *Kierkegaard and the Limits of the Ethical*, Oxford: Oxford University Press.

Taylor, Mark C. (1980) *Journeys to Selfhood: Hegel and Kierkegaard*, Berkeley, CA: University of California Press.

Weston, M. (1994) *Kierkegaard and Modern Continental Philosophy*, London: Routledge.

http://plato.stanford.edu/entries/kierkegaard/.

KARL MARX (1818–83)

> *Religious* distress is at the same time the *expression* of real distress and the *protest* against real distress. Religion is the sigh of the oppressed creature, the heart of a heartless world, just as it is the spirit of a spiritless situation. It is the *opium* of the people. The abolition of religion as the *illusory* happiness of the people is required for their real happiness. The demand to give up the illusion about its condition is the *demand to give up a condition, which needs illusions*.
>
> (Marx 1964: 42)

Karl Marx expressed this much quoted, harsh judgment about religion in the introduction of his 1844 essay "Contribution to the Critique of Hegel's Philosophy of Right." Opium is both a narcotic and hallucinogenic. It reduces pain while creating pleasant fantasies. The "real distress" is economic and is produced by the cruel exploitation of poor workers in capitalistic societies. The fantasy is the imaginary "pie in the sky by and by" offered by religion in general and Christianity in particular. It is no surprise that fantastic images of heaven include gates inlaid with pearl and streets paved with gold. The poor and exploited are told that all they have to do is work hard, do what they are told, and after they die God will reward them with a life of happiness and riches beyond their wildest dreams. Yet religion is also a protest and a real sigh of the oppressed and exploited.

Marx was the son of a German Jewish lawyer who had converted to Christianity largely for the sake of his career because Jews were barred from professional advancement by the government. Marx, although baptized as a child, seemed to have developed contempt for religion early in life. He went to Bonn at the age of seventeen to study law but soon transferred to Berlin where he joined a group of Young Hegelians called the "Doctors Club." These "left-wing" Hegelians found **Hegel**'s dialectical theory of history valuable for understanding the changes taking place in Europe as the industrial age entered history with a roar. However, they thought that **Hegel** had to be "turned on his head" in order to properly analyze what was happening and the historical events that led up to it. For Marx this reversal of the **Hegelian** dialectic meant that ideas do not determine economics but economics determines ideas. **Hegel**'s dialectical idealism needed to be replaced by a dialectical materialism. Contrary to **Hegel**, ideas do not make the world go round, the physical conditions of human existence do.

Feuerbach was a leading member of the Doctors Club when Marx joined. His ideas inspired much of Marx's early thought on religion. He basically agreed with **Feuerbach** that God is a projection of an idealized version of humanity and echoes that idea when he declared, "man makes religion." However, he thought that **Feuerbach** had not gone far enough with his critique of religion. The point of philosophical criticism should be to change the world, not just interpret it. That change had to include, for Marx, not only reinterpreting Christianity so its humanistic ethic was highlighted but also bringing about the complete elimination of all organized religion. For him religion functions as a compensator for deprivation, a support for an elitist and reactionary capitalist order. It blocks all social and economic reform.

Although Marx had hoped for an academic career, his radical views effectively barred him from any such appointment. He became a journalist instead and, along with his friend Friedrich Engels, began writing essays and books that would change the world. These writings sounded the themes of economic determinism (materialism), class struggle, alienation, revolution, and a communism that held out hope for a future classless society of economic equality and justice.

Marx maintained that there had been, at the beginning of the human race, a kind of primitive communism based on a barter system in which goods and services of equal value were exchanged. However, once private property had shattered this idyllic start, human history became a struggle between haves and have-nots. Those with the most private property not only had economic power, they also had the power to determine the lives of those who owned less or no private property at all.

If we are to understand the historical evolution of society, we must distinguish between base and superstructure. Base refers to economic or material conditions of human life and superstructure refers to culture (art, politics, law, religion, philosophy, etc.). Marx argued that base conditions determine or cause the superstructure in which humans live and work. The primary function of the superstructure is to contain or provide controlled release for the bitter tensions and conflicts that arise from the inevitable clashes between the rich and the poor. While governments often use force (police, military) to control the poor, philosophers, theologians, and moralists use persuasion to control the poor. The primary mechanism of persuasion is the development of an ideology that provides justifications, which serve the interests of the rich ruling classes by masking the real truth with a fictionalized version of the "truth." The real truth, for example, is that there is no life after death in which the poor will enjoy riches. The fictionalized "truth" is the myth about heaven and hell spun by priests in order to keep people somewhat happy with their lot in life. Religion, in other words, is an ideology devised to allow the rich to control and exploit the poor.

In 1848 Marx settled in London where the industrial revolution was in full swing. He observed great poverty (including his own) and appalling living conditions among the workers who toiled day and night, often along with their families, in unsafe factories for inadequate wages. He also observed the fabulously rich owners of the factories living in baronial splendor, often in large country estates complete with servants to attend their every need. According to the labor theory of value, the value of a product is equivalent to the labor and resources needed to produce it. So from where, Marx asked, did this great disparity in wealth come? His answer was that it came by underpaying the workers, thus creating a "surplus value" that the capitalist could enjoy.

Marx agreed with **Feuerbach**'s contention that self-alienation is a basic problem of human existence but argued that its causes were economic. Alienation is a social and economic problem, not just an individual problem. If religion robs us of our best human qualities, as **Feuerbach** contended, capitalism steals our labor by making it a mere commodity to be bought and sold. Work is a fundamental expression of human existence and when it is objectified as a commodity and taken from us by the capitalist in return for inadequate wages, an unhappy self-alienation is the result.

Although Marx devoted many more articles and books to economic and historical analysis than to religion, his ideas about religion have proved widely influential. His focus on how religion functions to console people in distress helped to spur interest in how religious beliefs function. The focus of scholars began to shift from asking questions about the truth of religious ideas to concentrating on what they do. Scholarly studies of religion also began to pay more attention to the complex relationships between economic conditions and religion.

While Marx has been severely criticized for his atheism and negative assessment of religion, he did acknowledge that it also constituted a *"protest* against a real distress." Subsequent scholars influenced by Marx have pursued that idea and subsequent research has shown the ways in which religion can also function as an agent of social change inspiring people to seek economic and social justice. Ironically, Marx's views inspired such religious movements as the Social Gospel, Liberation Theology, Christian Socialism, and Christian Realism. Perhaps this is because Marx's thought provides the basis for an economic reinterpretation of major themes in Judaism, Christianity, and Islam such as sin (alienation and economic injustice) and the kingdom of God (the classless society of economic and social justice).

Religion for Marx was entirely a part of the superstructure of culture. He posited a one-way causality between economic conditions and religious beliefs. Subsequent scholarship, albeit inspired by Marx, has shown that the relationship between religion and economics is far more complex. **Max Weber**, for example, found evidence that religion may also cause economic changes. While there are limitations to Marx's views of both economics and religion, there can be little doubt that religious scholarship since Marx had to take seriously the relationship between religion and economics.

See also: **Berger, Eliade, Foucault, Geertz, Gross, Smart, Troeltsch**

Major writings

(1964) *Karl Marx and Friedrich Engels On Religion*, New York: Schocken Books.

(1975) *Collected Works*, 50 vols., New York: International Publishers.

(1994) *Selected Writings*, ed. Lawrence H. Simon, Indianapolis, IN: Hackett Publishing Company.

Further reading

Berlin, Isaiah. (1974) *Karl Marx*, New York: Time Inc.

Carver, Terrell, ed. (1991) *The Cambridge Companion to Marx*, Cambridge: Cambridge University Press.

Dupré, Louis. (1967) *The Philosophical Foundations of Marxism*, New York: Harcourt Brace.

Wheen, Francis. (2001) *Karl Marx: A Life*, New York: W. W. Norton.

http://www.marxists.org.

F. MAX MÜLLER (1823–1900)

He who knows one [religion], *knows none.*

(Müller 1873: 12)

With this assertion from his *Introduction to the Science of Religion* (1873), Max Müller, a pioneer in the comparative study of religions, indicated one important reason to engage in the academic study of religion. Knowing only one religion, while possibly deepening one's own piety, tells us little about the nature of religion, let alone its history. Hence use of the comparative method in the study of religion was essential to establishing it as a "science."

Müller was born in Dessau, Germany and educated at the University of Leipzig, where he studied philosophy and philology. His father, who died when he was four, was a renowned German poet of the **Romantic** school and his mother, Adelheid, came from a prominent political family. Abandoning a career in music, he eventually made his way to England and began a lifelong teaching career at Oxford University where a chair of comparative philology was created for him after he failed to get the chair in Sanskrit. Because Müller was one of the leading Sanskrit scholars of his day, many suspected that he was turned down because he was "too liberal" in his politics and in his interpretation of Christianity. After his retirement he oversaw the publication of the *Sacred Books of the East*, a project that was crucial to introducing the texts of Asian religions to an English-speaking audience.

Like many linguists of his day, he was convinced that there was an original language (*Ursprache*) from which all Indo-European languages derived. A careful comparative analysis of the development of words could lead one, layer by layer, back to the roots from which modern words were derived and were as close to this original language as one could get. Just a century before philologists had thought that Hebrew was the original language of humans and had been revealed by God. Now, thanks to scientific philological research (in particular the discovery of the close relationship between Sanskrit, Greek, and Latin), that theory could no longer be maintained.

The study of language and the derivation of words were not only important for philological reasons. It held the key, Müller thought, to cracking the code of ancient myths and to the earliest religion of the human race. He noticed that linguistic roots relating to the sun were prevalent in many myths. This led him to posit what is called "solar mythology" or the theory that most if not all myths derived from our early ancestors' experience of the sun. This theory reflects a more general idea called "nature mythology" because it holds that myths are stories told about personified natural events, which, according to Müller, inspired awe and even worship among early people. So, for example, myths about gods rising from the dead or journeying in an underworld derived from the experiences of sunrise and sunset.

Whatever one may think about nature mythology in general or solar mythology in particular, such theories do not answer the question of why natural things like the sun are personified in the first place. One can understand why stories were told about the "birth" of the sun once it was personified, but why think of the sun as if it were a person in the first place?

Müller used the term "disease of language" to try to answer this question. Language, he claimed, by the use of masculine and feminine cases (the neuter case arising much later according to his research) inevitably caused people to think of natural events as if they were persons (see **Boyer**). Further, lacking any abstract concept of causality, this personification of nature had the added benefit of explaining why things happen by introducing the idea of agency. For example, positing a "Rainer" as a powerful force that controlled when, where, and how much it rained could explain rain. The step from "Rainer" to "rain god" is, according to Müller, a short one. Stories about such a god were inevitable because the nature of language, particularly the use of gender, makes it inevitable.

However, it is not simply the gender ascribed to words that facilitates a misleading personification of the natural events. We must dig deeper to understand how mythology arises from language because, Müller contends, originally every word is a radix that has no inflectional ending and every radix signified a certain characteristic. The linguistic phenomena of homonymy (different objects having ostensibly the same name), polynomy (different names for the same object), and synonymy (words with similar meanings) contribute to the rise of mythology. Language is such that one word can easily substitute for another word. Thus "warming" and "burning" might come to designate fire because they name qualities of fire. Two names for the same thing can become mythologized as "brothers" and "sisters" giving rise to stories about how they came to be and how they are related to other gods and goddesses.

Mythology, however, is not religion even if it contains stories about gods and goddesses. Religion proper lurks behind these stories. Religion, at least for Müller, has to do with unconditional adoration of the Infinite. We can dimly glimpse early people groping for the idea of the Infinite in the stories they told about the gods of sun, moon, stars, and storm. Under the influence of **Hegel**, Müller thought that careful comparison of languages, myths, and religions could reveal the story of the slow but progressive ascent of humans to ever more sophisticated ideas of God as the Infinite source of all life and of Christianity as the highest expression of religion. As Müller made clear in his Gifford Lectures (1888–92), he did not mean by "nature religion" that humans worshiped the sun or other natural phenomena as somehow divine but they worshiped, as he put it, the Infinite as manifested in nature. His point was that the idea of the Infinite beyond the world did not arise through some divine revelation but out of human reflection on nature.

Although Müller believed that Christianity was the apex of religious development up to his time, he emphasized the need for objectivity and tolerance in the study of all religions. The purpose of comparison was knowledge, not proof that one religion was superior to another. He constantly drew analogies between comparative philology and comparative religion, pointing out that both involve careful examination and collection of documents, classification systems to organize the data, and inductive reasoning to establish general "laws of thought."

Müller opposed Darwin's ideas, which were becoming increasingly influential in his day, because he thought that the ability to use language clearly showed that humans had not evolved from the "brutes." He also criticized the idea of "natural selection." Yet he did admit that history showed a general evolutionary tendency as human thought progressed from polytheism to monotheism. This was due, however, not to any blind natural selection but to what he called "rational selection" by a hidden divine will that guided human thought to ever more sublime ideas of the divine.

Müller's scholarly achievements were impressive. He edited and wrote more than a hundred books and gained the reputation of a scholar's scholar because of his great learning and impressive philological research. Among his many achievements were the first critical edition of the *Rig Veda*, and some two-dozen volumes of lectures and essays on language, mythology, and religion. People flocked to his public lectures and many regarded his ideas as the last word on comparative religion and mythology. However, even before his death his ideas were under attack.

Andrew Lang (1844–1912), a Scottish anthropologist and folklorist, was a relentless critic of Müller (among others). He ridiculed his ideas by pointing out that the attempt to explain Indo-European mythology on the basis of Indo-European philology was nonsense since the same solar mythic themes could be found in other parts of the world. He also pointed out that Müller almost completely ignored the important role of ritual in his account of religion. Other critics joined the fray, calling nature mythology into question as well as the notion that all myths are in one way or another about the sun, with the result that today, this pioneer (some claim founder) of the comparative "science of religion" is seldom read and usually receives little more than an aside in textbooks on religious studies.

See also: **Dumézil, Evans-Pritchard, Harrison, J. Z. Smith, Tylor**

Major writings

(1867) *Chips from a German Workshop: Essays on the Science of Religion*, Vol. 1, London: Longmans, Green and Company.

(1873) *Introduction to the Science of Religion*, London: Longmans, Green and Company.

(1897) *Contributions to the Science of Mythology*, 2 vols, London: Longmans, Green and Company.

(1901) *My Autobiography: A Fragment*, New York: Charles Scribner's Sons.

(1902) *The Life and Letters of the Right Honorable Friedrich Max Müller*, edited by his wife, 2 vols, London: Longmans, Green and Company.

(1909) *Comparative Mythology: An Essay*, New York: Charles Scribner's Sons.

Further reading

Chaudhuri, Nirad C. (1974) *Scholar Extraordinary: The Life of Professor Rt Hon. Friedrich Max Müller*, London: Chatto and Windus.

Stone, Jon. R., ed. (2002) *The Essential Max Müller: On Language, Mythology, and Religion*, New York: Palgrave.

Voigt, Johannes H. (1967) *Max Mueller: The Man and His Ideas*, Calcutta: K. L. Mukhopadhyay.

http://en.wikipedia.org/wiki/Max_Müller.

E. B. TYLOR (1832–1917)

> Thus animism, in its full development, includes the belief in souls and in a future state, in controlling deities and subordinate spirits, these doctrines practically resulting in some kind of active worship.
>
> (Tylor 1889: Vol. I, p. 427)

How did religion begin and how has it evolved? E. B. Tylor, the "father of British anthropology" devoted his career to answering these questions. His answer, as the above quotation from his monumental work *Primitive Culture* (1871) indicates, is animism – a word derived from the Latin *anima* meaning spirit. Religion starts as a simple belief in souls and evolves through various stages, but it remains fundamentally animistic in its understanding of the world.

Edward Burnett Tylor was born in London and raised as a member of the Society of Friends (Quakers), which is a Christian denomination that emphasizes getting in touch with the spiritual divine light of Christ within the soul. He went to work in his father's brass factory at the age of sixteen. After his health broke down, he traveled to America in search of a cure. Under the influence of the archeologist Henry Christi, he began a study of Mexican culture and published his first book, *Anahuac: Or Mexico and the Mexicans, Ancient and Modern* (1861), on that subject. He did not enter university after his return to England but continued to study what were then called "primitive" cultures, publishing his second book *Researches into the Early History of Mankind and the Development of Civilization* in 1865. The work for which he is best known, *Primitive Culture*, followed in 1871 and merited an honorary doctorate from Oxford University in 1875. In 1896 he was appointed the first professor of anthropology in Britain.

Charles Darwin's *Origin of Species* (1859) and *The Descent of Man* (1871) had taken the world by storm in Tylor's day and people waged battle (as they do today) in favor of evolution or against it. Although Tylor denied he was a "Darwinian" he, along with others, extended the idea of evolution to the study of culture and religion, inspiring a hunt for the origin of religion and an account of its development that would last well into the next century. His contribution to these debates centered on a theory of "survivals" and a theory of "animism."

We live nowhere near the time when religion began, so how can we know how religion got its start? Archeology can provide material artifacts, but without knowing something about a culture how can we tell what they meant to early peoples? Philologists like **Max**

Müller can provide evidence about the development of Indo-European languages, but inferences to other linguistic groups are problematic. What we need, Tylor thought, is a new "science of culture." This new science of anthropology can study "survivals" or the leftovers from more remote times among groups that the stream of evolutionary change "left behind" as well as survivals of super-stitions in our own cultures whose origins have long been forgotten. When we do, we discover what he called animism and defined as "the belief in spiritual beings."

If we assume primal humans (what Tylor called "primitives") had a reasoning capacity similar to our own, we can infer that like us they sought explanations for their experiences. The experiences of dreaming and death are surely among those requiring some explanation.

> It seems as though thinking men, as yet at a low level of culture, were deeply impressed by two groups of biological problems. In the first place, what is it that makes a difference between a living body and a dead one; what causes waking, sleep, trance, disease, death? In the second place, what are those human shapes which appear in dreams and visions? Looking at these two groups of phenomena, the ancient savage philosophers probably made their first step by the obvious inference that every man has two things belonging to him, namely, a life and a phantom as being its image or second self; both, also, are perceived to be things separable from the body. ... The second step would seem also easy for savages to make, seeing how extremely difficult civilized men have found it to unmake. It is merely to combine the life, and the phantom ... the result is that well-known conception ... the personal soul, or spirit.
>
> (Tylor 1889: Vol. I, p. 429)

If the concept of souls or spirits explains dreaming and visions of the dead, why should humans not extend it to other natural phenomena such as plants and animals? Maybe spirits moved the rivers and the wind too. Assuming our imagined primal philosophers observed the stars, then there is no reason why the spirit "hypothesis" could not be used to make sense of the heavens as well. If souls animate people, then it is logical to assume that spirits animate the whole world. Thus the animistic theory is born and over time evolves into polytheism (belief in many gods) and eventually monotheism (belief in one god).

Tylor knew that he had no firsthand, direct proof of his animistic theory of the origin and development of religion. Such proof is, by the nature of the case, impossible. Nevertheless it is, he thought, a plausible theory and, like any good theory, it explains a number of religious ideas that can be found across "primitive" cultures world-wide, and that still survive in the "higher" religions. It explains, for example, how beliefs about life after death came to be and it explains what many call idol worship. The material out of which an idol is made is not worshiped, but the spirit that it represents and that dwells within it. Animism can also explain the widespread use of fetishes—sacred objects—especially in healing ceremonies and other rituals. If we want to know why American Indians talk to animals, why healers ritually exorcise evil spirits, why gifts are left for the dead or why gods have human personalities and stories are told about their various exploits—if we want to know the answers to these and many more questions we have a simple theory at hand to explain it all, the theory of animism. If spirits are modeled on the souls of human persons, as Tylor's theory maintains, then it should come as no surprise that they are thought of as persons and treated accordingly.

Although Tylor regarded so-called primitives as children, he nevertheless saw them as rational human beings who were trying to explain and gain control of their world, even if they were wrong to think that spirits controlled natural events. This was certainly a step beyond those who simply dismissed such people as irrational, even if such views still supplied some justification for the so-called higher cultures to colonize and exploit them. However, one did not have to reflect very long to see that Tylor's ideas applied to all religion, not just primitive religion. At the heart of all religion is the "animistic hypothesis" and insofar as animism is a mistaken understanding of nature, all religion is caught in the grips of this colossal mistake. However plausible animistic explanations were to our ancestors, the advances of modern science provide demonstrably better explanations. Yet the so-called "higher religions" such as Judaism, Christianity, and Islam, while more morally advanced in Tylor's mind, are still largely survivals of an animistic mentality.

Although Tylor's ideas became popular among many and laid the foundations on which the study of primal religions was built for more than a century, they have not been without their critics. In his own day, theologians criticized him for allowing his atheism to influence his theory, and Andrew Lang (1844–1912) presented evidence of early beliefs in a "high god" that called into question all evolutionary schemes that placed monotheism at the end of a long developmental line. Tylor's intellectualism reduces religion to belief and largely ignores the ecstatic and communal elements that are vital to any religion in the full sense of the term. His intellectualism is combined with an individualism that supposes religion began with a mistaken inference of some "savage philosophers" and somehow caught on with others. There is, it must be said, no concrete evidence for this apart from Tylor's imagination and the citing of examples out of context that are at best only loosely associated. Many scholars also reject Tylor's assumption that things develop from a simple to a complex state. Not all evolution is that simple. Nor can we assume, as Tylor does, that all evolutionary developments are necessarily "improvements" on less advanced precursors.

Tylor presented his ideas as a "new science," but unlike natural scientific theories his theory of the origin and evolutionary development of religion cannot be proved or disproved. However, in spite of all these limitations, Tylor spurred on the quest for a "science of religion" that did not appeal to divine revelation or rest on theological premises. Like all scientists he appealed to observation and formulated a theory to organize and make sense of the data.

See also: **Asad, Bellah, Boyer, Durkheim, Evans-Pritchard, Harrison, Lévy-Bruhl, Malinowski, Radcliffe-Brown**

Major writings

(1889) *Primitive Culture*, 2 vols, New York: Henry Holt and Company.
(1994) *The Collected Works of Edward Burnett Tylor*, London: Routledge.

Further reading

Burrow, J. W. (1970) *Evolution and Society*, Cambridge: Cambridge University Press.
Marett, R. R. (1936) *Tylor*, London: Chapman and Hall.
Stocking, George W., Jr. (1987) *Victorian Anthropology*, New York: Free Press.
http://en.wikipedia.org/wiki/Edward_Burnett_Tylor.

WILLIAM JAMES (1842–1910)

> Now in these lectures I propose to ignore the institutional branch entirely, to say nothing of the ecclesiastical organization, to consider as little as possible the systematic theology and the ideas about the gods themselves, and to confine myself as far as I can to personal religion pure and simple. ... Religion, therefore, as I now ask you arbitrarily to take it,

shall mean for us the feelings, acts, and experiences of individual men in their solitude, so far as they apprehend themselves to stand in relation to whatever they may consider the divine.

(James 1997: 41–42)

With these words William James launched his Gifford Lectures of 1901–2 subsequently published in 1902 as *The Varieties of Religious Experience: A Study in Human Nature*. He also launched a new branch of the academic study of religion called the psychology of religion. This book was destined to influence generations of scholars and with its call for a "scientific" study of religion pointed in new and fertile directions.

James was the son of Mary Robertson Walsh and Henry James Sr., an independently wealthy would-be scholar who dabbled in Swedenborgianism (a kind of mysticism). His brother Henry achieved distinction as a novelist and his sister Alice as a diarist, while William became famous as a philosopher, psychologist, and lecturer.

His early education was unconventional and broad as his father moved the family around Europe and brought a steady flow of the leading intellectuals of the day into their home for lively discussions and debates around the dinner table. James developed an interest in both art and science and studied painting for a time before entering Harvard to study medicine. While on a scientific expedition to Brazil in 1865 he fell ill with smallpox, which complicated other physical ailments as well as James's bouts with depression. He received his medical degree in 1869, but never practiced medicine. He began teaching physiology and anatomy at Harvard, eventually moving into the fields of psychology (then just getting a foothold in the United States) and philosophy. He founded one of the first psychological laboratories in the United States and wrote the most definitive textbook of the day (*The Principles of Psychology*, 1890). He married in 1878 and became a full professor of philosophy at Harvard in 1885. He retired from a distinguished teaching career in 1907 but continued to write and publish until his death from heart disease in 1910.

James developed a number of distinctive ideas that have had a wide influence. Among them are "stream of consciousness," the James-Lange theory of emotion, pragmatism, radical empiricism, pure experience, and the will to believe.

Awareness, James argued, flows like a stream of water rather than coming in jerky sets of individual snapshots. This idea stimulated subsequent developments in literature, film, and the study of consciousness. James's famous bear example illustrates his views on emotion. Common sense tells us that we see a bear, feel afraid, then run. But in this case common sense is wrong. We see a bear, run, and then feel afraid. In other words, emotions follow actions and the physiological responses (in this case higher adrenaline) in our body that the stimulus triggers and our brains register as feeling fear come after the fact (the James-Lange theory of emotion).

James is famous for his pragmatic theory of truth, a theory that repudiates static concepts of truth and instead provides a dynamic view of truth as ideas that "work" in the Darwinian sense of contributing to survival. Some work to guide our sensations to further confirming sensations and some facilitate our thoughts that in turn lead to new ideas. James credited the philosopher Charles Peirce (1839–1914) with the original idea of pragmatism, but Pierce thought that James had misinterpreted what he meant so renamed his theory pragmaticism.

Unlike classical **empiricism**, which emphasized ideas as deriving from sensations of individual and unrelated things, James's radical empiricism is based on the claim that we experience not just individual, atomic-like things (the sensation of red for example) but the relations between and among things such as conjunctions, oppositions, and the like.

James was still working on the idea of pure experience at the time of his death. However, the concept was introduced in an essay, "A World of Pure Experience," first published in 1904. In that essay James was grappling with the mind/body problem. He argued that mind and matter are both aspects of something more fundamental, a something he called "pure experience" that is (despite the term experience) neither physical nor mental. He characterizes it as "the immediate flux of life which furnishes the material to our later reflection with its conceptual categories ... a *that* which is not yet any definite *what*, tho' ready to be all sorts of whats ..." (James 1967: 93). These pure experiences become categorized as "mind" or "matter" depending on the relations they enter. The philosopher Bertrand Russell (1872–1970) developed this idea into a theory now called "neutral monism." It was also picked up by Japanese philosophers interested in developing certain ideas that came out of the Zen Buddhist meditation tradition, such as the experience of "suchness."

James's essay "The Will to Believe" (1896) presented an argument in support of religious faith that was widely criticized in an age when agnosticism was all the rage among many intellectuals. James later regretted the title because critics thought he meant that people could believe whatever they wanted. It would have been better, James thought, to title it "The Right to Believe."

The agnosticism of James's day was based in evidentialism. William K. Clifford, an English mathematician, had famously argued in 1897 that we have both an intellectual and moral duty never to believe anything as true *beyond* the evidence (Clifford 1897: 177). The evidence for God is, at best, inconclusive. It follows, Clifford claimed, that we should withhold belief in God just as we would not believe a shipowner's claim that his ship was safe if he did not have evidence that it was safe.

James countered that we had a right to believe beyond the evidence in *certain situations*. If humans did not exercise such a right, many useful truths would never be discovered because some belief options are "genuine options" that are "living, forced, and momentous." We either act on them now, or risk losing the opportunity altogether (for example, getting married or going on a Polar expedition). In some cases failure to act guarantees that the evidence itself will never appear. James gives the example of jumping from one ledge to another when we are uncertain we can make the leap but will die where we are if we don't try. James argued that the "religious hypothesis" is a genuine option whose truth will never be known if we don't exercise our right to believe it true. Clifford's evidentialism and agnosticism are based on an "irrational rule" that would prevent someone from acknowledging "certain kinds of truth if those kinds of truth were really there." In the philosophy of religion, the cogency of James's argument is still debated.

Scholars consider James's *Varieties of Religious Experience* a classic. It has been a rich source of ideas on a wide variety of topics still studied today. James, as our opening quotation indicates, focused his study on individual and personal religion, an idea that has had wide and deep influence both within academia and with the public at large. Genuine religion, many today would claim, is a matter of inwardness first and foremost. Organized religion, with its rituals and dogmas, is, as James put it, religion "at second hand." Although the notion that the "spiritual" aspect of religion is the most important part has been widely influential, many scholars have criticized what they see as James's overemphasis on the religious individual at the expense of the communal dimension of religion.

James was, unlike many scholars of his day, more interested in the function of religion than its origins. He broadened the notion of religious experience, which many at the time had narrowed to refer exclusively to conversion experiences. In addition to conversion,

James discussed saintliness, mysticism, and religious temperaments that he called "healthy-mindedness" and the "sick soul."

Healthy-minded religion is optimistic and positive in outlook. Evil, sin, and the darker side of human nature find little place in such an outlook. The sick soul, however, can become obsessed with evil, sin, guilt, and a pessimistic outlook on life.

James analyzed conversion experiences in terms of a "divided self" suddenly or gradually finding unification. He was, however, much more interested in mysticism, which he felt to be the key to understanding personal religion. Based on the analysis and comparison of many cases (the method he used throughout the *Varieties*) including drug-induced mystical states, he described four marks of mystical experience—ineffability, noetic quality, transiency, and passivity—that are still used in studies of mystical consciousness (see **Suzuki**).

One of the central functions of religion, James concluded, is the healing of the self through a connection with "higher powers."

> The warring gods and formulas of the various religions do indeed cancel each other, but there is a certain uniform deliverance in which religions all appear to meet. It consists of two parts: –
>
> 1. An uneasiness; and
> 2. Its solution.
>
> The uneasiness, reduced to its simplest terms, is a sense that there is *something wrong about us* as we naturally stand.
>   The solution is a sense that *we are saved from the wrongness* by making proper connection with the higher powers.
>
> (James 1997: 377)

Do such "higher powers" actually exist outside the self or only within the ever-fertile human imagination? With this question we enter the realm of what James called "over-beliefs." However, he did think that Frederick Myers' concept of the subconscious might be useful in explaining where the "fountain-head" that feeds religion might be located.

James was very much a believer in what he called a "pluralistic universe." Monisms of all kinds suffocated him religiously, morally, and intellectually. The universe in which he preferred to live is open, evolving, ever-changing, and full of many surprises. James thought that philosophies exhibited what he called "tender and tough" minded attitudes.

The artistic and mystical side of James was not always in harmony with his scientific side, but he tried to strike a balance in both his life and his thought. His ideas are still influential not only because they contribute to our understanding of religion, but also because there is a little bit of tough- and tender-mindedness in all of us.

See also: **Asad, Freud, Hick, Jung, Otto, W. C. Smith, Tillich**

Major works

(1967) *Essays in Radical Empiricism and A Pluralistic Universe,* Gloucester, MA: Peter Smith.

(1975–88) *The Works of William James,* Cambridge, MA: Harvard University Press.

(1997) *The Varieties of Religious Experience: A Study in Human Nature,* New York: Simon and Schuster.

Further reading

Clifford, William K. (1897) *Lectures and Essays,* Vol. 2, London: Macmillan.

Gale, Richard M. (1999) *The Divided Self of William James,* Cambridge: Cambridge University Press.

Perry, Ralph Barton. (1935) *The Thought and Character of William James,* 2 vols, Boston, MA: Little, Brown and Company.

Proudfoot, Wayne. (2004) *William James and a Science of Religions,* New York: Columbia University Press.

Suckiel, Ellen Kappy. (1996) *Heaven's Champion: William James's Philosophy of Religion,* Notre Dame, IN: University of Notre Dame Press.

Taylor, Charles. (2002) *Varieties of Religion Today: William James Revisited,* Cambridge, MA: Harvard University Press.

http://plato.stanford.edu/entries/james/.

FRIEDRICH NIETZSCHE (1844–1900)

Have you not heard of that madman who lit a lantern in the bright morning hours, ran to the market place, and cried incessantly, "I seek God! I seek God!" ... "Whither is God?" he cried. "I shall tell you. We have killed him—you and I. All of us are his murderers. But how have we done this? How were we able to drink up the sea? Who gave us the sponge to wipe away the entire horizon? What did we do when we unchained this earth from its sun? ... Do we not smell anything yet of God's decomposition? Gods too decompose. God is dead. God remains dead. And we have killed him.

(Nietzsche 1974: 95–96)

What on earth (and in heaven for that matter) could the philosopher and cultural critic Friedrich Nietzsche have meant by claiming that God is dead? How could humans kill him? On the surface it seems nonsense because one thing people normally mean by God is a being that is not only eternal, but also infinitely more powerful than humans. However, if we substitute the word Absolute for God, as **Hegel** had done in his philosophy, then the "madman" can be read as claiming that the comfortable absolutes of nineteenth century European culture are no longer viable. The age of relativism and a sense of ultimate meaninglessness have dawned. For Nietzsche the death of God is a cultural fact with profound implications because it forces humanity to confront nihilism (nothingness).

On October 15, 1844 a son was born to a Lutheran pastor, Karl Ludwig Nietzsche, and his wife Franziska in a small town near Leipzig, and was named after the Prussian King, Friedrich Wilhelm IV. At the age of four Friedrich Nietzsche's father died, and from fourteen to nineteen Nietzsche attended a boarding school located near Naumburg, where the family had moved. In 1864 he entered the University of Bonn, intent on studying theology and philology. After graduation, he won a teaching position at the University of Basel but his health (he had contracted diphtheria and dysentery during the Franco–Prussian War) forced his resignation in 1879. He spent the rest of his life traveling about Europe and writing, until he experienced a mental breakdown in 1889. Family members, especially his sister Elisabeth, cared for him for the rest of his life.

What are the implications of the "death of God"? It implies, Nietzsche argued, that the basic assumptions of art, philosophy, science, morality, and religion are without any ultimate foundation. If there are no absolutes, then the cultural products of human culture amount to little more than useful fictions. We hide this from ourselves by confusing human constructs with reality itself.

Culture, Nietzsche claimed, is an expression of two visions of reality. One is Apollonian (named after Apollo, the Greek god of reason), which values rationality, order, and restraint. It is linear, unemotional, prudential, and disinterested. The other vision Nietzsche called Dionysian (named after the Greek god of wine, Dionysus). It celebrates irrationality, chaos, freedom, and emotion. Both attitudes, the Apollonian love of discipline and the Dioynsian love of ecstasy, express our humanity, but European culture had repressed the Dionysian element and celebrated the Apollonian vision. Hence Western culture is unbalanced, distorted, and repressive.

Conventional morality is essentially Apollonian, imposing law and order on the passions. It takes two forms: a "master morality" that celebrates strength and bravery, and a "slave morality" that glorifies weakness and humility. Christianity promotes a slave morality and claims the authority of God, but this kind of morality is generated out of the resentment the slave feels for the master. Nietzsche called Christianity the "one great curse" that arises out of the instinct for revenge but masks this truth by preaching service and selflessness. It denies everything noble about being human.

Nietzsche applied his criticism with insight, passion, and anger, as he sought to show that the absolutes assumed by conventional practices are empty. European culture and society are deeply conflicted and in denial of a truth it cannot face—the center no longer holds. Values are made up, they have a history or genealogy, and a careful tracing of the genealogy of central concepts like truth, beauty, and goodness reveals no solid ground, but ever-shifting quicksand.

Numerous critics have accused Nietzsche of promoting a nihilistic philosophy, but he was trying to combat a nihilism he saw coming once comfortable assumptions and values began to crumble. For Nietzsche, the "death of God" implies more than a dawning sense of meaninglessness. It implies freedom and opportunity if only humans can admit the truth and seize the day. God's death is not only a source of our despair but also our liberation.

However, this liberation cannot be realized without a "transvaluation of values." For such a transvaluation to take place, we must honestly acknowledge the death of all concepts of the absolute, understand that a basic "will to power" or vital life-creating energy animates history and nature, and strive to become the "Overman" (*Übermensch*) who realizes and rejoices in absolute freedom.

Although the Overman can be interpreted in different ways, one way is to view it as a metaphor for a transformed humanity that has the courage to acknowledge that it is the source of all value and the discipline to control and sublimate its passions in harmony with the will to power. To be in harmony with this will is to live each moment authentically, that is, as if each moment would recur eternally. This "eternal recurrence," as Nietzsche called it, requires a courageous, joyous, and noble life lived with the full knowledge that this life is all there is. There is no meaning beyond this existence and no God to make things right. To go beyond the coming nihilism we must learn to live so authentically that we are willing to have our lives, just as they are, with all their ups and downs, pains and sorrows, repeated over and over again for eternity.

Many factors influenced Nietzsche's thinking. He lived during the industrial revolution when unfettered capitalism was creating great wealth among the few and horrible poverty among the many. Nationalism and imperialism were on the rise and a repressive Victorian morality ruled the day. The knowledge explosion in the sciences and the implications of Darwin's theory of evolution were showing the old established "truths" of religion to be suspect. Hegelianism was in retreat and new information about how the Christian church had created the Bible was spreading. Nietzsche's own reading of Christian history convinced him that the Church had distorted the message of Jesus by accommodating the gospel to cultural and political conditions. His study of classical Greek humanism showed him that the sources of Western civilization were at odds with its present state. His own rebellion against a harsh and strict Lutheran upbringing led him to see himself as a lonely rebel and prophet ahead of his time.

Critics find, among other things, a basic inconsistency between his attack on absolutes and his own advocacy for ideas like the Overman and will to power. Yet his ideas have stimulated artists, psychologists, sociologists, historians, philosophers, theologians, and religion scholars. His genealogical method of analysis (tracing the history of the development of a concept) and his perspectivism (denial of any God's-eye view from which all can be seen clearly) have proved particularly rich sources for scholars of religion to mine in rethinking more traditional theological approaches. In his notebooks of the 1880s, Nietzsche stated repeatedly, "there are no facts, only interpretations." Perhaps the multitude of differing interpretations and evaluations of his ideas provide evidence for the truth of that aphorism, a truth the aphorism itself seems to deny.

See also: **Asad, Buber, Derrida, Feuerbach, Foucault, Freud, Kierkegaard, Tillich, Turner**

Major works

(1966) *Beyond Good and Evil,* trans. Walter Kaufmann, New York: Random House.

(1967a) *On the Genealogy of Morals and Ecce Homo,* trans. Walter Kaufmann, New York: Random House.

(1967b) *The Birth of Tragedy and The Case of Wagner,* trans. Walter Kaufmann, New York: Random House.

(1967c) *The Will to Power,* trans. Walter Kaufmann, New York: Random House.

(1968) *The Portable Nietzsche*, trans. and ed. Walter Kaufman, New York: Viking Press.

(1974) *The Gay Science, with a Prelude of Rhymes and an Appendix of Songs*, trans. Walter Kaufmann, New York: Random House.

(1979) *Philosophy and Truth: Selections from Nietzsche's Notebooks of the Early 1870's*, trans. and ed. Daniel Breazeale, Atlantic Highlands, NJ: Humanities Press.

(1986) *Human, All Too Human: A Book for Free Spirits*, trans. R. J. Hollingdale, Cambridge: Cambridge University Press.

Further reading

Bataille, Georges. (1992) *On Nietzsche*, trans. Bruce Boone, London: Athlone Press.

Danto, Arthur C. (1965) *Nietzsche as Philosopher: An Original Study*, New York: Columbia University Press.

Kaufmann, Walter. (1975) *Nietzsche: Philosopher, Psychologist, Anti-Christ*, 4e., Princeton, NJ: Princeton University Press.

Solomon, Robert C. (2003) *Living With Nietzsche: What the Great "Immoralist" Has to Teach Us*, Oxford: Oxford University Press.

http://plato.stanford.edu/entries/nietzsche.

JANE HARRISON (1850–1928)

> Every religion contains two elements. There is first what a man *thinks* about the unseen ... second, what he *does* in relation to this unseen—his ritual. In primitive religions, though these two elements are clearly to be distinguished, they are never, or very rarely, separable. In all living religions these two elements are informed and transfused by a third impulse—that of each man's personal emotion towards the unseen, his sense of dependence on it, his fear, his hope, his love.
>
> (*The Religion of Ancient Greece*, 1905: 7–8)

With these words Jane Harrison, a classical scholar and member of the Cambridge Ritualists (see **Frazer**), succinctly stated her view that myths (what people think) are always or nearly always connected with rituals (what people do). Although strongly influenced by **Tylor**'s evolutionary theory of religion, she goes beyond his focus on belief by adding both action and emotion as key aspects of any complete theory of religion.

Jane Ellen Harrison was born in Cottingham, Yorkshire. Early in life she exhibited an aptitude for languages and eventually learned sixteen different languages including her specialties, Latin and Greek.

She was one of the first women to attend Cambridge University, where she studied classical art and literature. She helped to broaden classical scholarship by supplementing the traditional study of ancient texts with the study of art, archeology, anthropology, and sociology. Harrison was supportive of the suffragette movement and took as her motto Terence's statement, "I am a human being; nothing human is alien to me."

Among her many writings, three were the most influential: *Prolegomena to the History of Greek Religion* (1903), *Themis* (1912), and *Epilegomena* (1921). In the *Prolegomena*, Harrison described two forms of ritual, Olympian and Chthonic (of earth or underworld). The Olympian rites centered on sacrificial offerings to the gods with the hope of currying their favor. Its principle was *do ut des*, "I give in order that you give." The Chthonic rites had to do with the spirits of the underworld. Its principle was *do abeas*, "I give in order that you leave and stay away."

This distinction led Harrison to analyze three important festivals: Anthestoria, Thargelia, and Thesmophoria. The Anthesteria was celebrated in spring and centered on the placation of ghosts. Its goal was to purge evil forces so that fertility might flourish. The Thargelia, which was celebrated in summer, was primarily a fertility rite whose goal was to preserve and promote fertility. The Thesmophoria, celebrated in autumn, centered on the promotion of fertility by magical rites involving the handling of sacred objects thought to possess magical powers.

All three of these rites are, according to Harrison, concerned with the necessity of purification to remove the contamination of evil influences. If evil was not expelled from the community, then crops and animals would become infertile and the very life of people would be threatened.

On this substrate of Greek ritual life (centered as it was on aversion to evil and the promotion of fertility) a new missionary religion built a different set of rituals. The Dionysian cult took an old god of vegetation (Dionysus was the god of wine) and introduced the emotional element of enthusiasm. Initially, enthused states were induced by intoxication, but eventually other techniques were developed to induce ecstasy. This development was strongly influenced by the association of the god of music—Orpheus—with Dionysius. Orphism made possible the development of the notion that humans could attain the divine attribute of immortality by a mystical union with the god. The idea that purgation could banish evil expanded to include the notion that it could also issue in immortality for humans.

Previously, only a few exceptional individuals could attain divinity by becoming heroes. Now, via initiation into the divine mysteries (so called because initiates took a vow never to reveal the secret rites) of Orpheus, anyone could become immortal.

In *Themis*, Harrison made the case that the Eniautos-Daimon "lies behind each and every primitive god." Harrison created the term Eniautos-Daimon in order to label a spirit (*daimon*) that represents the periodic processes of decay, death, and rebirth. Her focus was on the "*dromenon*" (thing done and redone with magical intent) in spring rituals to insure the victory of life over death. Introducing the ideas of the French sociologist **Durkheim**, she argued that the Daimon represents the unity of the social group and stood behind two main features of Greek cultural life—athletic contests and drama. In both, death followed by rebirth was represented as a contest resulting in a victory. The *agon* connects both since it refers to the contest for a prize in athletic games such as the Olympics and the verbal contest between characters in Greek tragedies.

Harrison also found the Eniautos-Daimon behind the semi-divine heroes of Greek mythology. The mythic heroes are basically functionaries that represent the permanent life of the group. By performing heroic feats and overcoming great odds, they celebrate the ability of the social group to go on even as individual members die. Although she emphasized the social function of the Eniautos-Daimon, Harrison also reminded her readers that this figure represents not only the life of the group but also the life of nature, thereby exhibiting the unity of human life with the life cycles of the natural world.

In the course of her analysis of Greek rituals, Harrison underscored the contention of the Cambridge Ritualists who argued that myth and ritual go together. So Harrison declares in *Themis*, "The primary meaning of myth … is the spoken correlative of the acted rite, the thing done." (328). In other words, myths are like scripts for plays or librettos for operas. They are what is said over what is done and both have the magical intent of renewing the life of the community and nature on which the community depends. Sometimes she claimed myths and rituals arise together, and at other times she said that ritual actions precede myths. Whatever their relationship may be, she is certain that all of art, and especially dramas, were derived from religious rituals.

Harrison's contribution to the study of religion expands the horizons beyond **Müller**'s views about the "disease of language" giving rise to nature/solar mythology and **Tylor**'s views that religion evolved out of primitive animistic beliefs that found expression in mistaken attempts to explain the world, attempts we now call mythology. For Harrison religion involves more than beliefs and myths, it has both a ritualistic and emotional dimension that is prior to the formulation of beliefs and stories about gods and goddesses. She also took seriously psychological, archeological, and sociological theories, thereby expanding classical studies beyond a narrow focus on literature. Ultimately, however, the myth/ritual school's influence waned as it became increasingly obvious that not all myths are connected to rituals and vice versa.

Today few if any scholars of religion would subscribe to the ideas of the myth/ritual school. However, Harrison's studies remain valuable because they remind us that narrative and action are often closely connected in religion and that other cultural phenomena like literature, art, and drama have important, though often hidden, connections to the religious impulse to celebrate and control unseen forces.

See also: **Burkert, Dumézil, van Gennep, Nietzsche, Schleiermacher**

Major works

(1903) *Prolegomena to the Study of Greek Religion*, Cambridge: Cambridge University Press.
(1905) *The Religion of Ancient Greece*, London: Archibald Constable and Co.
(1912) *Themis: A Study of the Social Origins of Greek Religion*, Cambridge: Cambridge University Press.
(1913) *Ancient Art and Ritual*, London: Williams and Norgate.
(1921) *Epilegomena to the Study of Greek Religion*, Cambridge: Cambridge University Press.
(1924) *Mythology*, Boston: Marshall Jones Company.
(1925) *Reminiscences of a Student's Life*, London: Hogarth.

Further reading

Ackerman, Robert. (1991) *The Myth and Ritual School*, New York: Garland Publishing.
Robinson, Annabel. (2002) *The Life and Work of Jane Ellen Harrison*, Oxford: Oxford University Press.
Stewart, Jessie. (1959) *Jane Ellen Harrison*, London: Merlin Press.
http://en.wikipedia.org/wiki/Jane_Ellen_Harrison.

JAMES G. FRAZER (1854–1941)

> We have seen that on the one hand magic is nothing but a mistaken application of the simplest and most elementary process of the mind, namely the association of ideas by virtue of resemblance or contiguity; and that on the other hand religion assumes the operation of conscious or personal agents, superior to man, behind the visible screen of nature. ... Thus, if magic be deduced immediately from elementary processes of reasoning, it becomes probable that magic arose before religion in the evolution of our race, and that man essayed to bend nature to his wishes by the sheer force of spells and enchantments before he strove to coax and mollify a coy, capricious, or irascible deity by the soft insinuations of prayer and sacrifice.
>
> (Frazer 1900: 51)

With these words James G. Frazer, a British anthropologist and historian of religion, tried to capture not only the distinction between religion and magic but also their evolutionary relationship. For him, magic aims to control nature and thereby the welfare of humans by dealing with supposed impersonal forces. Religion, however, attempts to control nature by dealing with personal agents. Assuming what is simple comes before what is complex, he placed the origin of magic earlier than religion and both exist side by side today. Although he did not mention it in the above quotation, Frazer thought the progression does not stop with religion. Science follows as the next stage and while it shares with magic the idea that impersonal forces control nature, science unlike magic, has discerned the true nature of these forces and developed appropriate technology for dealing with them.

James George Frazer was born in Glasgow. His parents were devout members of the conservative Free Church of Scotland. He entered the University of Glasgow at the age of fifteen and eventually secured a position as fellow of Trinity College, Cambridge. In 1896 he married a writer, Elizabeth Grove. Although Frazer published many books throughout his life time, he is best known for the multi-volume *The Golden Bough* (third edition, 1911–15), which became the most influential work on religion for many years.

It was noteworthy because it did something never done before—it treated the classical religion of Greece and Rome as if it were "primitive," describing parallels selected from the vast array of anthropological data being amassed from around the world. Moreover, it read like a mystery novel, beginning with a dramatic description of a strange and ancient ritual combat that took place at the Temple of Diana (a goddess of the hunt, fertility, and childbirth) outside of Rome. This mysterious event raised a number of questions that Frazer set out to answer, and his answers have had a wide-ranging influence on modern scholarship, art, literature, and culture.

In a wooded grove at Nemi, the rule was that any runaway slave who managed to kill the "priest" who guarded the shrine would gain his freedom. There was, as is so often the case, a catch. The victorious slave would now become the guardian and either kill or be killed in turn. He watched over a temple and a sacred oak tree that had a yellow branch or "golden bough." This guardian was called the "King of the Wood" and, although obviously human, was also regarded as a divine lover of Diana and the animating spirit of the sacred oak tree. A "sacred marriage" was annually celebrated between the "King of the Wood" and a female spirit in order to induce fecundity. This sacred marriage ritually embodied the idea that sexual intercourse promotes vegetation.

According to Frazer, what we know about Roman religion could not explain this strange rite. It required comparative analysis with similar ritual combats around the world. This analysis showed that the guardian at Nemi was a priest-king who, because he represented the life of both nature and society, had to be kept well and alive as long as possible. If the priest-king should weaken and die, the fertility of nature and the life of the community would die unless his power was transferred to a successor. He not only ritually symbolized divine fertility, but also embodied that power within his person.

This analysis led Frazer into lengthy discussions of taboo, magic, sacrifice, and scapegoats because these constitute strategies adopted for protecting the priest-king. These discussions reveal that Frazer's primary concern is with how the "primitive mind" works, a topic of great curiosity in his day. He argued the he could uncover the laws by which the "primitive" reasoned because of the "law of similarity." Following **Tylor**'s idea of "survivals" and adopting his notion that humans have, both mentally and physically, evolved in a uniform fashion, Frazer reconstructed primitive mentality by comparing numerous examples from different times and places.

The struggle to survive played a central role in the life of "savages." Whenever animals or crops were needed to eat, ancient peoples sought ways to insure an abundant supply. Their efforts took the form of sympathetic magic. They assumed that nature works by "sympathies" or influences of one sort or another because they thought that if two things can be mentally associated, then they are also physically associated. Specialists (magicians) were enlisted to discover these influences and try to control them. The means devised centered on the principles that "like affects like" and "part affects part." Hence two types of magic were developed: imitative and contagious. Thus during a drought the magician pours water through a screen so that it *looks like* (imitates) falling water. Similar events should produce similar results. A voodoo priest puts the hair of his victim on a doll and pushes pins through it because at one time the hair was in contact with the victim. What is done to it is done to him because the items on the doll were once in contact (contagion) with the intended victim.

Frazer was fascinated by how "scientific" all this was. Like science, magic assumed certain invariant laws of nature such as cause and effect, and like science it developed technologies (spells, incantations, manipulation of material objects) in an attempt to exploit these laws for the benefit of people. In spite of the similarities, there is, nevertheless, a vast difference. Scientific understanding of the laws of nature is correct and the magician's understanding is mistaken. Magic is mistaken science. And because it is mistaken, it inevitably declines as more people begin to realize that it does not always work.

Religion arises with the decline of magic and the priest-king slowly replaces the magician-king. Religion rejects the idea of impersonal forces or influences and replaces it with the idea that the real power controlling nature is personal. Humans must now learn how to get these personal forces—spirits and deities—to do what they want. Prayers, supplications, vows, now become far more important to insure human welfare than spells and incantations. The power of the magician-king resides in his specialized knowledge of spells designed to compel the secret forces of nature, but the power of the priest-king resides in his ability to persuade the gods. It is not surprising then that priest-kings were often elevated to divine status and people came to see their very lives and the life of their world as dependent on the power of the priest-kings to influence the gods.

However, if it is so vital to keep the priest-king alive, why allow a ritual combat in which the priest-king was eventually slain? The short answer is because the "King of the Wood" (as Frazer called him) embodied the power of fertility and life in his very person so his strength had to be periodically tested. If he was infirm someone had to replace him who was strong enough to sustain the spirit of fertility. So the priest-king was either sacrificed, deposed, or killed in single combat by an incumbent. This action parallels the pattern of nature. Life is followed by decay followed by death followed by new life. The death and resurrection stories found in many religions including Christianity echo this theme. Better that one die so the many can live. And the shout still goes up, "The king is dead; long live the [new] king."

Frazer's massive study, covering far more topics than we can possibly discuss here, reinforced the growing consensus that religion and magic can be understood "scientifically" by careful comparison of diverse cases. Supernatural and theological explanations such as those that prevailed before are of little use in explaining religion. *The Golden Bough* supported the idea that we can explain religion by discovering its origin. Furthermore, we can *actually* discover it even though its beginnings have long faded into the mists of time.

Although Frazer's work was immensely influential at the time, its influence slowly waned (at least among scholars) as scholarly criticism mounted. Anthropologists found his method wanting because it ignored the social and historical context of his examples and thereby overlooked important differences. In addition, Frazer drew conclusions based on a limited number of similarities among his examples. He seemed to believe that every ancient story of death and resurrection must somehow relate to the strange goings-on in the ancient woods outside of Rome. As anthropological fieldwork grew in importance, Frazer eventually was used as the prime example of an "armchair anthropologist" to warn graduate students about how *not* to do anthropology. Nevertheless, many of his ideas became the springboard for other theorists, among them the so-called Cambridge Ritualists (also called the "Myth and Ritual School") who emphasized the importance of ritual and viewed it as the source of myth, drama, and literature.

See also: **Bellah, Burkert, Dumézil, Durkheim, Evans-Pritchard, Freud, van Gennep, Harrison, Lévy-Bruhl, Malinowski, Radcliffe-Brown, J. Z. Smith**

Major works

Macmillan (London) published all of the following.

(1900) *The Golden Bough: A Study of Magic and Religion.*
(1910) *Totemism and Exogamy: A Treatise on Certain Early Forms of Superstition and Society,* 4 vols.
(1911–15) *The Golden Bough,* 12 vols.
(1918) *Folklore in the Old Testament: Studies in Comparative Religion, Legend, and Law,* 3 vols.

Further reading

Fraser, Robert and Robert Ackerman. (1980) *J. G. Frazer: His Life and Work, and The Making of the Golden Bough*, New York: Palgrave Macmillan.

——(2002) *The Myth and Ritual School: J. G. Frazer and the Cambridge Ritualists*, London: Routledge.
Gaster, Theodor, ed. (1959) *The New Golden Bough: A New Abridgment of the Classic Work*, New York: Criterion.
http://en.wikipedia.org/wiki/James_Frazer.

SIGMUND FREUD (1856–1939)

> Religion would thus be the universal obsessional neurosis of humanity.
>
> (Freud 1965: 70–71)

With this bold statement, Sigmund Freud summed up one of many conclusions he drew about religion based on insights gained from his psychoanalytic studies. The parallels between the repetitive behaviors characteristic of neurotic obsessions and religious rituals convinced him that religion was a psychological illness that humans needed to outgrow. This insight, he thought, explains why people continue to hold strange religious beliefs and practice irrational rituals akin to magic even in a scientific age.

Sigmund Freud, best known as the father of psychoanalysis, was the son of a Jewish merchant of modest means. He was born in Freiburg, Moravia but his family moved to Vienna when he was four. He was educated in both classics and science. He entered the University of Vienna to study law, but his interests turned to medicine. He graduated in 1881 and married Martha Bernays. His early work on hysteria, with Dr. Josef Breuer, led to the development of a theory about the unconscious mind.

The unconscious is a name for those drives and forces, affecting both personality and behavior, that are unknown to the conscious mind. It contains repressed material that can be uncovered by psychoanalytic therapy. Making the unconscious conscious brings it under the control of the ego (Latin for "I") and hence under the control of rational thought.

The ego is one of three powers of the personality. It functions to integrate the other two powers, which Freud famously called the id (Latin for "it") and the superego (Latin for "above I"). The function of the id is to discharge energy in accord with the pleasure principle. When I am hungry, I want to find food and eat. The id urges me to do just that. But the function of the superego is to try to control this discharge of id-energy by imposing moral and social constraints on the natural pursuit of pleasure. It tells me that I cannot eat anything and everything whenever I am hungry. The superego is formed as we internalize the constraints and prohibitions of parents and society. Religion plays a key role in this process in most societies.

Inevitably conflicts arise between id energy seeking its pleasure and superego constraints. How can these conflicts be resolved without the complete disintegration of the personality? The answer lies in the ego. Its integrative role seeks to reconcile the demands of superego and id in the interests of the total personality according to the reality principle (what is physically and socially possible). The ego or choosing center of each of us has an inherently difficult problem balancing the desires of the id with the restraints of the superego in light of what is possible given the realities of life.

The exchange of psychic energy among the three aspects of personality—id, superego, and ego—is seldom perfect. Hence humans often become neurotic in their attempts to reconcile conflicting urges, especially if they have experienced a trauma early in life. A neurosis is a mental illness that does not seem to have an organic basis and does not result in a loss of contact with reality but does produce symptoms such as obsessive behavior, anxiety, and depression. Could it be that religion, with its repetitive rituals, guilt over sin, and obsessions with purity, is a kind of neurosis?

Freud touched on the topic of religion in a number of different writings and devoted three books to the topic. He regarded *Totem and Taboo* (1913) as one of his best but *The Future of an Illusion* (1927) is probably more widely read today. *Moses and Monotheism* (1939) was published in the year of his death and gathers essays written between 1934 and 1938.

In *Totem and Taboo* Freud turned his attention to developing a psychological understanding of "primitive" peoples. Like **Tylor** and **Frazer** he assumes that humans have not only evolved physically, but also mentally. Furthermore, he understood evolution as, however unsteady, a gradual upward progress of social institutions and intellectual abilities.

Freud focused his study on two practices that seem strange to modern thinking: taboos that forbid particular behaviors, and the worship of animals and plants as **totems** or ancestors of clans and tribes. One of the most widespread taboos was the incest taboo and the demand that marriage be exogamous or outside the family or clan. To this "horror of incest" were added rules forbidding the killing and eating of the **totem** animal. However, on certain ceremonial occasions this taboo was broken and the **totem** animal was killed and consumed. Freud asked why? What might explain such strange beliefs and behaviors? A clue to the answer can be found in the fact that it makes no sense to forbid what people do not desire to do. Although few would admit incestuous, murderous, and cannibalistic desires toward their kin, these are unconscious desires that emerge, albeit in symbolic forms, in dreams. Postulating such desires immediately makes sense of the elaborate rules, regulations, rituals, and taboos surrounding **totems** and marriage.

Freud postulated a primal horde at the beginning of the human race in which the father controlled all the females much as silverback gorillas dominate family groups. The sons, out of frustration, eventually band together, kill the father and eat him to gain his powers. This act of rebellion allows the sons to take possession of the females. There is, however, danger in this revolt, as the sons soon realize. They not only feel guilt arising from the murder of their father but also begin to fight for power. Spurred on by both guilt and rivalry, they form brotherhoods and renounce the ideal of any one of them possessing all the females. The results are the incest taboo and exogamy. The **totem** itself developed as a substitute for the father. The totemic feast of sacrificing and eating the totem unconsciously celebrates the victory of the sons over the father and provides an opportunity to appease the fear and guilt stemming from the primal murder. Emotional ambivalence—both hating and loving the same thing—can be found at the very beginning of human civilization.

Anyone familiar with Freud's notion of the Oedipus complex (the unconscious desire of sons to kill their fathers and sexually possesses their mothers) can immediately recognize how Freud applied it to explaining the origins of religion. However, it explains more than that. It also explains the origins of morality and society. The agreements among primal bands of sons constitute the first "social contract" as well as the origin of such taboos as "Thou shall not kill."

Even the development of the so-called higher religions can be understood as a natural development out of **totemism**. The **totemic** celebration obviously presupposes that the spirit of the primal father somehow lives in the **totem**. It is a short step to polytheism or the belief that the many spirits that animate nature and society are gods. Finally, the primal father is projected as one god living in the sky who is the creator of all things including all humans. With this step monotheism is born. While these steps may be short intellectually, they evolved over thousands of years in different places and times.

Dim reflections of the primal murder can still be seen in modern religious rituals that Christians celebrate, such as Holy Communion or Mass. In the Lord's Supper Christians celebrate the death of God's only son and share his body and blood, represented by bread and wine. Here we can see the partial return to consciousness of the original primal murder because the son of the father God is no less than God himself. Only this time the sons sacrifice one of their own in order to appease the wrath of the father and remove their guilt.

In *The Future of an Illusion* Freud argued that civilization could not exist without the sacrifice of some instinctual desires. If it is to sustain itself, it must provide some kind of recompense for such sacrifice. Religion is one of the means created by civilization to provide the necessary compensation. It does so by exorcising the terrors of nature (e.g. miracles), reconciling humans to the cruelty of inevitable death (e.g. eternal life), and rewarding people for moral behavior (e.g. social and divine approval).

Religious beliefs are not "delusions" because they *might* be true, but they are "illusions". They cannot be proved to be true or false by either empirical or logical investigation, they result from wishful thinking, and do not contradict reality (all features of neurosis). Civilization has needed this illusion in the past, but now, Freud was confident, science can assume the functions of religion without recourse to illusions. Science, in particular psychoanalysis, can finally free civilization of its religious neurosis.

In *Moses and Monotheism*, Freud explored the development of monotheism in more detail. He argued that Moses (who has an Egyptian name) was really an Egyptian who saw in the Hebrew slaves the possibility of restoring the religion of his mentor, the Pharaoh Iknaton. Iknaton had introduced monotheism to Egypt by proclaiming the sun god (Aton) the one and only god, much to the chagrin of the established priesthood whose power derived from polytheistic worship. Moses teaches monotheism to the Hebrews and leads a revolt against the Egyptian overlords. His Hebrew converts eventually kill him, having become disillusioned by the hardships of the journey to the Promised Land. These events rekindle the repressed memories of the primal murder and the "original sin" and guilt associated with the sons rebelling against the father. But the memories are distorted because the primal murder is too traumatic to be faced openly without a symbolic and religious disguise.

In explicating and developing his theory of religion as a group neurosis, Freud was careful to draw parallels with the genesis of neurosis he had discovered in his clinical work. First there is a trauma (primal murder) followed by the development of defense mechanisms (**totems** and taboos), which in turn is followed by a period of latency (development of polytheism). Eventually there is an outbreak and partial return of the repressed material but still in symbolic form (Moses, Monotheism, Christianity). Healing occurs through discovery of the true events behind the symbols because then the illusion that is religion will, once exposed, disappear.

Freud's theory of religion, and the analogy he draws between religion and neurosis, sparked both controversy and converts. One persistent criticism is the limitations of the theory. It purports to be a theory of religion, but at best it is primarily a theory of monotheistic religions, in particular Judaism and Christianity. His theory of the development of religion relies heavily on an analogy between historical events and the development of neurosis in individuals. Not only is that analogy doubtful, but also it is circular. He wanted to show that religion is a neurosis and, in order to do so, he looked at people who are psychologically ill and then argued by analogy to religion. It is little wonder that this results in the conclusion we quoted at the outset.

In spite of the problems with his theory of religion, it is difficult to underestimate Freud's impact on the modern world. He is one of a handful of thinkers who transformed the way people think of themselves. Just as Albert Einstein's idea of relativity transformed physics, so Freud's idea of the unconscious opened up hidden dimensions of the human psyche. His ideas influenced **C. G. Jung**, among others, although **Jung** came to see the positive benefits of religion in helping people overcome their problems, and broke with Freud.

See also: **Boyer, Burkert, Dumézil, Durkheim, Eliade, Feuerbach, Geertz, James, Malinowski**

Major works

(1953) *The Standard Edition of the Complete Psychological Works of Sigmund Freud*, trans. and ed. James Strachey in collaboration with Anna Freud, London: Hogarth Press.

(1965)*The Future of an Illusion*, trans. W. D. Robson-Scott, Garden City, New York: Doubleday and Company.

Further reading

Gay, Peter. (1987) *A Godless Jew: Freud, Atheism, and the Making of Psychoanalysis*, New Haven, NJ: Yale University Press.
——(1988) *Freud: A Life for Our Times*, New York: W. W. Norton.
Herzog, Patricia. (1991) *Conscious and Unconscious: Freud's Dynamic Distinction Reconsidered*, Madison, CT: International Universities Press.

Robinson, Paul. (1993) *Freud and His Critics*, Berkeley, CA: University of California Press.
www.iep.utm.edu/f/freud.htm.

LUCIEN LÉVY-BRUHL (1857–1939)

> The reality surrounding the primitives is itself mystical.
>
> (Lévy-Bruhl 1966: 25)

What might this statement mean? Who are the so-called "primitives?" Are they somehow inferior to "civilized" people? And what does "mystical" mean? Does Lévy-Bruhl want to imply that modern people are not mystical? These and a host of other questions surround Lévy-Bruhl's claim that so-called primitives thought very differently from the way we do and consequently experienced the world differently. His goal was to explain the difference.

Lévy-Bruhl was born on April 10, 1857 in Paris. Torn between a career in music or in philosophy, he finally decided on the latter course of study, graduating in 1879 from the École normale supérieure. He earned his doctor's degree in 1884 and was appointed to the Sorbonne in 1896. He wrote several important works on philosophy but eventually became interested in the then emerging field of sociology, which, along with anthropology, was probing the way of life and thought among people very different from educated "civilized" Europeans. Ironically, just as Europeans were becoming more secularized and less religious they became more fascinated by what appeared to be the intense religiosity of what they called "primitives," that had been colonized by European countries in their relentless search for resources.

In his first two books, translated into English with the titles *Primitive Mentality* (1923) and *How Natives Think* (1926), Lévy-Bruhl criticized the work of **Tylor** and **Frazer** and set off in a new direction, a direction that placed less emphasis on evolutionary continuity and more emphasis on basic differences between what he called the "primitive mentality" in contrast to "civilized thought."

The key to understanding the differences is to recognize the role that emotion plays in primitive mentality. Primitives are no less rational than moderns, nor should we think of them as childlike precursors of the "higher" European civilizations. Both civilized and primitive peoples are rational, but their interests and concerns move in a different direction because they allow a larger role for emotions. This leads to a mystical orientation in the sense that invisible powers often represented as spirits or gods color their experiences of the world. Hence visions and dreams play a larger role in their lives and hidden, less "objective" associations often determine how they evaluate and react to objects and events. Observations that might refute their beliefs such as the failure of magical healing rites to bring health do not disturb their beliefs because the evidence of sight, so important to the scientist, is not their primary concern. They revere tradition and if tradition says that a certain ritual works, then it works no matter what others may say.

The law of causality plays a crucial role in civilized societies but not in primitive societies. There is another law, which Lévy-Bruhl called the "law of participation," that trumps concerns with discovering causal connections. According to this law, humans participate in the life of other humans and even non-human animals and inanimate objects to the point of virtual identity. So a stone can be both itself and a spirit. If a man and a tiger arouse the same emotional association, then that man is a tiger. Things and events are linked not by causality but by mystical participation.

This mystical orientation leads to an indifference to logical contradictions. So the primitive is not much concerned when someone objects to his claim that a powerful sorcerer can be in two places at the same time. Unfortunately Lévy-Bruhl labeled this "indifference" as a "pre-logical mentality," a term widely associated with his views on religion. He does not, however, mean that primitive peoples are unable to recognize contradictions. Nor does he mean that their religion is prior to the development of logical reasoning and hence illogical. Rather he means that the law of participation takes precedence over the law of causality and of contradiction. However, persistent misinterpretations of the term "pre-logical" eventually led him to abandon its use.

The myths and rituals of primitives seem so strange to moderns that many have come to think of them as irrational or at least so simple and childlike as to be inferior to civilized peoples. They and their religious beliefs and practices are on a lower rung of the evolutionary ladder. Lévy-Bruhl was at pains to say "not so." Rather, unlike moderns who separate themselves from the world and seek to master it through science, primitives see themselves in communion with the world and seek to feel its interconnections. The anthropologist Robin Horton summarizes this sense of communion as follows:

> In the first place, because primitive man's every perception is so heavily invested with emotion, he does not so much perceive the world around him as feel it. Secondly, because this emotion arises

within him as well as investing what he perceives, he himself is involved in a continual participation in the world. Finally, because men, animals, plants and inert things are equally associated with mystical influences, there is a tendency to confront all categories of such objects as though they were in some sense personal—i.e. in some sense fellow subjects. Primitive man, then, is more accurately described as communing with the world about him than as perceiving it.

(Horton 1993: 66)

Although some criticized Lévy-Bruhl for nearly ignoring the sociology of primitive thought, he did place the ideas of participation and communion in a social context. One of his key concerns was with the role "collective representations" play in the primitive's experience of the world. The mentality of individuals is derived from the common notions found in their society. In primitive societies individuals are subordinated to the community and its aims because the cooperation of the whole community is necessary for survival. Therefore it is not surprising that beliefs about gods, witches, the effectiveness of rites and so on are acquired by accepting the authority of socializing agents rather than independent and critical scientific thought. Nor is it surprising that ideas of participation should derive from the experience of being immersed in a larger community. The result is less independence of thought than characterizes industrial societies that place a high premium on the individual. Indeed the transition from "primitive" to "civilized" thought might be explained sociologically as a transition from a community orientation to an individualistic orientation.

Among the many criticisms of Lévy-Bruhl's ideas, the most common is that he makes too much of the differences between so-called primitive peoples and civilized ones. Primitives hunt, fish, build homes, raise families, and live together in complex communities. They could not do all of this and learn how to live in very challenging environments while lost in some mystical world of visions and occult participations. Further, among "civilized peoples" there are visionaries, mystics, and traditional healers of one sort or another. We should not portray those we call "primitives" as more superstitious than many people living in a "civilized" society.

It is to Lévy-Bruhl's credit that he did recognize that there subsists in every human mind, however modern, a fund of "primitive" mentality. **C. G. Jung**'s idea of the **collective unconscious**, which **Jung** used to develop his psychoanalytic theory of religion, owed a debt to this idea.

Although Lévy-Bruhl is not read much today, his ideas have had, and continue to have, an important influence. His discovery of the "law of participation" and his abandonment of the quest for the origins of religion have led scholars of religion to focus more intently on the role of society in forming religious beliefs. The issue of exactly how and why some societies changed from a communal outlook to a more individual orientation and the impact of this change on religion still excites considerable discussion.

See also: **Buber, Evans–Pritchard, Malinowski**

Major works

(1923) *Primitive Mentality*, trans. Lilian A. Clare, New York: The Macmillan Company.

(1928) *The "Soul" of the Primitive*, trans. Lilian A. Clare, New York: The Macmillan Company.

(1935) *Primitives and the Supernatural*, trans. Lilian A. Clare, New York: E. P. Dutton.

(1966) *How Natives Think*, trans. Lilian A. Clare, New York: Washington Square Press (first English translation published in 1926).

Further reading

Cazeneuve, Jean. (1972) *Lucien Lévy-Bruhl*, trans. Peter Rivière, New York: Harper and Row.

Evans–Pritchard, E. E. (1965) *Theories of Primitive Religion*, London: Oxford University Press.

Horton, Robin. (1993) *Patterns of Thought in Africa and the West: Essays on Magic, Religion and Science*, Cambridge: Cambridge University Press.

http://www.bookrags.com/biography/lucien-levy-bruhl.

ÉMILE DURKHEIM (1858–1917)

> A religion is a unified system of beliefs and practices relative to sacred things, that is to say, things set apart and forbidden—beliefs and practices which unite into one single moral community called a Church, all those who adhere to them.
>
> (Durkheim 1915: 47)

With this definition of religion, the famous and influential sociologist Émile Durkheim both challenged previous approaches to the study of religion and set off in a new direction, a direction that was destined to become the sociology of religion. The focus of study now shifted from trying to understand beliefs about supernatural matters to the social function of religion. How do beliefs and practices related to "sacred things" create "moral" communities? What makes something sacred? What is a moral community?

Durkheim was born in the town of Epinal, located near Strasbourg. His father was a rabbi, and expected his son to follow that vocation. However, Durkheim's education and interests led him in a different direction. He was admitted (after two failed attempts) into the prestigious and rigorous École normale supérieure where he studied both philosophy and history. After completing his studies he taught secondary school, then studied in Germany for a year and in 1887 married Louise Dreyfus. He became a professor at the University of Bordeaux and eventually took a position at the University of Paris at the age of forty-four. In 1916 his son was killed in the First World War and Durkheim was overcome with grief. He suffered a stroke soon after receiving the news of his son's death and died a year later.

Throughout his career he wrote many influential books on a wide variety of topics and with others founded *L' année sociologique*, which published new scholarly work in the emerging field of sociology. In *The Division of Labor* (1897) Durkheim noted that individuals are born into pre-existing groups and hence the group or society, not the individual, is of primary importance in understanding human behavior. Groups are much more than a mere collection of unrelated individuals; they include the connections or relations among the members. We cannot understand human behavior unless we understand these connections, and we cannot understand religion until we understand the role it plays in promoting social solidarity.

In *The Rules of Sociological Method* (1895) Durkheim introduced the idea of "social facts." Just as the physical sciences study physical facts of nature, so sociologists study the social facts of human behavior. These facts include laws, customs, languages, traditions, and values that influence what people believe and do. People experience these facts as external and as a constraint on behavior just as they experience physical facts. Sociology is the science of social facts and like all science it involves gathering evidence, comparison, classification, theorizing, inferring hypotheses, and testing.

In his seminal study *Suicide* (1897), Durkheim discovered that social conditions play a decisive role in certain kinds of suicides. Suicide rates increased during periods of social stress. He named this type "anomic suicide" (from the Greek *anomia* meaning "lawless"). During periods of dislocation, social instability, and economic distress, people often come to feel that nothing is certain and there are no clear guidelines on how to live. The power of traditions to control human behavior begins to break down and suicide rates increase as more people come to the conclusion that life is no longer worth living.

The Elementary Forms of the Religious Life (1912) is Durkheim's most important and influential work. In this book he focused on "simple" societies, such as Australian aborigines and Native American tribes. He applied the idea of the influence of society on the individual by developing a theory of the connection between society and the sacred, which he regarded as a basic religious category, as well as a sociological theory of human knowledge.

Instead of defining religion in terms of the difference between supernatural and natural, an approach popular in his day among the followers of **Tylor** and **Frazer**, he argued that the real dichotomy at the heart of religion was the opposition between sacred and profane. In order to understand the sacred, we need to grasp its function in society because, "The idea of society is the soul of religion" (Durkheim 1915: 419).

The idea of the sacred only makes sense in contrast to the notion of the profane. Sacred objects are those that are surrounded and protected by taboos that forbid certain uses. For example, the animal or plant that some Australian aborigine clans regard as their ancestor cannot be killed or used for food except under certain carefully controlled ritual conditions. Profane animals or plants can be used as needed. The sacred is the forbidden in the sense that its use is ritually controlled while the profane is not controlled by ritual rules. The sacred animal or plant constitutes the **totem** of the clan. The **totem** is not only the ancestor or first member of the clan, it is also the clan itself. If one is a member of the crow clan, one is a crow.

Totemic beliefs are so fundamental to life in "simple" societies that they shape every belief and practice of any importance. For instance, they govern the basic perceptions of nature. Some aboriginal peoples place the sun in the clan of the white cockatoos, while the clan of the black cockatoos contains the moon and stars. This shows that classification, a primary function of thought, has its roots in the **totemic** coding of clans.

More importantly, cognitive generalization is rooted in this classification system. All the clans have different **totems** yet they recognize that each of these **totems** shares something in common. This indicates, Durkheim argued, that there is recognition of what he called the "totemic principle"—an impersonal force that exercises power over the thought and life of the clan.

If we grant that the earliest form of religion and systems of classi-fication that we can discover is **totemism**, a mystery still remains. What does the **totem** symbolize in addition to the "totemic principle?" We can find a clue if we think of the **totem** as a kind of emblem. It is like a flag or logo that constitutes a visible image of the clan, much as the American eagle or "Old Glory" is a visible and concrete image of the United States. In short the **totem**, the earliest sacred object we can discover, is nothing less than the society of the clan, and hence the "totemic principle" must be nothing less than society itself. If we think of this sacred **totemic** principle as a kind of god, then the sociological analysis of religion has uncovered a startling truth; God symbolizes society.

If this seems like an overly bold conclusion, one needs to reflect on the similarity of feelings that **totems**, gods, and societies arouse. Durkheim listed the following: a sense of perpetual dependence, respect, security, support, meaning, and identity. Both **totems** and society arouse these feelings and so Durkheim concluded that the sacred power symbolized by the **totem** is none other than the collective life of the society.

Further corroboration can be found in **totemic** rituals as well as beliefs. Important celebrations centering on the **totem** occur when the various clans get together for communal rites. Normally life is routine and dull but special occasions of collective celebration become times of excitement. A sense of renewal binds the participants toge-ther as they celebrate their corporate and individual identity. Energy, joy, and commitment to a larger cause animate the participants just as secular collective rituals in more complex societies (e.g. sports events) energize the audience and participants. The whole becomes greater than the sum of its parts and individuals transcend themselves as they become swept up in the celebration of that whole, which gives life meaning and purpose.

The importance of the ritual life of Australian religion is a clue to understanding the whole of religion. Religion is not only a matter of beliefs but also a matter of ritual. The "cult" (corporate rituals of worship) is the very core of religion. Just as cultic worship among the aborigines is a way to promote consciousness of the clan, so too religious worship in general is a way to promote a sense of belonging to and dependence on (see **Feuerbach**) something larger and greater than the mundane and profane world that dominates so much of life. Religious ritual provides a way for individuals to connect with something greater than themselves—something that they understand to be divine but in reality is the larger society of which they are members.

Although Durkheim's views on religion have been and remain widely influential, they have not been without their critics. Numerous scholars have questioned his ideas concerning the sacred/ profane dichotomy and the evidence on which he relied. Perhaps the most prevalent criticism is the charge of causal and functional **reductionism**. His theory, critics claim, is built around the idea that the relation between religion and society is primarily a one-way street. Society is what determines religious beliefs and practices. While few would question the claim that religion and society are connected, many would regard the connection as a two-way street and defenders of Durhkeim would claim that he did too.

Defenders have, as well, raised the issue of why we should think that **"reductionism"** is so obviously wrong. We understand chemistry by reducing substances to the elements that make them up. We understand physics by "reducing" matter to ever-smaller forms of energy. Why should not the same hold true for human endeavors such as religion? Does the charge of **reductionism**, a charge leveled at many theorists, as we shall see, disguise a lingering supernaturalism on the part of the critic that rejects the whole enterprise of viewing religion as a natural human undertaking?

The critics and defenders of Durkheim, however, do not distract from the importance and influence of his ideas. Today good academic studies of religions are careful to place them in their social context. They also employ, as Durkheim advocated, the scientific method in order to foster as much as possible an objective understanding of religious beliefs and practices. Although it remains controversial, some form of sociological functionalism continues to prove immensely illuminating in study after study of religion. Society may not be, as Durkheim claimed, the "soul" of religion, but it is certainly an important part of that soul.

See also: **Bellah, Berger, Burkert, Douglas, Dumézil, Eliade, Evans-Pritchard, Freud, Geertz, van Gennep, Lévi-Strauss, Malinowski, Radcliffe-Brown, Weber**

Major works

(1915) *The Elementary Forms of the Religious Life*, trans. Joseph Ward Swain, New York: The Macmillan Company.

(1952) *Suicide: A Study in Sociology*, trans. John A. Spaulding and George Simpson, Glencoe, IL: Free Press.

(1982) *The Rules of Sociological Method*, trans. W. D. Hall, London: Macmillan.

(1984) *The Division of Labour in Society*, trans. W. D. Hall, London: Macmillan.

Further reading

Alexander, Jeffrey C. and Philip Smith, eds. (2005) *The Cambridge Companion to Durkheim*, Cambridge: Cambridge University Press.

Jones, Robert Alun. (1986) *Émile Durkheim*, Beverly Hills, CA: Sage Publications.

Lukes, Steven. (1972) *Émile Durkheim, His Life and Work: A Historical and Critical Study*, New York: Harper and Row.

Pickering, W. S. F. (1984) *Durkheim's Sociology of Religion*, London: Routledge and Kegan Paul.

http://en.wikipedia.org/wiki/%C3%89mile Durkheim.

MAX WEBER (1864–1920)

> For of the last stage of this cultural development, it might well be truly said: "Specialists without spirit, sensualists without heart; this nullity imagines that it has attained a level of civilization never before achieved."
>
> (Weber 1996: 182)

With these words Max Weber brought to a close his masterful classic *The Protestant Ethic and the Spirit of Capitalism* (1904–5) and scholars have been arguing about it ever since. The "cultural development" to which he referred is the result of a complex interaction between what he called the "Protestant ethic" and the "spirit of capitalism." But what precisely is this Protestant ethic? How is it connected to the capitalistic spirit?

Karl Emil Maximilian "Max" Weber was born to a wealthy and well-connected family. His father was an influential lawyer and politician who served as a representative in the Reichstag. Max seemed destined for a career in law and politics. In 1882 he began his university studies and by the time he graduated in 1886 had studied law, history, and theology at several universities including Heidelberg and Berlin. In 1893 he became a professor of law at the University of Berlin and in 1897 a professor of political science at Heidelberg University.

In 1903 Weber had a "nervous breakdown" that forced him to resign his academic position. He eventually began a new life as a private scholar writing on a variety of topics including the relationship between religion and economics. He died on June 14 of pneumonia with his major research program on economics and religion still unfinished.

Before we discuss his views on the relationship between religion and economics, we need to look briefly at his sociological methodology. Central to his approach is the idea that human behavior cannot be understood until we realize that people do not respond to their environment directly, but to the *meaning* that their environment holds for them. Unless we understand what people *think* events mean, sociology can do little more than scratch the surface of explaining human social behavior.

Understanding the meaning people attribute to events requires the practice of *Verstehen* or "understanding" (see **Schleiermacher**). To answer the question of what meaning people attribute to the world as they experience it requires understanding their perspective. In emphasizing the need to understand beliefs and practices from the perspective of the actor, Weber signaled a break from the materialistic and functional reductionism of **Marx** and **Durkheim**. The goal of the sociology of religion is not only to uncover the external causes of religious ideas but also to grasp the subjective factors that contribute to their development.

In addition to the idea of *Verstehen*, Weber introduced the notion of "ideal-types." Ideal-types are not generalizations but abstractions of the ideal characteristics associated with particular social types. No actual historical instance of an ideal-type will have all the characteristics associated with that type, but enough of them to both identify the type and compare it to other types. For example, if we study religious leaders, we can discern at least three major types: magician, priest, and prophet. If we think of religion as rooted in ecstatic states, then the magician is one who knows how to manage such states on demand. For instance he or she can go into trance and draw on "spirit guides" to heal people when called upon to do so. Magicians are, in Weber's words, "permanently endowed with charisma." Charisma refers to the power some people have to influence others.

The priest also has charisma, but of a different sort. Priests have professional status and their charisma derives from their office. Unlike magic, which tends to be an occasional activity performed when needed, priests perform their functions on a regular basis at fixed times and places and usually according to a ritual routine. Their concern is with stability and structure and the rise of priesthood is a key factor in the development of ideas like cosmic order and a universal ethic.

Prophets, in contrast to priests, are individual bearers of charisma like the magician, but unlike magicians, prophets have a mission to proclaim some important message. Their activity is not centered on securing everyday benefits for clients but on spreading a life-changing message or practice. Unlike priests, the prophet's charisma is not derived from an official office, but from the power of the message to effect change, often revolutionary change, such as the founding of a new religion.

Historically there have been two main types of prophets: "ethical prophets" and "exemplary prophets." Ethical prophets see themselves as emissaries from the divine with a message that others should believe. It is, the prophet proclaims, "an ethical duty to believe what I say." Exemplary prophets are not primarily emissaries, but people who by their personal examples show others the path to wisdom and truth. The exemplary prophet preaches, "Do as I do." Muhammad is a good example of an ethical prophet and Gautama the Buddha is a good example of an exemplary prophet.

Prophets, as I remarked above, are often founders of new religions or redirect elements in existing religions in new directions. When this happens, there is great excitement among the first disciples. Over time, however, this high energy level is difficult to maintain. Funds need to be raised, leaders appointed, and a host of organizational problems solved. The charisma of the beginning slowly succumbs to the routine of running an organization. Weber called this process the "routinization of charisma." When routinization has so overwhelmed a religious movement that the original vitality seems all but lost, reform movements develop, claiming to recover the original message and power of the founder.

It should be emphasized that no actual historical instances necessarily have all of the characteristics of these ideal-types. Some priestly activities do shade off into magic (exorcism) and some ethical prophets share qualities with exemplary prophets (Jesus). It should also be noted that the analytic and comparative concepts Weber developed in his study of religions have their secular counterparts. The routinization process applies to political movements and business enterprises as well as religion.

Weber applied the ideas of *Verstehen* and ideal-types in *The Protestant Ethic and the Spirit of Capitalism* in order to show that early modern capitalism might not have developed when and where it did if it were not for the impact of Protestant ideas on culture and society. Weber noted that after the Protestant Reformation the carriers of capitalism (bankers, merchants, skilled tradesmen) were mostly Protestant and that a capitalistic economy more rapidly replaced a feudal economy in Protestant countries than in Roman Catholic countries. He asked why and found the answer in what he termed the Protestant ethic.

Martin Luther (1483–1546) led the "protest" against Roman Catholicism by democratizing the religious idea of calling or vocation. At the heart of Catholicism was a distinction between clergy and laity. The work of priests, monks, and nuns was spiritual work because God had "called" them. Luther's claim that God blessed *all* honest labor, secular or religious, unleashed a flood of social and economic energy that eventually destroyed the feudal system.

John Calvin (1509–64), the second most influential Protestant reformer after Luther, added to Luther's reinterpretation of vocation the idea that whether one's vocation was secular or religious, the work it entailed should be done in such a way as to glorify God. Honest, hard work glorified God while dishonest, lazy work did not. In addition Calvin emphasized the doctrine of predestination. In order to preserve Luther's insistence that only God has the power to save, Calvin taught that God from all eternity elected some but not all people to be saved.

In time, Weber argued, followers of Calvin began to experience anxiety over their fate. If the sacraments and prescribed good works of the Catholic Church could not be relied upon to lead to heaven and if even before one was born one's fate was sealed, how could one know if he or she was among the elect or the damned? Protestant pastors, in order to provide spiritual comfort, begin to emphasize "signs" of election. Among these signs was success in business. Virtues such a thrift, hard work, and frugality had to be signs of election because surely God would not bless the damned in such ways. Wealth should not be used for pleasure or extravagant lifestyles but reinvested in order to make more money, thereby witnessing to God's glory.

Making money became, in effect, an ethic or moral obligation. Weber named this ethic "inner-worldly asceticism" and contrasted it with "other-worldly asceticism." Practices of self-denial (asceticism) should be focused on changing this world for the better, not on gaining one's entry into heaven. Unlike the monk who leaves the world to devote his life to God, the pious Protestant should engage the world. The ethic of inner-worldly asceticism is an important factor in the rise of the *spirit* of capitalism because it reinforced the kind of work ethic demanded by capitalism—the accumulation of surplus wealth that could be invested. Even after the religious meaning of this ethic began to fade, the ethic continued to inspire the capitalistic spirit as the popularity in colonial America of Benjamin

Franklin's secular aphorisms ("A penny saved is a penny earned") reveal.

Over time, this capitalistic spirit sheds most of its ethical constraints and making money by any legal, or often not so legal, means becomes an end in itself. Getting rich in order to show the glory of God eventually becomes getting rich in order to enjoy the power wealth brings. What began as a religious reformation in Christian ideas had the unintended economic consequence of promoting capitalism and the unintended social consequence of creating "sensualists without heart."

Weber's study of Protestantism's economic/social impact was just the first stage in an ongoing research project aimed at clarifying the relationship between the major world religions and economic development. Weber wanted to know the "economic ethic" that emerged in the religions of China, India, Judaism, and Islam. He never lived to complete this project. Although his conclusions with regard to Judaism and the religions of Asia are nuanced, and controversial, he found that the "inner-worldly asceticism" that developed in Protestant Christianity did not develop in other religions. Thus modern capitalism as we know it did not develop in those societies until it was carried there by Western expansionism.

Weber's work covers a vast amount of historical, religious, and cultural material so it is not surprising that one of many criticisms is the charge of inconsistency. Sometimes Weber argued for recognizing the causative role of religious ideas in social development. At other times he argued for recognizing the causative role of social developments in the origins of religious ideas. For example, he acknowledged that the idea of ethical monotheism reflects the Middle Eastern notion of an all-powerful king. Weber did not see the inconsistency his critics claimed because he viewed causation as a complex, interactive process in which ideas shape society and society in turn shapes ideas.

His alleged "inconsistency" on the causal relationship between religion and social factors does not, in the end, detract from the enormously important contributions he made to the sociological study of religion. It serves to emphasize the complexity of explaining religious behavior and to caution those who would oversimplify theories of religion by assuming a one-way causal street. It can plausibly be argued that he was not so much interested in refuting **Marx**'s analysis of religion, as he was in balancing it by pointing out the complexities of the interaction between religious ideas and economic factors.

See also: **Bellah, Berger, Buber, Geertz, van der Leeuw, Troeltsch**

Major works

(1951) *The Religion of China: Confucianism and Taoism*, trans. Hans H. Gerth, New York: The Free Press.

(1951) *The Religion of India*, trans. Hans H. Gerth and Don Martindale, New York: The Free Press.

(1952) *Ancient Judaism*, trans. Hans H. Gerth and Don Martindale, Glencoe, IL: The Free Press.

(1963) *The Sociology of Religion*, trans. Ephraim Fischoff, Boston, MA: Beacon Press.

(1978) *Economy and Society: An Outline of Interpretive Sociology*, trans. Guenther Roth, and Claus Weittich, Berkeley, CA: University of California Press.

(1996) *The Protestant Ethic and the Spirit of Capitalism*, trans. Talcott Parsons, Los Angeles, CA: Roxbury Publishing Company.

Further reading

Radkau, Joachim. (2009) *Max Weber: A Biography*, Cambridge: Polity Press.

Turner, Stephen, ed. (2000) *The Cambridge Companion to Weber*, Cambridge: Cambridge University Press.

Wrong, Dennis, ed. (1970) *Max Weber*, Englewood Cliffs, NJ: Prentice Hall. http://en.wikipedia.org/wiki/Max_Weber.

ERNST TROELTSCH (1865–1923)

> The Church is that type of organization which is overwhelmingly conservative, which to a certain extent accepts the secular order, and dominates the masses: in principle, therefore, it is universal, i.e. it desires to cover the whole of humanity. The sects, on the other hand, are comparatively small groups; they aspire after personal inward perfection, and they aim at a direct personal fellowship between the members of each group.
>
> (Troeltsch 1960: 331)

What exactly did Ernst Troeltsch have in mind by designating some religious groups churches and some sects? Do the characteristics he listed describe the basic features of these ideal-types (see **Weber**)? How do the differences between these two types of religious organization influence Christian ideas on social ethics? Are there additional types?

Ernst Troeltsch was born in Southern Germany and spent his youth in Augsburg. He was the son of a wealthy physician and, although interested in medicine and science, decided to study

Christian theology and history at several different universities before becoming a professor first at Bonn (1892), then Heidelberg (1894), and finally Berlin (1914). Throughout his career he was active in progressive political movements and strongly supported democratic and economic reforms aimed at breaking down class barriers. His publications were voluminous but he is best known today for his monumental study *The Social Teaching of the Christian Churches* (1911).

Troeltsch is often associated with the *Religionsgeschichtliche Schule* ("History of Religions School") because of his support for studying Christianity as one would study any other religion by situating it firmly in its historical, social, and cultural context. This study, he argued, ought to be thoroughly empirical, adhering to the best principles of historiography. These include criticism, analogy, and correlation. By criticism he meant to indicate that all historical judgments, like all scientific conclusions, are more or less probable. The method of analogy is based on the assumption that our own experiences are not totally unlike the experiences of other people even though they may live in different times and places. The principle of correlation is based on the premise that no event is totally isolated and hence can only be understood as part of a web of social, cultural, historical, economic, and religious events.

He also claimed that the rigorous use of comparison should not have as its goal proving the superiority of Christianity, but describing the differences and similarities among religions. He argued that for Europe and America, the Christian religion was entirely appropriate. But there is no way to prove empirically the universal superiority of Christianity for all people. Hence Christians must take other religions seriously and understand how they are appropriate for their time and place. These views clearly anticipate the problems associated with cultural relativism and pluralism that scholars still wrestle with today. They also reveal that Troeltsch did not fully anticipate the adaptability of Christianity to other cultures as it spread around the globe. They do, however, undermine **Hegel**'s claim that Christianity is the final goal of the human spiritual quest.

In *The Social Teaching of the Christian Churches*, Troeltsch focused on the tension between the ethical teachings contained in the Gospels and the social order. Jesus' injunctions to love your neighbor as yourself and his emphasis on a fellowship of loving care for even one's enemies stand in marked contrast to the "ways of the world." How could such teachings lead to anything like a realistic social ethic? The quest for such an ethic produced three different types of social ethics associated with three different types of social organizations. The

Church or ecclesiastical type emphasizes the unity of the Christian church with society. This reached its highest expression in the Roman Catholic Church during the Middle Ages.

The sectarian type emphasizes the separation of Christians from a sinful society. Although sectarian tendencies were there from the beginning, they became more pronounced and organized into diverse sects during and after the Protestant Reformation.

The mystical type emphasizes the spiritual development of the individual. Because of its emphasis on "direct inward and present religious experience" it never fully developed a robust social ethic and never organized itself into sociologically distinct organizations. Like the sects its tendency is to withdraw from the secular social order, but the dualistic emphasis of the sects on the distinction between the "saved" and the "damned" did not gain much of a foothold among mystical groups. Instead there is an emphasis on a "universal spiritual brotherhood" of all human beings.

Troeltsch's analysis of the church/sect typology has received the most attention from sociologists of religion. He borrowed the distinction from his friend **Max Weber** but refined it. While **Weber** thought the salient difference is that one is born into a church but one voluntarily joins a sect, Troeltsch went on to add a number of other descriptors. Sects usually have a restrictive membership policy while churches are more inclusive. Sects often think that salvation is achieved by moral purity and churches emphasize the grace of God as mediated by the sacraments. Sects are often hostile to secular society and churches tend to support existing social values. All of these characteristics lead to different kinds of social ethics.

Troeltsch thought that **Karl Marx**'s analysis of economic factors as causes of different kinds of religious ideology should be taken seriously. However, he also thought that economic factors provided only a "concrete stimulus" and that the causes of the different kinds of social ethics were generated from within Christianity itself. In the final analysis religion is self-generating even though it is caught in a social web of differing social, economic, and historical influences.

Scholars since Troeltsch have worked to generalize his findings to religions other than Christianity without a great deal of success, and Troeltsch himself was skeptical about the cross-cultural usefulness of his typology. Those working with the typology have also discovered another problem. The empirical utility of his version of the typology is limited because he suggests many different variables that mix sociological and theological elements. It also fails to provide much information about the social conditions likely to generate different kinds of groups. Nevertheless the church/sect typology has become standard fare in most sociology of religion textbooks. It inspired H. Richard Niebuhr in *The Social Sources of Denominationalism* (1957) to develop Troeltsch's ideas by identifying the social conditions that give rise to each type of group.

Troeltsch had hoped that one result of his study of the history and sociology of Christian social ethics would be a new theological synthesis of Christian teachings and modern culture. He sought a new social ethic for his time but had to admit that while the older forms had "spent their force" he could discover no certain direction for the future. The creeping secularization of European society appeared to make Christianity increasingly irrelevant to social concerns, at least in Europe.

See also: **J. Z. Smith**

Major works

(1958) *Protestantism and Progress: A Historical Study of the Relation of Protestantism to the Modern World*, Boston, MA: Beacon Press.

(1960) *The Social Teaching of the Christian Churches*, 2 vols., New York: Harper and Brothers.

(1971) *The Absoluteness of Christianity and the History of Religions*, trans. David Reid, Atlanta, GA: John Knox Press.

(1991) *Religion in History*, trans. J. L. Adams and W. F. Bense, Minneapolis, MN: Fortress Press.

Further reading

Chapman, Mark D. (2001) *Ernst Troeltsch and Liberal Theology: Religion and Cultural Synthesis in Wilhelmine Germany*, Oxford: Oxford University Press.

Drescher, H. (1992) *Ernst Troeltsch: His Life and Work*, London: SCM.

Rubanowice, Robert J. (1983) *Crisis of Consciousness: The Thought of Ernst Troeltsch*, Gainesville, FL: University of Florida Press.

http://people.bu.edu/wwildman/bce/troeltsch.htm.

RUDOLF OTTO (1869–1937)

> I shall speak, then, of a unique "numinous" category of value and of a definitely "numinous" state of mind, which is always found wherever the category is applied. This mental state is perfectly *sui generis* and irreducible to any other; and therefore, like every absolutely primary and elementary datum, while it admits of being discussed, it cannot be strictly defined.
>
> (Otto, 1958: 7)

With these words, Rudolf Otto introduced the central concept of his popular and widely discussed book, *Das Heilige* (The Holy, 1917). In retrospect his comments seem paradoxical, since the numinous cannot be defined. Yet this idea managed to inspire generations of scholars who argued that the central idea of religion (holy, sacred, numinous) is unique (*sui generis*) and hence cannot be reduced to any other more fundamental category such as economics, society, or culture. This idea helped convince some colleges and universities in America to start departments of religious studies rather than incorporate the study of religion into departments of history or sociology.

Rudolf Otto was born on September 25 in Peine, Germany. He studied at the Universities of Erlangen and Göttingen, intending to enter the Lutheran ministry. However, the conservative Lutheran establishment regarded his views as too liberal so he embarked on an academic career in theology at Göttingen, where he encountered the work of Jakob Friedrich Fries (1773–1843). Fries's interpretation of **Kant** influenced the direction of his thought. In 1904 he was overtaken by a deep depression and considered abandoning the teaching of theology, but in 1907 he recovered and resumed a career of both teaching and comparative research. In 1911 he traveled to India and studied Sanskrit and Hinduism, which piqued his interest in mysticism and comparative religions. In 1936 Otto fell from a tower (unconfirmed rumor had it that it was a suicide attempt) and suffered major injuries. He died of pneumonia in March of 1937.

Otto's most influential book was *Das Heilige*. Unfortunately this was translated into English as *The Idea of the Holy*. This is a misleading translation for two reasons. First, Otto is not primarily concerned with an idea but with a feeling. Second, *heilige* can mean "holy" or "sacred" in English and a good case can be made for using the English sacred rather than holy, which has moral implications that Otto did not intend.

Otto began with a discussion of the rational and non-rational. The traditional attributes of God such as purpose, reason, spirit, good will, and the like are all concepts that can be defined. However, to think of these qualities as the essence of divinity is "seriously misleading" because they imply a "non-rational or supra-rational" subject. Orthodox Christianity has constructed dogmas and doctrines that obscure rather than reveal the non-rational dimension of religion. This has led to an overly rationalistic interpretation of religion. Otto hoped to correct this imbalance by explicating the unique non-rational essence of religion—the holy or sacred.

The holy or sacred is not primarily a moral category. It means more than that. It contains an "overplus of meaning" that is non-rational and it is this overplus that we must understand if we are to grasp what is distinctive and irreducible in religion. Otto coined the term "numinous" to characterize this overplus of meaning. The word is derived from the Latin *numen*, which means a "spirit," and the key to religion is understanding the numinous experience that stands at its heart. This is an "intrinsically religious feeling" and to grasp it people must have some sense of it based on their own religious experiences such as the feelings aroused by "solemn worship." However, if we subtract the moral and rational elements from the term holy, what is left?

Religious experience holds the possibility for an empirical grounding of God's existence in some sort of immediate experience. **Schleiermacher** thought this was the case. However, Otto thought he had missed the mark. Although **Schleiermacher** had identified a key feature of religious experience (the feeling of absolute dependence) the existence of a divine cause of that feeling had to be inferred. There may well be other natural causes. Otto proposed "creature-consciousness" or "creature feeling" as a more accurate description. It is more accurate because *within* the experience itself an object is given. Creature-feeling is the sense of being overwhelmed by one's own nothingness. In the face of an overwhelming power one's own importance, indeed one's own existence, seems trivial. "The numinous is thus felt as objective and outside the self" (Otto 1958: 11).

What is felt in the numinous experience Otto calls "*mysterium tremendum.*" He used the Latin for this "tremendous mystery" not to obscure, but to indicate he was using the words mystery and tremendous in a technical sense. We can only understand this sense by analogy with more common experiences, and we can only express it in language using symbols and metaphors. Otto cited experiences of solemn ceremonies or the atmosphere that clings to ancient temples. These experiences arouse a sense of something unfamiliar, hidden, and even extraordinary.

In spite of the linguistic difficulties of using conceptual language in analyzing and describing what is essentially non-rational, Otto believed we could identify five distinct but related elements. If we focus first on the *tremendum* we can draw an analogy to the experience of fear. But this is not ordinary fear, it is a dreadful fear such as occurs when we are aghast, shudder, or feel horror. It is like the experience of fright night on television when the hairs on the back of our necks tingle. We are left in awe at the awe-fullness of what we have just encountered. Otto claimed that it is just such an experience of dread and awe that the Bible is talking about when it speaks of the wrath of God.

There is more to the *tremendum* than awe. There is also a sense of being overpowered and overwhelmed by a force so great it is absolutely unapproachable. Otto called this aspect "*majestas*" thereby suggesting that it is like the feeling of being in the presence of a great king or emperor. In its more mystical expression, this sense of being overpowered leads to feelings of self-annihilation. I am nothing and the transcendent is the sole and entire reality.

The third element of the *tremendum* that Otto identified is energy or urgency. There is vitality, excitement, activity, passion, and the like, associated with the numinous object. It is alive, more alive than anything we have ever experienced. These three elements (awe, majesty, and urgency) constitute the basic features of that part of the numinous experience that Otto named the *tremendum*.

If we turn our attention to the *mysterium* element in the numinous, we can only make "hints and suggestions." This mystery leaves us stupefied and in a state of blank wonder and absolute astonishment. Otto could think of no better designation for this mystery than "wholly other." As the name implies, it is beyond the intelligible and familiar.

> The truly "mysterious" object is beyond our apprehension and comprehension, not only because our knowledge has certain irremovable limits, but because in it we come upon something inherently "wholly other", whose kind and character are incommensurable with our own, and before which we therefore recoil in a wonder that strikes us chill and numb.
>
> (Otto 1958: 28)

Otto thought the "Void" of Eastern mysticism and the "Nothing" talked about by some Western mystics stemmed from this aspect of the numinous experience. We can feel it but lack the capacity to clearly express it because it is the opposite of "everything that is and can be thought."

The reader may, by now, be wondering whether religious experiences of mercy, forgiveness, love, grace, and blessedness have any basis at all in the numinous experience. They do, Otto claimed, in the fifth element of the numinous experience. He named it the element of fascination and called it the "strangest and most noteworthy phenomenon in the whole history of religion" (Otto 1958: 31). This element entrances, captivates, enraptures, and excites, yet can also produce great calm and transport into "the peace that passes all understanding." Ecstasy can be so exciting one is not sure one can stand it and yet it can produce a great serenity and sense of comfort. For example, the excitement of dancing to a throbbing and persistent beat can, strangely enough, lead to such transport and forgetfulness of self that a calm envelops the dancer even in the midst of near-frenzied activity.

Otto provided a number of examples that contain elements of the numinous experience, pointing in particular to Moses' encounter with the burning bush. A bush is on fire, yet it is not consumed. A voice from the burning bush is heard announcing, "I AM the God of your fathers." Moses is afraid yet he is transfixed, fascinated, and overwhelmed by the power and mystery of the experience. Such is the heart of religion.

Otto wrote other books on comparative religion, among them *Mysticism East and West* (1926) and *India's Religion of Grace and Christianity Compared and Contrasted* (1930) but none gained the attention or had the impact of *The Idea of the Holy*. However, several criticisms have emerged, among them Otto's failure to properly contextualize his evidence. His tendency to universalize elements that best fit Christianity and his failure to pay careful attention to historical, cultural, and social environments meant that his analysis of the numinous experience had limited usefulness.

There are also methodological problems. If the numinous experience cannot be understood by anyone who has not had the experience or close analogues, then the evidence supporting Otto's claims is only available to those who through introspection of their own conscious experiences have similar experiences. The subjective nature of introspection severely limits any objective verification.

In spite of these criticisms, Otto's descriptive accounts had a deep impact on theorists who believed that religion is an expression of a *sui generis* experience of the sacred. His most significant impact was on a form of the comparative study of religion known today as the **phenomenology** of religion, especially as it was practiced by people like **Mircea Eliade**. Also, **Paul Tillich** made use of his ideas in developing his philosophical theology.

See also: **Douglas, Hick, James, Jung, van der Leeuw, Radcliffe-Brown, Radhakrishnan, Smart, J. Z. Smith, Suzuki**

Major works

(1930) *India's Religion of Grace and Christianity Compared and Contrasted*, trans. Frank Hugh Foster, New York: Macmillan.

(1932) *Mysticism East and West: A Comparative Analysis of the Nature of Mysticism*, trans. Bertha L. Bracey and Richenda C. Payne, New York: Macmillan.

(1958) *The Idea of the Holy: An Inquiry into the Non-rational Factor in the Idea of the Divine and its Relation to the Rational*, trans. John W. Harvey, New York: Oxford University Press.

Further reading

Almond, Philip. (1984) *Rudolf Otto: An Introduction to His Philosophical Theology*, Chapel Hill, NC: University of North Carolina Press.

Davidson, Robert F. (1947) *Rudolf Otto's Interpretation of Religion*, Princeton, NJ: Princeton University Press.

Gooch, Todd A. (2000) *The Numinous and Modernity: An Interpretation of Rudolf Otto's Philosophy of Religion*, Berlin: Walter de Gruyter.

http://epages.wordpress.com/2009/02/14/an-outline-of-rudolf-ottos-the-idea-of-the-holy-by-michael-w-clark-phd.

D. T. SUZUKI (1870–1966)

> *Satori* may be defined as an intuitive looking into the nature of things in contradistinction to the analytical or logical understanding of it. Practically, it means the unfolding of a new world hitherto unperceived in the confusion of a dualistically-trained mind.
>
> (Suzuki 1956: 84)

Satori is the Japanese term for **enlightenment** or awakening. It is, according to D. T. Suzuki, the essence of Zen Buddhism. But it is more than that; it is also the essence of a spirituality that transcends the boundaries of religions and cultures. But what exactly is this experience of "waking up" like? How is it achieved? And is it, as Suzuki maintains, the essence of spirituality?

Born Suzuki Teitaro in Kanazawa, he was given the name Daisetsu ("great simplicity") by one of his Zen teachers. His family belonged to the Rinzai sect of Zen Buddhism, but his high school mathematics instructor sparked his serious interest in Zen. His father was a physician who died when he was five, forcing his son to leave school due to financial problems. He made a living for a time teaching English, which he had taught himself, but eventually started his studies at Waseda University and later at the Tokyo Imperial University, although he never earned a college degree. He underwent Zen training under the direction of Shaku Soen (1859–1919) but he was never ordained in the Buddhist tradition.

Suzuki went to America in 1897 to assist Paul Carus (a German philosopher and founder of Open Court Press) in the translation and publication of Asian philosophical works. He studied literature and philosophy at the University of Chicago and came to admire the work of Ralph Waldo Emerson, Henry David Thoreau, and John Dewey. In 1921 he became professor of Buddhist philosophy at Otani University but returned to the United States to offer a widely acclaimed series of lectures at Columbia University (1951–57) that greatly influenced the "beat generation." He became the leading interpreter of Zen Buddhism for the West and is largely responsible for spreading both popular and scholarly interest in Japanese culture and Buddhism in Europe and North America. He was a prolific writer, publishing over 30 books.

Some (Victoria 1998) have accused Suzuki of supporting Japanese militarism in the 1930s and 1940s, and his claim that Japanese culture was more spiritually advanced than other Asian cultures seems to give some credibility to the charge. Suzuki, however, denied the charge and private letters written to friends prior to World War II show that he had grave reservations about Japanese militarism.

Like both **Schleiermacher** and **Otto**, Suzuki thought spirituality originates in a unique and distinctive experience. However, his description of that experience is different in important ways. Unlike **Schleiermacher** and **Otto**, whose views on religion and spiritual experience were strongly influenced by Christian theism, Suzuki's views were shaped by the non-theistic Zen Buddhist experience of *satori* as well as Emerson's mystical transcendentalism, theosophical monism, and **William James**'s concept of pure experience. Although he touched on other religions in some of his writings, he did not try to prove his ideas by presenting vast amounts of comparative evidence. Instead he focused his energies on making information about Buddhism available to a wider public. It was largely through his efforts that concepts like *satori*, *zazen* (seated meditation), *koan* (riddle), and a host of others entered the vocabulary of the West.

Suzuki characterized *satori* in different ways. He likened it to the sudden harmonizing of opposites into an organic whole, an intuitive "Eureka" experience, picking a hidden lock that unleashes new creative insights into the "way things are," a "seeing into one's own nature," and a "mental clicking or opening" leading to a new point of view on oneself and the nature of reality. While *satori* often occurs unexpectedly (Suzuki's happened while cycling in fields outside of

Chicago) it is proceeded by an intense personal effort of one's whole being in which the mind becomes completely identified with its object to the point that even "the consciousness of identity is lost."

Although Suzuki characterized the *satori* experience with different metaphors and analogies, he summarized his views by identifying eight chief characteristics. The first one is *irrationality*. He meant by this that *satori* is not a conclusion reached by reasoning and cannot be intellectually determined. It is characterized by "inexplicability, and incommunicability" (Suzuki 1956: 103).

The second chief characteristic is *intuitive insight*. Suzuki referred to **James**'s claim that mystical experiences have a noetic quality to explain what he meant. There is a sense that knowledge of great importance is attained in the experience, even though it is not possible to communicate clearly what this knowledge is. However, he does say it "is the knowledge of an individual object and also that of Reality which is, if I may say so, at the back of it" (Suzuki 1956: 104).

This noetic sense of "knowing something" comes with *authoritativeness* (third characteristic). It is the final truth that "no amount of logical argument can refute." While this truth cannot be rationally stated, it is not something negative. It is an *affirmation* (fourth characteristic) of life *just as it is*. It engenders an attitude of acceptance and patience that goes beyond the common dualism into which we categorize things such as right and wrong. Reality is not good or bad, it just is.

And yet there is also a *sense of the Beyond* (fifth characteristic) that may be described differently in different religions but at its heart is the feeling that while the experience is indeed my own experience it is "rooted elsewhere." Constraints on individuality explode and one feels a melting away into something indescribable. There is both the sense of release and of coming to rest.

But who does the releasing and where does one come to rest? Many religions would say the divine, but Suzuki was emphatic that *satori* has a decidedly *impersonal tone* (sixth characteristic). There is no hint of God, divine love, or a union with the divine so typical of much Christian mysticism. In comparison to the exalted words theistic mystics use extolling unspeakable joys of a spiritual marriage, *satori* appears gray, commonplace, and barren. When the "doors of perception" burst open there is no God in all his glory on a throne but as one Zen master put it, "the old man in all his homeliness."

Nevertheless, there is a *feeling of exaltation* (seventh characteristic). This is due to the sense of release and the breaking up of restrictions we impose on ourselves based on mistaken views of what is real.

Once we realize that the world of oppositions and divisions is only one way of seeing the world, a feeling of intense liberation and exaltation overcomes the person having the experience.

James claimed that one of the marks of mystical experience is that it is transient. It only lasts a short time and Suzuki identified this as the eighth characteristic of *satori*. It is not, however, the duration alone that is important but also its abruptness. He goes so far as to claim that if it is "not abrupt and momentary" it is not *satori*. This abrupt experience opens up in one moment "an altogether new vista." *Satori* startles one and comes and goes as if in a flash.

Obviously not all religious experiences have all these characteristics, nor do they have them to the same degree. However, they are universal enough that Suzuki was confident in affirming a trans-historical and trans-cultural significance for *satori*. And Zen Buddhism, as presented by Suzuki, was exotic enough and different enough from the traditional Christian emphasis on faith and belief in doctrines that a whole generation of Americans became interested in undertaking a serious study of Japanese Buddhism and Asian religions. However, when they put in the effort to learn Japanese and travel to Japan to study Buddhism, they were shocked. The Buddhism that Suzuki had taught them resembled Japanese Buddhism in only the most general sense. For one thing, *satori* was far less important to Japanese Buddhism than Suzuki had led them to believe. Hence his version of Buddhism is sometimes called "*satori* Buddhism" and, while it most resembles the Rinzai school, it differs markedly from the Soto school of Zen Buddhism. Suzuki began to appear less like a scholar of Buddhism and more like a missionary of a particular version of Buddhism, a version he created from many different sources.

Today Suzuki is considered to be more of a popularizer of Buddhism than a reliable scholar. Nevertheless he did make important scholarly contributions with his translations of important texts and even though his popularizing of Zen Buddhism suffered from the twin sins of all popularization—oversimplification and selective reading—he sparked an interest that was to change and broaden American and European perceptions of the nature of religion.

See also: **Jung**

Major works

(1956) *Zen Buddhism: Selected Writings of D. T. Suzuki*, ed. William Barrett, Garden City, NY: Doubleday and Company.

(1959) *Zen and Japanese Culture*, Princeton, NJ: Princeton University Press.

(1960) *Manual of Zen Buddhism*, New York: Grove Press.
(1961) *Essays in Zen Buddhism: First Series*, New York: Grove Press.
(1963) "Lectures on Zen Buddhism," *Zen Buddhism and Psychoanalysis*, New York: Harper and Brothers.
(1964) *An Introduction to Zen Buddhism*, New York: Grove Press.
(1968) *Zen and Japanese Buddhism*, Tokyo: Japan Travel Bureau.

Further reading

Abe, Masao. (1986) *A Zen Life: D. T. Suzuki Remembered*, New York: Shambhala.
Leonard, George J. (1999) "D. T. Suzuki and the Creation of Japanese American Zen," *The Asian Pacific American Heritage: A Companion to Literature and Art*, George J. Leonard, ed., New York: Garland Publishing.
Switzer, Irwin, and John Snelling. (1985) *D. T. Suzuki: A Biography*, London: Buddhist Publishing Group.
Victoria, Brian. (1998) *Zen at War*, Boston, MA: Weatherhill.
http://en.wikipedia.org/wiki/D._T._Suzuki.

ARNOLD VAN GENNEP (1873–1957)

> Our interest lies not in the particular rites but in their essential significance and their relative positions within ceremonial wholes. ... The underlying arrangement is always the same. Beneath a multiplicity of forms, either consciously expressed or merely implied, a typical pattern always recurs: *the pattern of the rites of passage.*
>
> (van Gennep 1960: 191)

Masked intruders take boys from their homes. They are herded to an underground dwelling and, in the flickering light, gods appear to reveal sacred secrets. The boys emerge to the world above and return to their families. Their community no longer regards them as boys, but as men. What does this mean? Might this be part of a **rite of passage**?

Arnold van Gennep was born in Germany, but his father was descended from French emigrants. His parents divorced when he was six and his mother returned to France with him. She remarried a doctor who had a practice in Savoy, a region of France van Gennep came to regard as home. He developed an interest in folklore and began traveling through the villages of Savoy collecting stories.

He had larger interests than folklore, as evidenced by his university studies. He had a gift for languages and studied general linguistics, Egyptology, Arabic (ancient and modern), Islam, and the religions of "primitive" peoples. For a time he taught ethnology at the University of Neuchâtel until he expressed skepticism about the Swiss claim to neutrality during World War I and was "asked" to leave. This was the only academic position he would hold. He began a life as a private scholar, earning his living from books and articles. His most important and influential work was *The Rites of Passage* (1908).

Rites of passage mark transitions from one stage of *social* life to another. Some examples are ceremonies centering on the transition from boy to man, girl to woman, single to married, and life to death. These are often considered dangerous times for the community and the individual because the established social order is potentially threatened if such transitions are not properly managed.

Van Gennep thought that seasonal and calendrical rituals should also be included in the category "**rites of passage**" because they also mark transitions such as winter to spring and spring to summer. Although these rites mark transitions in nature, they also affect the social life of the community and show similar patterns and perform similar functions as rituals marking social passages.

By comparing a number of ceremonies that mark transitions or passages from one social status to another or from one season to another, van Gennep discerned three stages: the time before (marked by rites of separation), the time during (marked by rites of transition) and the time after (marked by rites of incorporation). For example, in the Navaho initiation ceremony partially described above, boys are taken from their homes (separation) to a sacred underground *kiva*. There masked figures dressed as gods or spirits (*katchinas*) teach them songs and dances and finally take off their masks, revealing themselves as ordinary men (transition). After these rites the initiates are led back to their homes and assume the duties and responsibilities of men (incorporation). Van Gennep remarked, "although a complete scheme of rites of passage theoretically includes preliminal rites (rites of separation), liminal rites (rites of transition) and postliminal rites (rites of incorporation) in specific instances these three types are not always equally important or equally elaborate" (van Gennep 1960: 11). The use of the word **liminal** (threshold or doorway) indicates that van Gennep pictured this structure as similar to passing through a door from one space to another.

Van Gennep noted that these rites indicate, contrary to **Durkheim**'s views, that the sacred is not absolute but relative to particular circumstances. Ordinarily the *katchinas* are sacred beings, but during this particular rite their humanness is revealed. He further noted that marking changes in social identity or nature functions socially to reduce whatever harmful and disturbing effects on the social order such passages might have. Crossing boundaries (physical or social) is always a potentially dangerous activity because it threatens to disrupt the social order. Ritualizing such crossings helps the individual and the community to reduce the anxiety associated with such transitions and reassures people that order, although perhaps of a new kind, can be reestablished.

Van Gennep used his threefold schema to analyze rites accompanying territorial movement, pregnancy and childbirth, betrothal and marriage, funerals and initiations. His longest chapter is devoted to initiation rites such as circumcision and baptism. Although many of these are often called "puberty rites," he emphatically denies that the connection to biology is determinative. Rites of initiation can and do occur at different ages and are not necessarily tied to birth or puberty. It is society, not biology, that is determinative in constructing social identity.

In his conclusion to *The Rites of Passage*, van Gennep argued that although rites differ in detail and emphasis among different religions and cultures, their function is similar. They both draw social boundaries and facilitate the crossing of social boundaries in order to change and maintain the social order. The transitional phase of such rites is significant and often stands independently of the other stages. It denotes a special time of **liminality** when humans are "betwixt and between" normal social conditions. The rites both justify violations of the sacred order and reinforce the underlying sense of order the violation transgresses. They also link transitions in the community to cosmic changes. The social world is linked to the cosmic world, thereby grounding the meaning of human life and death in a larger and greater pattern.

Although van Gennep's analysis of **rites of passage** has inspired and still inspires continuing research, he is not without his critics. One common criticism is that he universalized the tripartite pattern when in fact it is far more local than he thought. For example, a close examination and comparison of women's initiation with men's by Bruce Lincoln (1991) notes that they often follow a different pattern. Instead of separation, transition, and incorporation, Lincoln discovered a pattern better characterized by enclosure, metamorphosis, and emergence. Others have argued that van Gennep's emphasis on passage misses the disjunctive aspects of rites. Rituals of initiation may instill anxiety rather that resolve individual and social tensions. Finding out that what you have been taught were gods are only masked humans can create a new set of tensions and questions that may remain unresolved.

Criticism of theories often leads to further advances in understanding. Whatever problems and shortcomings exist with van

Gennep's concept of **rites of passage**, it has influenced scholars like **Mircea Eliade**, **Victor Turner**, **Carl Jung** and others to further develop the idea of **liminality**, apply his analysis to understanding pilgrimage rituals, and explore the psychological as well as social implications of such rites.

Van Gennep pointed to new interpretations of the symbolism of rebirth and regeneration made famous by the myth and ritual school (see **Jane Harrison** and **James Frazer**). His rethinking of the idea of the sacred opened ways for scholars to explore how ritual can create the sacred rather than just react to something already established as sacred. This appreciation for the creative aspects of ritual has prompted others to explore the connections between ritual, play, and the performing arts.

See also: **Douglas, J. Z. Smith**

Major works

(1904) *Tabou et totémisme à Madagascar: Étude descriptive et théorique*, Paris: E. Leroux.

(1906) *Mythes et legends d' Australie*, Paris: Guilmoto.

(1960) *The Rites of Passage*, trans. Monika B. Vizedom and Gabrielle L. Caffee, Chicago, IL: University of Chicago Press.

Further reading

Belier, Wouter W. (May 1994) "Arnold van Gennep and the Rise of French Sociology of Religion," *Numen* 41: 141–62.

Belmont, Nicole. (1978) *Arnold van Gennep: The Creator of French Ethnography*, trans. Derek Coltman, Chicago, IL: University of Chicago Press.

Lincoln, Bruce (1991) *Emerging from the Chrysalis: Rituals of Women's Initiations*, rev. ed., New York: Oxford University Press.

Zumwalt, Rosemary Lévy. (1988) *The Enigma of Arnold van Gennep (1873–1957): Master of French Folklore and Hermit of Bourg-la-Reine*, Helsinki: Suomalainen Tiedeakatemia.

http://www.bookrags.com/research/gennep-arnold-van-eorl-05.

CARL JUNG (1875–1961)

"Religion," it might be said, is the term that designates the attitude peculiar to a consciousness which has been altered by the experience of the numinosum. Creeds are codified and dogmatized forms of original religious experience.

(Jung 1938: 6)

Like **Schleiermacher**, **Otto**, **Suzuki**, **Eliade**, and others, Jung located the heart of religion in a unique type of experience. He makes reference to **Otto**'s idea of the numinous but, as we shall see, he has very different ideas about where this experience comes from. It wells up from the **collective unconscious**.

Carl Gustav Jung was born in Switzerland into the family of a country parson in a small village on the shores of Lake Constance. Jung's mother Emile was warmhearted but unpredictable and at times frightening. His parents' marriage was not a happy one and Jung felt the tension between them from an early age. When he was four, his father accepted a position as Protestant chaplain of the Friedmatt Mental Hospital near Basel. Jung developed interests in both science and the humanities but finally decided on the study of medicine because he thought it would best allow him to combine both interests. In 1900, after completing his studies at the University of Basel, he took a position at a psychiatric hospital in Zurich. He married Emma Rauschenbach in 1903 and eventually devoted most of his energies to private practice.

Jung traveled widely and collaborated with scholars in many different fields ranging from Chinese studies to mythology. His most famous association was with **Sigmund Freud**, but as their views on a variety of subjects including religion began to diverge, Jung started his own school of analytic psychology. He resigned his presidency of the International Psychoanalytic Society in 1914 and embarked on his own path.

Jung published a number of influential works on religion that are gathered together with his other psychological writings in his *Collected Works*. His most important writings on religion include *The Secret of the Golden Flower* (1931), *Psychology of Religion* (1938), *Introduction to a Science of Mythology* (with Karl Kerényi, 1951), *Psychology and Alchemy* (1953), *Answer to Job* (1956), and *Psychology and Religion: West and East* (1958).

According to Jung, the unconscious can be divided into two layers – the personal or individual unconscious and the collective or shared unconscious. The contents of the personal unconscious are determined by one's past experiences and are either repressed because they are too painful to face or go unnoticed because they are unimportant. The **collective unconscious** consists of material that has been formed during the whole history of the human race. It is, if you will, a kind of species unconscious. Jung was led to posit this controversial idea when he began to notice that his patients' dreams and fantasies were filled with ideas and images that could not be traced to past personal experience. He also noted the resemblance of this material to religious and mythical themes that were universal and could not be explained by cultural contact. Jung called these shared "primordial images" archetypes. Archetypes are inherited patterns that Jung posited to account for recurring themes in myths, dreams, art, and literature. They function to condition and filter experience and can appear in a variety of forms.

Two pairs of significant archetypes that are keys to Jung's psychology of religion are *persona/shadow* and *anima/animus*. The word *persona* in Latin means "mask." Jung used it to refer to our public or social self. It is that side of our personality that we are willing to allow others to see because we regard it as socially acceptable. But a mask both reveals and conceals. What is concealed Jung calls the *shadow*. It is that aspect of ourselves that we consider unacceptable and therefore hide from public view and, in many cases, from our selves. It often appears in religion as original sin, a devil, demons, or an evil twin. People develop neuroses when they identify themselves with their *persona* or when they deny their *shadow* by projecting it onto others.

The *anima* is the archetype of femininity present in the unconscious of men. It is an inherited collective image of women and is associated with feeling and intuition. Men who think of themselves as very masculine often deny, repress, or devalue their feminine side. The *animus* is the masculine in women and is the inherited collective image of men usually associated with thinking and rationality. Women who regard themselves as very feminine often deny or repress their "tomboy" qualities. The failure of men to accept their feminine side or the failure of women to accept their masculine side can often lead to inner conflicts and turmoil in relationships.

The self is the most important archetype. The ego is the actual center of consciousness and the self is the potential center. It is an ideal of a balanced and psychologically healthy person who has overcome inner conflicts. In religion saints and holy persons like Buddha or Christ often symbolize the self. Geometric figures such as crosses visually represent the reconciliation of opposites that is characteristic of the self. Quaternities like the cross represent the self because they visually show the reconciliation of opposites.

Life is a journey toward self-realization. This journey is a process that Jung called individuation. The journey begins in an undifferentiated state in which individuals cannot distinguish between themselves and other things. Slowly consciousness emerges from this relatively unconscious state and eventually the ego develops as differentiation of our selves from others becomes stronger. The first stage of undifferentiation (from conception to roughly the age of six) is often represented in creation myths by water or a chaotic state. The movement to the stage of a differentiated ego (roughly puberty to young adulthood) is told in both religious and secular stories involving a hero. It is a story of facing and overcoming obstacles in order to establish one's own unique identity and place in the world. In the last stages of life (middle age to death) the need to reexamine one's life and the values by which it has been lived develops. It is a time to reconcile conflicts, harmonize opposites, and pursue wisdom about the meaning and purpose of life. The opportunity arises to realize a higher, more inclusive, self beyond the ego.

The symbols and images of archetypes like the Mother, the Child, the Wise Old Man, and the Self appear in dreams and in other ways along the course of this journey of individuation to either help or hinder our passage to full humanity depending on how we use them and how well we discern the messages they send. In the modern, secular age, people are in particular peril of failing to successfully complete the path of self-realization because religious mythology and ritual no longer play, as they once did, an influential role in peoples' lives. Jung does not mean by this that the metaphysical information about an alleged supernatural reality provided by religious representations of archetypes needs to somehow regain its authority. What is required is the psychological reinterpretation of religion in order to benefit from its inherited and collective wisdom for living a full and meaningful life. Religious myths and rituals, rightly understood, can be aids on the path to self-realization. The source of religious wisdom is within us, buried in the deepest recesses of our psyches.

Jung's *Psychology and Religion* contains three lectures delivered at Yale University in 1937. The first lecture establishes the "Autonomy of the Unconscious Mind." Jung insisted that psychology is a natural science and as such does not deal with the truth of religious claims but with the human side of religion. Hence it is a **phenomenological** or an empirically descriptive science, and its primary focus should be on religious experience and secondarily on religious creeds and dogmas that provide theological but not psychological interpretations of experience.

Jung argued that religious experiences have their origin in the unconscious mind. They intrude into ego consciousness from the unconscious and thus the subject feels that they come from a source beyond his/her control. This should not lead us to dismiss them as mere imaginings but to take them seriously as influences on human thought and behavior. Their source lies deeper than the personal unconscious. It lies in the **collective unconscious**.

In the second lecture, titled "Dogma and Natural Symbols," Jung presented evidence from his clinical practice that the **collective unconscious** speaks to consciousness via what he called "natural symbols." These symbols represent archetypes and their meanings can be discerned by careful analysis of collections of dreams and by comparative studies in religion, mythology, and art. Such natural symbols can be at odds with official religious teachings even though those teachings influence them. For example, the natural symbol for wholeness and integration is a quaternity. Yet the Christian dogma of the Trinity asserts that God is three persons in one, the Father, the Son, and the Holy Spirit. This dogma integrates several important insights about the relationship of fundamental processes such as creation (father), self-realization (son) and integration (Holy Spirit). However, the Trinity doctrine is an incomplete quaternity because the feminine (anima) is not represented, nor is the shadow side of reality (evil). Evil does appear in Christian dogma but is personified in a Satan figure that exists separately from the Trinity. This shows, Jung argued, that the demands of orthodoxy can restrict and hence misrepresent the natural symbols through which the **collective unconsciousness** speaks.

In the final lecture, titled "The History and Psychology of a Natural Symbol," Jung turned his attention to *mandalas* as symbols of quaternity. These are geometric images that we find in all cultures and religions that suggest integration, often by picturing some type of squared circle. The circle represents cosmic wholeness and the square in conjunction with the circle suggests the integration of opposites. Jung observed in both his own dreams and in the dreams of others that *mandalas* would spontaneously appear when some inner conflict was about to be resolved. In religious *mandalas* (often used as objects of meditation, particularly in Asian religions) the center usually contains an image of a deity. Yet the centers of some modern *mandalas* are empty. Is this a symbol of atheism? Jung argued it is not a denial of God's existence. Rather the empty *mandala* symbolizes that the quest for human wholeness has taken the place of more traditional spiritual quests.

Jung's views have not gone unchallenged. Theologians have accused him of atheism and psychological **reductionism** while those who see psychology as a science are quick to point out that there is no way to experimentally verify or falsify many of his theories. They may be interesting in a kind of poetic sense, but they are not science.

At one time Jung's influence was felt in a wide range of fields, from psychology and literature to religious studies and mythology. His influence has waned in the last few decades but his ideas have impacted pop culture (*Star Wars*) and comparative mythology. His claim that religion is a unique psychological reality still informs one important segment of present debates about **reductionism** in the study of religion.

See also: **Dumézil, van Gennep, James, Lévy-Bruhl**

Major works

(1938) *Psychology and Religion*, New Haven, CT: Yale University Press.
(1959) *The Basic Writings of C. G. Jung*, ed. Violet Staub De Laszlo, New York: The Modern Library.
(1967–79) *Collected Works of C. G. Jung*, 18 vols., ed. Sir Herbert Read, et. al., trans. R. F. C. Hull, Princeton, NJ: Princeton University Press.

Further reading

Bair, Deirdre. (2004) *Jung: A Biography*, Boston: Little Brown.
Hauke, Christopher. (2000) *Jung and the Postmodern: The Interpretation of Realities*, New York: Routledge.
Homans, Peter. (1979) *Jung in Context: Modernity and the Making of Psychology*, Chicago, IL: Chicago University Press.
Rowland, Susan. (2002) *Jung: A Feminist Revision*, Cambridge: Cambridge University Press.
http://en.wikipedia.org/wiki/Carl_Jung.

MARTIN BUBER (1878–1939)

> And in all the seriousness of truth, listen: without It a human being cannot live. But whoever lives with only that is not human.
>
> (Buber 1970: 85)

What is "It"? What does this cryptic remark mean? Why cannot humans live without It and why does living only with It detract from their humanity?

Martin Buber, a Jewish philosopher and educator, was born in Vienna but raised by his grandparents when his parents' marriage broke up. He studied at universities in Vienna, Leipzig, Zurich, and Berlin, obtaining his PhD in 1903. He married the German writer Paula Winkler in 1899, and they had two children. Buber became active in Jewish cultural life and began teaching at the University of Frankfurt in 1923. In 1938 he left Germany because of the rising power of the Nazis and began teaching philosophy at Hebrew

University in Jerusalem. He was active in Israeli politics and worked to improve Jewish/Arab relations, arguing strongly for a bi-national state in which Jews and Palestinians shared equal power. His argument did not carry the day, and he reluctantly endorsed a Jewish state knowing that this could lead to serious problems.

During his teenage and early university years, Buber felt alienated from Judaism. When he got involved with the Zionist movement to establish a homeland for the Jews, his sense of belonging to the Jewish community returned. This sense of belonging was intensified when he started to study Hasidism, a mystical branch of Judaism. Buber believed that Hasidism exemplified a spiritual power that could help the disillusioned youth of his day overcome alienation. Hasidic Judaism was, he argued, a way of life rather than a system of ritual practices and theological concepts. He thought that religion, at its best, could restore meaning and purpose to a world rapidly drowning in the impersonality of technological domination and suffering from the morally corrosive effects of war. In addition to Zionism and Hasidism, Buber was influenced by the existentialism of **Kierkegaard** and of **Nietzsche**, as well as the sociology of **Max Weber**.

Buber's basic insight, which runs through his many books on religion, is the idea that there are two fundamental ways of relating to nature, other people, and the divine. One of these ways he labeled I–It and the other he called I–You (Thou). His most influential book, *I and Thou*, describes these two types of relationship in poetic and moving prose.

The I–It mode of relating is, for moderns at least, the most common. It is characterized by an instrumentalist, practical, and goal-oriented point of view. People in this mode relate to nature as an object to be used and manipulated for their own ends. Trees are seen as so much wood to be harvested and used in construction or for other purposes. People also relate to other people as if they were "Its." With a detached and impersonal perspective, they evaluate others in terms of their usefulness for their own ends. Other people are not seen as ends in themselves but as means to further goals (see **Kant**). In effect the I–It mode is a one-way relationship (if we can call it a relationship at all) because there is no mutuality. We relate to the other with only a part of ourselves and relate to only part of the other. We take no risks but seek a security that assures our own interests will prevail. There is no genuine and authentic listening to the other and hence no authentic relationship. Nor is there open and honest communication. Words are used to conceal and not to reveal.

Genuine participation and relation is the mark of the I–You relationship in contrast to the I–It. In this type of relationship, we relate to nature as if it were alive and take heed of our responsibilities to nurture it. The so-called primitives lived in an enchanted forest and the mythic stories they told of talking trees and animals indicate an I–You mode of connection and participation (see **Lévy-Bruhl**). When the relationship is one of I–You we relate to other people in a personal mode and with our whole being rather than only part of our being. We listen receptively and do not seek to manipulate others for our own ends. Our attitude is not one of objective detachment but of engagement and dialogue. By dialogue Buber meant an open and honest relationship that does not speak or listen according to predetermined values and categories but speaks and listens in the present moment open to the new and unexpected. It is communication at the deepest levels of our being.

Buber was well aware that I–It relationships are necessary to life. We cannot always live in the world of I–You. It is fleeting and fluid. But if we only live in an I–It mode, we can never realize our full humanity. Buber was concerned that the I–It mode of relating was becoming the dominant mode in the modern world because of the influence of technology, science, and economic rationalization. He wanted to champion an alternative way of living that he believed allowed people to live a more complete and humane life. This, he thought, was a more spiritual way of life that made religion a real and effective power rather than a system of strange ideas, boring rituals, and repressive morality.

Buber drew the connection between I–You and religion by arguing that the fleeting moments of I–You intimacy awaken the desire for a more permanent and genuine relationship. However, the I–You moments eventually transition into I–It and then transition back to I–You again. I–You cannot be sustained indefinitely in the world in which we live. So some come to long for an eternal You unconditioned by the flux of life. When humans encounter the eternal You, the exclusive You who by its very nature can never become an It, they enter the realm of religion even if this eternal You is not called God. Religions, as we know them historically, call the eternal You by many names. Even if someone rejects all names including the name God, "and fancies that he is godless—when he addresses with his whole devoted being the You of his life that cannot be restricted by any other, he addresses God" (Buber 1970: 124).

Buber was convinced that the fundamental reality in which humans live is the reality of relations or of the "in-between" as he called it. This applies not just to nature and other people, but also to the divine. If we think of religion as centering on the experience of absolute dependence or mystical claims about absorption into the divine, we miss a vital element. Religion is about relationships and in particular about a relationship with an eternal You. The history of religion is a history of humans trying to turn an eternal You into an It. Hence religions come and go, wax and wane, for all attempts to change what cannot be changed are bound, sooner or later, to fail.

Although organized religion has its limitations, it can offer glimpses of an I–You relationship with the divine. The eternal You summons us to dialogue and sends us on a mission to relate authentically to others. Glimpses of the eternal You can also be had in ordinary I–You relationships. However, religion offers a unique opportunity to engage the divine in an ongoing dialogue.

Critics of Buber often complain that his poetic prose is vague and ambiguous. Those seeking a more precise philosophical analysis are often disappointed. It can be very difficult to know exactly what he is talking about in many passages of his books. His attitude about the limitations of science and scholarship, which by its very nature objectifies what it studies, can inspire an anti-science mentality and undermine rather than promote a more objective understanding of religion. Hence the usefulness of his ideas for academic religious studies appears limited. However his views have proved both influential and useful in the analysis and interpretation of ancient civilizations (see Henri Frankfort's *Before Philosophy*).

In Buber's defense, we need to understand that his intention was to edify and inspire, not to dissect and objectify. The ambiguity of his prose often succeeds in causing readers to rethink their lives and find meaning in their relationships. This may not make them better scholars (though hopefully it would), but it can make them better human beings. Buber reminds us of the positive role religion can play in humanizing our world.

See also: **Schleiermacher, Scholem, Tillich, Turner**

Major works

(1951) *Two Types of Faith: A Study of Interpretation of Judaism and Christianity*, New York: HarperCollins.

(1952) *Eclipse of God: Studies in the Relation Between Religion and Philosophy*, New York: Harper and Row.

(1953) *Good and Evil*, New York: Scribner's.

(1967) *On Judaism*, ed. Nahum H. Glatzer, New York: Schocken Books.
(1965) *Between Man and Man*, trans. Ronald Gregor Smith, New York: The Macmillan Company.
(1970) *I and Thou*, trans. Walter Kaufmann, New York: Charles Scribner's and Sons.

Further reading

Frankfort, Henri A., Wilson, John A., Jacobsen, Thorkild, Irwin, William A. (1966) *Before Philosophy: The Intellectual Adventure of Ancient Man*, Baltimore, MD: Penguin Books.
Friedman, Maurice. (2002) *Martin Buber: A Life of Dialogue*, 4th ed., New York: Routledge.
Gorden, Haim and Jochanan Bloch, eds. (1984) *Martin Buber: A Centenary Volume*, New York: Ktav.
Silberstein, Laurence. (1990) *Martin Buber's Social and Religious Thought*, Albany, NY: New York University Press.
http://plato.stanford.edu/entries/buber.

A. R. RADCLIFFE-BROWN (1881–1955)

> Stated in its simplest possible terms the theory is that an orderly social life amongst human beings depends upon the presence in the minds of the members of a society of certain sentiments, which control the behaviour of the individual in his relation to others.
>
> (Radcliffe-Brown 1952: 157)

With these words Alfred Reginald Radcliffe-Brown, one of the founders of English social anthropology, summarized his theory of what religious rituals do. That theory is not just a theory of the function of rituals, but a theory of religion as well. But what does he mean by "certain sentiments?" How does religion produce and maintain them?

Radcliffe-Brown was born in Sparkbrook, Birmingham and began his advanced education as a premedical student at Birmingham University. After a year he transferred to Trinity College, Cambridge and took his bachelor's degree in mental and moral science. He went on to study anthropology and in 1906 spent two years doing fieldwork among the people of the Andaman Islands. After some delays due to World War I, his fieldwork was finally published in 1922 as *The Andaman Islanders* and helped establish fieldwork as an essential component of anthropology. He also carried out fieldwork in Australia, which led to an interest in **totemism** and the theories of **Émile Durkheim**.

Radcliffe-Brown had an illustrious and influential teaching career establishing programs in social anthropology in a number of countries. He occupied chairs in Cape Town, Sydney, Chicago, and Oxford. His writing and thinking made major contributions to what some call structural functionalism (see below). Many of his more important essays on method and theory were published in 1952 as *Structure and Function in Primitive Society*. As the title indicates, he was not only interested in how religion functions to produce and maintain social unity but also in how function was related to social structure. He was a pioneer in establishing a scientific comparative social anthropology in the face of entrenched social evolutionary approaches to the study of religion.

In a chapter titled "Religion and Society," (*Structure and Function in Primitive Society*) Radcliffe-Brown noted that a common way of viewing religion is as a group of illusory beliefs and practices. This is particularly true when it comes to so-called primitive religions. If we pursue this line of inquiry then the problem of how such erroneous beliefs and ineffective rituals were created and so widely accepted must soon be addressed. He made it clear that he did not think this sort of approach would yield any real understanding of religion.

He proposed another approach that recognizes that religion, like morality and law, is an essential part of a complex social system that allows humans to live together by maintaining a social order. However ineffective a rainmaking ritual may be when it comes to actually producing rain, such practices may have other effects that are socially valuable. Hence they persist even in the face of failure. Discovering their social value and describing it is the work of social anthropology, a task bequeathed by **Durkheim** whose ideas deeply influenced Radcliffe-Brown's understanding of the "sentiments" inspired by religion and their social significance.

Anthropologists have been influenced by the Protestant Christian emphasis on belief. Hence they tend to define religion in terms of beliefs and concentrate their energy on discovering how beliefs are formed and adopted (see **Asad**). There is, Radcliffe-Brown argued, no clear cause and effect relationship between belief and action. Religious practices and religious beliefs are formed together but it is action (rites, ceremonies, rituals) that controls and inspires beliefs. The actions should be viewed as "symbolic expressions of sentiments." Social anthropologists should concentrate their attention on rites rather than beliefs if they want to further our understanding of religion. Rituals have a specific social function because they "transmit from one generation to another sentiments on which the constitution of society depends" (Radcliffe-Brown 1952: 157).

But what are these sentiments? There are many different senti-ments, but the most basic one, Radcliffe-Brown suggested, is "a sense of dependence on a power outside ourselves, a power which we may speak of as a spiritual or moral power" (Radcliffe-Brown 1952: 157). At this point one would expect him to evoke **Schleiermacher**'s views on the feeling of absolute dependence or **Otto**'s notion of creature-feeling but instead he cites (among others) an ancient Chinese philosopher, Hsün Tzu, and his analysis of rites as functioning to bind people together and to regulate human feelings.

There are two sides to this sense of dependence. One side is oriented to the past, the other side to the present. For example, in the cult of ancestor-worship people acknowledge their dependence on those who have gone before and are responsible for their existence. But they also acknowledge that the ancestors watch over their conduct in the present. If they fail to do their duties, the ancestors will punish them, perhaps with sickness or some other misfortune. If they fulfill their duties, the ancestors will send blessings, perhaps giving them many children or increasing their wealth. Taken together these two aspects of the sentiment of dependence send the message that people can and must depend on the ancestors and hence on one another. So-called advanced religions like monotheism send and reinforce similar messages. One can and must rely on God. "[W]hat makes and keeps a man a social animal," wrote Radcliffe-Brown, "is not some herd instinct, but the sense of dependence in the innumerable forms that it takes" (Radcliffe-Brown 1952: 176).

Examining different societies and seeing if there is a correspon-dence between the religion and the social structure of that society can test this theory of the social value of religion. For example, ancestor-worship is correlated with societies in which family lineage is a significant part of the social structure. Rejecting the idea that religion causes social structure, Radcliffe-Brown, like **Durkheim**, argued that society causes religion. In other words, the sense of dependence people feel is not really to spirits but to society, or at least to society as expressed in some particular social structure such as family, clan, tribe, or nation.

Radcliffe-Brown not only made contributions to social anthropology by collecting data on the Andaman Islanders and by contributing to the development of **Durkheim**'s theory of religion as a reflection of society, but also by devoting a significant amount of attention to problems of method and definition. He conceived of social anthro-pology as a science and developed his ideas by drawing parallels with biology and linguistics. Biology studies the structure and function of organisms and linguistics studies the structure and function of language. Both use the methods of observation, classification, and comparison (see **J. Z. Smith**). Social anthropology studies the structure and function of society and it too uses the methods of observation, classification, and comparison.

Social anthropology can be divided into three parts—social morphology, physiology, and the processes by which social structures change and new forms arise. Morphology is the study of types or forms of structural systems. Structural systems consist of social structures that are in turn complex networks of social relations. Social physiology focuses on explaining how structural systems persist. Just as biological physiology seeks to explain the persistence of an organism by describing how it functions, so social anthropology must describe how social structures function to preserve social continuity even when the parts of the system change. Religion is just one kind of social structure and it functions, according to Radcliffe-Brown, by creating social solidarity through creating and maintaining sentiments of dependence.

The processes by which social structures change and new forms are created are many and varied but one process that gives us some starting points for investigation is organic evolution. Biological evolution is based on two basic ideas, namely, diversification (a small number of kinds of organism give rise to a larger number of kinds) and increasing complexity. Both of these occur because of the necessity of an organism to adapt to changing environments. By analogy, we might think of social evolution as a process by which social structures adapt to changing environments, leading to social diversification and increasing social complexity. We can understand changes in religion and the creation of new religions as a process of diversification and increasing complexity.

Although Radcliffe-Brown talks about religious evolution, his approach to the study of religion is not primarily evolutionary (see **Tylor** and **Frazer**). The study of religion is like the study of other social structures. It is made up of the investigation of the structures and functions of religious practices and the processes by which they change.

One of the ways Radcliffe-Brown extended **Durkheim**'s interpretation of ritual was by suggesting a more systematic correlation between social structure and types of religion. For example, lineage social systems are usually correlated with ancestor-worship. Unfortunately, as critics have pointed out, this is not always the case. Different types of religion are not always correlated with the social structure one would expect. Indeed some types, Christian and Islamic monotheism for example, have spread to and been successful in many different societies that have very different social systems.

Critics have remarked that the functionalism of Radcliffe-Brown seems inherently conservative. Religion functions to promote and maintain social order. While this may be true, it is not always true. Religion can also be a revolutionary force (e.g. the Protestant Reformation) that divides and fragments social unity by creating competing ideologies.

Even though there are limitations to Radcliffe-Brown's views, he developed a more sophisticated social anthropology by making field-work essential. He also turned attention away from trying to discover the origin of religion and to reconstruct a schema of religious evolution, which largely had been based on speculation, toward more empirically grounded tasks centering on observation, description, and classification of existing forms of religious life in so-called primitive societies. He also influenced future developments by laying some of the groundwork for the structuralism of **Claude Lévi-Strauss**.

See also: **Evans-Pritchard**

Major works

(1952) *Structure and Function in Primitive Society*, Glencoe, IL: The Free Press.

(1964) *The Andaman Islanders*, Glencoe, IL: The Free Press.

(1977) *The Social Anthropology of Radcliffe-Brown*, ed. Adam Kuper, London: Routledge and Kegan Paul.

Further reading

Câmara, J. L. Bettencourt da. (1995) *Radcliffe-Brown and Lévi-Strauss: A Reappraisal*, Lisbon: Instituto Superior de Ciências Sociais e Políticas.

Fortes, Meyer, ed. (1963) *Social Structure: Studies Presented to A. R. Radcliffe-Brown*, New York: Russell and Russell.

Kuper, Adam. (2004) *The Social Anthropology of Radcliffe-Brown*, London: Routledge.

http://en.wikipedia.org/wiki/Alfred_Radcliffe-Brown.

BRONISLAW MALINOWSKI (1884–1942)

> We have taken for our starting-point a most definite and tangible distinction: we have defined, within the domain of the sacred, magic as a practical art consisting of acts which are only means to a definite end expected to follow later on; religion as a body of self-contained acts being themselves the fulfillment of their purpose.
>
> (Malinowski 1954: 88)

With these words, the "father" of social anthropology, Bronislaw Malinowski, answered a question about what distinguishes religion from magic. Magic is a means to a definite end (e.g. a cure) while religious worship is an end in itself. Both are sacred. Science (see below) is part of the profane and while having similarities to magic is based on different convictions.

Bronislaw Kasper Malinowski was born in Cracow, Poland to an aristocratic family. He studied physics and mathematics at Jagiellonian University in Cracow and studied the social sciences at the London School of Economics where he received his DSc in 1916. He attributed his shift from the natural sciences to the human sciences to reading **Frazer**'s *The Golden Bough*. However, while **Frazer** is known as an "armchair" anthropologist, Malinowski insisted that anthropological study must involve fieldwork and participant observation. The introduction of fieldwork as the *sine qua non* of anthropology revolutionized the discipline.

In 1914–15, Malinowski spent time among the Mailu on Toulon Island off the southern coast of New Guinea. In 1915 he started a twenty-one month study in the Trobriand Islands. His most famous book, *Argonauts of the Western Pacific* (1922) details his research. He became the first professor of anthropology at the University of London in 1927. In 1938 he accepted a visiting professor position at Yale University. He died in 1942 from a heart condition.

One of Malinowski's more popular books was *Sex and Repression in Savage Society* (1927) in which he argued against both **Freud**'s assertion that the Oedipus complex is universal and his claims about the origin of religion and culture in a primal, Oedipal act of murder. He contended not only that these claims are beyond any empirical verification, but also that the evidence he gathered from his Trobriand fieldwork did not support them.

Two basic ideas pervade Malinowski's work: **empiricism** and functionalism. His empirical orientation led to a distrust of theoretical appeals to entities that may exist beyond experience and to a preference for intellectual constructs consisting of observables. Biology inspired his functionalism, which was built on the claim that the functions of social institutions such as religion can be discovered in the human needs they satisfy.

The introduction to *Argonauts* deals with fieldwork methods and reflects Malinowski's empirical bent. The social anthropologist is advised to learn the native language and live among the natives for an extended period of time collecting data on tribal organization, types of behaviors, and such elements as myths, magical practices, religious rituals, marriage practices, and folklore. The goal, he famously said, is "to grasp the native's point of view" (Malinowski 1961: 25).

Malinowski's functionalism assumed that culture is a closed system of social relations whose internal dynamism is powered by social mechanisms that function to maintain the system. Religious rituals, for example, are viewed as a way of stabilizing society by maintaining group ethos and restoring harmony after a disruption. Unlike **Durkheim**, Malinowski thought religion was rooted in individual experiences rather than in society. His version of functionalism stressed the idea of a hierarchy of human needs ranging from basic biological needs, through cultural or social needs, to normative or integrative needs. Human culture plays a role at all these levels by creating mechanisms for satisfying such needs.

Although other anthropologists treated myths as a kind of poetry or, like **Tylor**, as mistaken explanations of natural events, Malinowski argued that their function was to validate the social order. Myths strengthen social and religious traditions by appeal to an idealized past when supernatural beings first established the practices and beliefs central to the life of the group. They function as a kind of supernatural "charter" that provides authority for what people believe and do. Myths do not explain but "vouch for." They do not function to satisfy curiosity but to validate beliefs. For example, the Trobriand Islanders maintain that magic came from underground, or was handed down by ancestors, or given by non-human but powerful beings. According to their myths, it was definitely not invented by humans and, in that sense, has "always been there."

Malinowski began *Magic, Science, and Religion* (1925), from which our opening quotation comes, by distinguishing between sacred and profane. Magic and religion belong to the realm of the sacred, while science is part of the profane. He rejected **Lévy-Bruhl**'s notion that primitive thought is "prelogical" and "mystical" along with **Frazer**'s theory of evolutionary progression from magic to religion to science. His fieldwork showed him that the Trobriand Islanders were practical people with a great degree of technical knowledge about building canoes, sailing them, and about agricultural techniques. They used magical spells when they faced dangerous and unknown situations where their practical knowledge, their "science," was limited. The evolutionary scheme of **Frazer** was without empirical support and, by its very nature, could not be empirically verified since we can never get back to the origins of human culture. The evidence was simply not available and to infer from presently existing "primitive" cultures to an unknown past was little more than guesswork.

What magic does, according to Malinowski, is provide psychological support for cooperative group activities in those cases where lack of knowledge endangers success. It is a supplement to but not a substitute for practical endeavors such as fishing. Religion is not magic, although in some respects they are akin. Religion functions in a way magic does not by providing psychological consolation in the face of tragedy and anxiety aroused by uncertainty.

The relationship of magic to religion is complex. Both function in situations of stress and crises. They both open avenues of escape from such situations. Both are based on a mythological tradition and are surrounded by taboos. However, magic is a practical art that aims to accomplish certain specific goals but religion is not a practical art. It is not instrumental and does not aim at any specific outcome such as a good harvest. It does, however, have a function. It "establishes, fixes, and enhances all valuable mental attitudes, such as reverence for tradition, harmony with the environment, courage and confidence in the struggle with difficulties and at the prospect of death" (Malinowski 1954: 89).

When we turn our attention to science, we can see certain similarities with magic as well as important differences. Both magic and science are practical endeavors aimed at specific ends. Both develop special techniques. However, science is based on experiences stemming from everyday life and not, like magic, on special emotional states of stress or crisis. Its theories are based on observation, logic, and testing, and not on the association of ideas influenced by desire. It is based on the conviction that rational efforts will prevail in solving problems. Magic is based on the belief that "hope will not fail."

Malinowski's quest to see the world from the native viewpoint led him to pay particular attention to language. Language is the means by which we filter our experiences and communicate them. It is also culture-dependent in important ways, which makes it very difficult for someone from another culture to comprehend all the nuances of another language, especially one arising from a worldview so very different from one's own. What he called the "symbol situation" is the place to begin to understand because meaning is context dependent. Unless we can grasp the context in which words are used, we cannot grasp their meanings. Further, the meaning of words is rooted in what he called their "pragmatic efficiency" and is not magically contained in the sounds and symbols.

Malinowski identified what he called a "phatic" function of language (later called the performative function). This is particularly important when trying to grasp ritualized uses of words. Language can create a social reality that did not exist before. Pronouncements made in marriage ceremonies are good examples. People are transformed into husband and wife, along with a new set of social roles, by such ritualized language.

For all his contributions to an anthropological understanding of magic and religion, Malinowski has not been without his critics. He has been charged with overgeneralizing based on limited samples rather than careful comparative work. Sociologists have complained that his use of the concept of function is ambiguous and more geared to identifying psychological functions than sociological ones. In his reaction to the "arm chair" anthropologists who tried to reconstruct the history of religion in cultures long since gone, Malinowski almost completely neglected the historical.

Perhaps the most prevalent criticism has centered on his assumptions about society. For Malinowski, an integrated, stable society is the norm and social conflict is abnormal. However, conflict is a normal part of any society and religion plays as much a role in stabilizing a society as in changing it and in creating conflict. Rituals may function to decrease anxiety but they may also function to increase it.

Whatever shortcomings his ideas may have, there is no denying that Malinowski played a vital role in the advancement of social anthropology, particularly in regard to the role of fieldwork. His ideas concerning magic inspired later theories and his notions of language anticipated the revolutionary ideas of **Wittgenstein**.

See also: **Eliade, Evans-Pritchard, Lévi-Strauss**

Major works

(1923) "The Problem of Meaning in Primitive Languages," in C. K. Ogden and I. A. Richards, eds, *The Meaning of Meaning: A Study of the Influence of Language upon Thought and of the Science of Symbolism*, New York: Harcourt, Brace and World.

(1927) *Sex and Repression in Savage Society*, London: Routledge and Kegan Paul.

(1929) *The Sexual Life of Savages in North-Western Melanesia: An Ethnographic Account of Courtship, Marriage and Family Life Among the Natives of the Trobriand Islands*, London: G. Rutledge.

(1935) *Coral Gardens and Their Magic: A Study of the Methods of Tilling the Soil and of Agricultural Rite*, London: Allen and Unwin.

(1954) *Magic, Science and Religion*, Garden City, NY: Doubleday and Company.

(1961) *Argonauts of the Western Pacific: An Account of Native Enterprise and Adventure in the Archipelagoes of Melanesian New Guinea*, New York: E. P. Dutton.

Further reading

Firth, Raymond, ed. (1964) *Man and Culture: An Evaluation of the Work of Bronislaw Malinowski*, New York: Harper and Row.

Gellner, Ernest. (1998) *Language and Solitude: Wittgenstein, Malinowski and the Habsburg Dilemma*, Cambridge: Cambridge University Press.

Gluckman, Max. (1949) *An Analysis of the Sociological Theories of Bronislaw Manlinowski*, New York: Oxford University Press.

Young, Michael W. (2004) *Malinowski: Odyssey of an Anthropologist 1884–1920*, New Haven, CT: Yale University Press.

http://en.wikipedia.org/wiki/Bronislaw_Malinowski.

PAUL TILLICH (1886–1965)

> Religion is the state of being grasped by an ultimate concern, a concern which qualifies all other concerns as preliminary and which itself contains the answer to the question of the meaning of our life.
>
> (Tillich 1963: 4)

This very broad definition of religion is at the core of Paul Tillich's understanding of the importance of religion in human life. Ultimate concerns can be almost anything. If we call them gods, we speak of religion and if they are things we normally regard as secular, such as the nation or nature, Tillich proposes we call them quasi-religions. Humans turn to religions and/or quasi-religions at those times when the question of life's meaning presses upon them.

The father of Paul Johannes Tillich was a Lutheran pastor in Brandenburg, Germany. It was only natural for Paul to pursue an education that would lead to ordination in 1912 after completing his PhD at the University of Berlin and his ThD at the University of Halle. In World War I he served as a military chaplain and his war experiences challenged his faith to the core.

After the war he began teaching philosophy and sociology at the University of Frankfurt and in 1933 he published a book (*The Socialist Decision*) that got him into trouble with the Nazi party because it contained criticism of National Socialism. In the same year he immigrated to the United States and began teaching at Union Theological Seminary in New York. After he retired from Union in 1955, he was invited to serve as University Professor at Harvard University and in 1962 he was appointed Nuveen Professor of Theology at the University of Chicago. Both of these appointments were significant honors and reflected the fact that his ideas had, over the years, influenced in important ways the direction of Christian thought in Europe and North America.

Tillich lived through two world wars, as well as the Cold War. He characterized that time as an "Age of Anxiety" and tried to show how anxiety was rooted in the human condition of finiteness and related to estrangement (his word for sin). Humans are alienated from the "Ground of Being" (the Infinite) and this alienation results in many of the problems that plague human life such as anxiety and a sense of meaninglessness. Religions, including Christianity, address this situation, as do the quasi-religions, by offering ways in which humans can live fulfilled and meaningful lives. However, not all alleged "ultimates" are truly ultimate (such as the nation or wealth) and hence quasi-religions offer, in the end, little permanent satisfaction.

If religion seeks to speak to the human condition, how are we to understand the human situation? Tillich drew on religious sources, but also on such existential thinkers as **Kierkegaard** and **Nietzsche** among others, to show that anxiety is rooted in the ontological condition or basic structure of being human. Humans exist in "finitude" and this situation gives rise to anxiety, which expresses itself in guilt, fear of death, and a sense that life is, in the last analysis, without meaning or purpose. We tend to think of fear, guilt, and anxiety as psychological and treat them as such. But if Tillich is right about their foundation in the very structure of human existence, then they are never merely psychological. Fear, guilt, and meaninglessness run deeper, and so a solution that goes beyond psychology is required.

The human condition would not give rise to anxiety if humans were not estranged or alienated from the Infinite. This estrangement is symbolized in the Christian myth (sacred story) of the Fall and expulsion from the Garden of Eden. It is symbolized theologically by the concept of "original sin." Other religions symbolize this situation in other ways. For example, Buddhism talks about suffering.

In addition to finitude, existence is structured in polar opposites such as individualization and participation, dynamics and form, freedom and destiny. For example, political movements often reveal tensions between the need for individual freedom (individualism) and the need for community (participation). Humans find themselves in a constant struggle to harmonize these polar opposites because they have "finite freedom." Such freedom is a "dreadful freedom" because it demands that we take responsibility for how we live our lives. Religions recognize this by placing moral demands on humans to live their lives in certain ways.

Religion, however, is not just another cultural institution preaching morality. It is the "depth dimension" underlying all structures of existence. Hence human culture (art, literature, science, economics, and the like) is to a greater or lesser degree an expression of the religious impulse to find meaning and purpose in life and to overcome the problems associated with finitude. Religions recognize that humans must live by faith, that is, by embracing some ultimate concern. However, the great danger of religion is idolatry.

Idolatry is mistaking something finite for the Infinite and hence becoming ultimately concerned about that which is not truly ultimate. The advantage of religion is genuine faith or a living authentic relationship with what is truly ultimate. There are dangers, however, because faith can be distorted in different ways. In *Dynamics of Faith*, Tillich described three common distortions of genuine faith—the intellectualistic, voluntaristic, and emotionalistic. The first distortion confuses faith with "believing that" certain propositions are true. On this account of faith as belief, the believer is required to give intellectual assent to the truth of such statements of faith as creeds and dogmas. The second distortion confuses faith with an act of will. According to this distortion, one should will oneself to believe even if one is not intellectually convinced. The final distortion confuses faith with emotion. Faith is a warm feeling akin to feelings of love and devotion. Faith is reduced to a good feeling.

The reason that confusing faith with belief, or an act of will, or an emotional feeling, amounts to a distortion is because in each case faith is reduced to one or another of its dimensions. Authentic faith arises from an integrated center of one's self. It is, as Tillich put it, the "acceptance of being accepted." It is the existential realization that in spite of our shortcomings, anxieties, and alienation there is a sure foundation for courageous living. Genuine faith gives us the "courage to be" even in the face of doubts, fear, and guilt. It allows us to acknowledge honestly our limitations and yet affirm the possibility of transcending finitude.

In his three-volume *Systematic Theology*, Tillich turned his attention to reinterpreting the basic teachings of the Christian church. His goal was to show how these teachings correlate to questions that arise from the existential conditions of human existence. He called his method of analysis the "method of correlation." The central symbols of Christianity are God the Father, God the Son, and God the Holy

Spirit. All of these are symbols and should not, if idolatry is to be avoided, be taken literally. But what do they mean and how are they correlated with the human condition?

The symbol God answers the ontological question of the meaning of being. It tells us why there is something rather than nothing. God is best understood as "being-itself." The claim that ultimate reality is being-itself implies that God is not just one more being among a long list of beings but is the source, power, or "ground of being." God is the theological symbol for the priority of being over nonbeing or nothingness.

However, humans are concerned with more than just abstract metaphysical questions about why there is something rather than nothing. They are also concerned with finding fulfillment and meaning. The question about the meaning of human existence arises from the estrangement of human existence. Why are things not as they ought to be? The symbol of Christ (God the Son) shows us the meaning of human existence by offering the possibility of bearing the meaninglessness and contradictions of human existence without being overwhelmed by despair. Christ is the "New Being" that offers the possibility of a new beginning.

In addition to the question of the meaning of being and the meaning of human existence, humans face the question of the meaning of life. Why are we here living in an ambiguous world with its mixture of joy and suffering? Why are we thrust into ambiguous situations in which it is far from clear what is the best course of action? The symbol of the "Holy Spirit" assures us that there is an unambiguous meaning and purpose that faith can discern in and through the ambiguities of life.

When Tillich spoke of God, Christ, and Spirit as symbols for something deeper, he used the word symbol in a technical sense. Symbols are different from signs. Signs are conventional and interchangeable because they do not participate in the reality to which they point. Symbols do participate in the reality to which they refer. Hence the symbols God, Christ, and Spirit actually make present in this world the ultimate meaning of human existence. However, he did maintain that there was one central non-symbolic designation for God, namely, "God is being-itself."

Although Tillich was first and foremost concerned with reinterpreting Christianity for the "Age of Anxiety," near the end of this life he began to pay more attention to other religions. Our opening quotation comes from the first chapter of the lectures he delivered in Japan on the encounter of the world religions. In those lectures he advocated open and honest dialogue that acknowledges both the differences and similarities of the many religions in a spirit of tolerance. He rejected Christian exclusivism while acknowledging that each of the world religions had much to learn from the others. However, as his definition of religion indicates, he thought his understanding of faith as ultimate concern could further our understanding of all the many different religions.

Tillich, at the height of his career, was the most popular philosophical theologian in North America and much of Europe. He did, however, have critics. Conservative theologians accused him of being an atheist because he argued that it was as absurd to claim that God existed as a being among beings as it was to assert that God did not exist. Many philosophers found his claims about the symbolic nature of religious language incoherent and historians of religion argued that his definition of religion as ultimate concern was too broad to be useful.

At one time Tillich's ideas were widely influential. He appealed to the religious and nonreligious alike. Since his death his influence has waned and few appeal to his ideas today. Perhaps that has resulted from the steady decline of existential philosophy, to which his views were closely tied, or from the fact that the academic study of religion has taken a turn toward historical and social scientific studies. In any case, he is still read and some of his ideas, such as ultimate concern, have proved quite useful in understanding religion.

See also: **Bellah, Berger, Buber, Eliade, Geertz, Gross, Hegel, James, Otto, Radhakrishnan, Schleiermacher, W. C. Smith, Turner, Wittgenstein**

Major works

(1951–63) *Systematic Theology*, 3 vols. Chicago, IL: The University of Chicago Press.
(1952) *The Courage to Be*, New Haven, CT: Yale University Press.
(1957) *Dynamics of Faith*, New York: Harper and Brothers.
(1959) *Theology of Culture*, New York: Oxford University Press.
(1963) *Christianity and the Encounter of World Religions*, New York: Columbia University Press.

Further reading

Edwards, Paul, (1965) "Professor Tillich's Confusions," *Mind*, Vol. 74, 192–214.
Kegley, C. W. and R. W. Brettal. (1956) *The Theology of Paul Tillich*, New York: Macmillan.

Pauck, Wilhelm and Marion Pauck. (1976) *Paul Tillich: His life and Thought*, New York: Harper and Row.

Taylor, Mark K. (1987) *Paul Tillich: Theologian of the Boundaries*, London: Collins.

http://people.bu.edu/wwildman/WeirdWildWeb/courses/mwt/dictionary/mwt_themes_755_tillich.htm.

SARVEPALLI RADHAKRISHNAN (1888–1975)

> It [religion] is the reaction of the whole man to the whole reality. We seek the religious object by the totality of our faculties and energies. Such functioning of the whole man may be called spiritual life, as distinct from a merely intellectual or moral or aesthetic activity or a combination of them. The spiritual sense, the instinct for the real, is not satisfied with anything less than the absolute and the eternal.
>
> (Radhakrishnan 1980: 69–70)

With these words Sarvepalli Radhakrishnan, the most famous and influential Indian philosopher of religion of the last century, states what he takes to be the essence of religion. His views reflect an idealist approach to religion that deftly weaves together elements from both Eastern and Western philosophy.

Radhakrishnan was born in South India to a Brahmin family. He went to a Christian missionary school for twelve years, graduating from Madras Christian College in 1908. His teachers tried to convince him that Christianity was superior to Hinduism but he did not accept their arguments. However, the tension between his Hindu piety and the Christian doctrine he was taught sparked a lifelong interest in comparative philosophy and religion and a search to overcome the tension.

Shankara (eighth or ninth century) and his Advaita Vedanta (non-dualistic) school of Indian religious philosophy, along with **Hegel**'s absolute idealism, strongly influenced Radhakrishnan's understanding of religion. He became a renowned teacher, serving as a professor of philosophy at Calcutta University and as the Spalding Professor of Eastern Religions at Oxford University. In addition to teaching, he established careers in both academic administration and politics. He was elected the second president of modern India in 1962.

Radhakrishnan wrote extensively and published papers and books on both Eastern and Western philosophy and religion. Among his best-known and most influential works are *Indian Philosophy* (1923 and 1927), *The Hindu View of Life* (1926), and *An Idealist View of Life* (from which the above quotation comes), first published in English in 1932. In his writings he sought to convince his readers that at their core all religions are the same, that philosophical idealism offers the best understanding of reality, and that materialistic and scientific thinking that excludes religion cannot adequately meet the needs of the human quest for meaning.

Radhakrishnan characterized the philosophy of religion in **Hegelian** fashion as religion coming to "understanding itself." It can and should become "scientific" by focusing on the universal characteristics of religious experience and discovering how religious convictions "fit in" with the principles of the universe and "tested laws." Philosophy of religion should be distinguished from dogmatic theology because it is open to all religious experience and does not assume the truth of the particular teachings of any one tradition.

As the opening quotation indicates, Radhakrishnan defined religion very broadly and rather vaguely. He regarded its essence as a quest for the ideal possibilities of human life and argued that it cannot be reduced to any particular function of the human mind, nor can it be reduced to a particular emotion (see **Tillich**). It is independent in the sense that it is unique reality.

If a unique experience is at the heart of religion, how can we characterize it? Radhakrishnan described it as both mystical and revelatory. It is an undivided, integrated, and unitary consciousness in which any division between subject and object melts away. In addition, it is self-authenticating, leading to a sense of absolute certitude. Echoing **James**'s analysis of mysticism, he asserted that words are inadequate to describe it and we must make a distinction between what mystics say and what they mean. What they say is never adequate to express what they mean.

This linguistic shortcoming is due not only to the limitations of human language and symbols, but also due to the "wholly other" character of the divine (see **Otto**). The frame of reference used to interpret the experience is determined, at least in part, by heredity and culture. Thus all religions draw on their traditions to make sense of the experiences reported by sages, seers, saints, and prophets. Nevertheless, Radhakrishnan claimed there is a fundamental agreement among mystics behind the diversity of expression. He wrote, "The consubstantiality of the spirit in man and God is the conviction fundamental to all spiritual wisdom" (Radhakrishnan 1980: 81).

What humans generally symbolize as God is both within the human spirit and without. The mystic finds the source of the divine within and the worshipper or devotee finds it without. Contrary to appearances, these forms of spirituality are not basically different, but two different ways of symbolizing the absolute ground of all reality. "All religion is symbolic, and symbolism is excluded from religion only when religion itself perishes. God is a symbol in which religion cognized the absolute" (Radhakrishnan 1980: 85).

If the absolute is one and is the core of reality, what about the many things we experience? Are they illusions? Radhakrishnan maintained "the many" is not an illusion because the "one reveals itself in the many." Spiritual seers, he argued, acknowledge this when they speak of seeing the harmony of the world and the interconnectedness of all things. Hence he denied that Eastern religions are "world-denying" (a popular criticism in his day) and reinterpreted Shankara's concept of *maya* (magic play) that Advaita Vedanta uses to characterize the world of the senses as referring to the mutability of the world not its illusory nature.

Radhakrishnan argued that his theory of religion leads to some important conclusions. First, none of the world's great religions can really contradict one another, even if they appear to do so on the surface (see **Hick**). Each is an incomplete vision of one truth. Second, it follows that religious intolerance makes no sense. The aim of religion is to get us beyond our "momentary meaningless provincialism" so we can enjoy a larger, more inclusive, vision of life. It may take a long time to get to this more tolerant outlook, but it is a goal worth pursuing and religions should help us get there, not hinder or block our attempts by insisting on their exclusive possession of spiritual truth. Third, he was a strong and tireless supporter of religious freedom and urged others to be the same. He claimed that every religious tradition was valuable insofar as it can awaken the divine in all of us.

Central to Radhakrishnan's philosophy of religion is the notion of intuition. While perception and inference are valid ways to arrive at truth, so is intuition. Intuition takes different forms, such as scientific and ethical insight, but in its religious form it is the immediate apprehension of the divine in nature, the self, and in history. Intuition needs to be strengthened by the practice of meditation and the pursuit of moral goodness. We need not retreat from society in order to practice meditation, but should engage society by working for the improvement of the human condition.

Radhakrishnan read widely and deeply in the Scriptures and other religious literature of the world but, his critics point out, he often "cherry picks" the evidence without regard for historical and cultural context. His scholarship was immense, but he tended to focus only on material that reinforced his predetermined theory of absolute idealism. Whatever fit he found a place for and whatever did not he reinterpreted until it did. Some have complained that he avoided the hard questions of truth and incompatibility among the religions in his desire to show that all religions are somehow one at their core.

There is little doubt that Radhakrishnan greatly contributed to our knowledge of Eastern religions, particularly Hinduism. His translations of Hindu classics, his lectures, and his articles and books helped to make the study of comparative religions truly comparative. The widespread popular opinion that all religions are basically the same bears witness to his ability to cross the divide between scholarship and popular culture. While most scholars today find such claims oversimplified, they applaud his strong support of religious tolerance, freedom, and understanding.

See also: **Eliade**

Major works

(1923 and 1927) *Indian Philosophy*, 2 vols. New York: Macmillan Company.
(1926) *The Hindu View of Life*, London: Oxford University Press.
(1940) *Eastern Religions and Western Thought*, 2nd ed. New York: Oxford University Press.
(1980) *An Idealist View of Life*, London: Unwin Hyman.

Further reading

Pappu, S. S. Rama, ed. (1995) *New Essays in the Philosophy of Sarvepalli Radhakrishnan*, Columbia, MO: South Asia Books.
Schilpp, Paul Arthur, ed. (1952) *The Philosophy of Sarvepalli Radhakrishnan*, New York: Tudor Publishing.
http://en.wikipedia.org/wiki/Sarvepalli_Radhakrishnan.

LUDWIG WITTGENSTEIN (1889–1951)

> It strikes me that a religious belief could only be something like a passionate commitment to a system of reference.
>
> (Wittgenstein 1980: 64)

In his typically cryptic style, Ludwig Wittgenstein, one of most influential philosophers of the twentieth century, states something profound with deep implications for understanding religion. But his remark is obscure. What is a "system of reference"? Why is religious belief "something like a passionate commitment" to such a system? Why could it "only be" that? The story behind this remark is complex, with many twists and turns and at least one about-face.

Ludwig Josef Johann Wittgenstein was born in Vienna, the youngest of eight children whose father had organized the first Austrian steel industry and whose grandfather had converted from Judaism to Roman Catholicism. He was educated at home until the age of fourteen, then embarked on a study of engineering. In 1908 he went to England and entered the University of Manchester but while there his interests shifted from engineering to mathematics. After reading Bertrand Russell's work on logic, he decided to study logic with Russell, entering Trinity College, Cambridge in 1912.

Wittgenstein could be very charming, but he was often moody and depressed, even, at times, entertaining thoughts of suicide. In 1913 he moved to Norway and lived in seclusion in order to focus his tormented mind on logical problems. During World War I he volunteered for the Austrian Army and served with distinction in an artillery unit. He kept philosophical notebooks that became the basis for the *Tractatus Logico-Philosophicus* (1922), the first of his major publications. After the war he became a teacher at a small village school.

He gave up schoolteaching in 1926 and moved to Vienna, where he came in contact with the famous Vienna Circle of philosophers led by Moritz Schlick. The Vienna Circle is famous for developing **logical positivism**, which centered on the verification theory of meaning. This theory claimed that only those statements that scientific methods could "in principle" verify yield knowledge about reality. Metaphysical claims, including religious statements about unverifiable entities, although grammatically correct, were nonetheless meaningless. Wittgenstein is often associated with this theory, but he did not endorse it.

In 1937 Wittgenstein returned to Cambridge, submitted the *Tractatus* for his PhD thesis, and received a research appointment at the university. He assumed the prestigious G. E. Moore Chair in Philosophy in 1945 but found the life of a professional philosopher too artificial for his taste. He resigned his position, lived for a time in Ireland, was diagnosed with cancer and spent the last two years of his life staying with friends in Oxford.

There are only two published works of Wittgenstein that deal directly with religious matters: *Lectures on Religious Belief* (1966) and *Remarks on Frazer's "Golden Bough"* (1979). Nevertheless, the impact of his ideas on the philosophy of religion were revolutionary. He was primarily concerned with the nature of language, which, he thought, is of fundamental importance because it is through language that human life and the world become comprehensible. Although philosophy, unlike the natural sciences, discovers no new information about the world, it can clarify how language works, thereby dissolving metaphysical problems and calming anxieties that misunderstandings about the possibilities of language create. If we demand that "God-talk" make empirical sense, it would seem that much religious language is either false or meaningless babble. There may, however, be other possibilities.

The *Tractatus* changed the way philosophers thought about logic, language, and the very nature of philosophy. Wittgenstein was concerned with how a sentence can tell someone that such and such is the case in the world. What makes it possible for words to represent facts? Wittgenstein answered with the "picture theory" of language. "A proposition," he maintained, "is a model of reality as we think it to be" (*Tractatus*, 4.01).

At first this claim seems rather strange. How can a sentence on the printed page or spoken by a human voice picture (rightly or wrongly) "what is the case" in the real nonlinguistic world? The word "tree" is very different from the physical tree to which it refers. For a picture to represent something, it must have something in common with what it purports to represent. What do words and things have in common?

The thing sentences have in common with what they represent is logical form (also called the form of reality). Sentences state the *possibility* that things in the world are as they are pictured in a sentence. It is, Wittgenstein argued, logical form that connects sentences and the world.

There are, however, some things that cannot be said. The last thesis of the *Tractatus* famously admonishes, "Whereof one cannot speak, thereof one must be silent." Among the things that cannot be spoken are the existence of metaphysical entities such as God and of moral qualities like good and evil. Wittgenstein referred to this realm collectively as the "mystical." Talk about such things is nonsensical because the logical form pictured in human language is the logical form of the world, not of otherworldly things. While some have interpreted this claim to mean that Wittgenstein did not believe that metaphysical entities existed, this is not the case. There may well be a metaphysical and moral realm; however, it is just not possible to picture it in human language.

It is rare for a philosopher to develop two very different philosophies in one lifetime but Wittgenstein did exactly that. Moreover, both of his philosophies had immense influence. The so-called early

Wittgenstein of the *Tractatus* established what many thought were limits of what can be meaningfully said, and the later Wittgenstein of the *Philosophical Investigations* broke through those limits. The early Wittgenstein spoke about linguistic meaning in terms of pictures, as we have seen above. The later Wittgenstein spoke about meaning as use (see **Malinowski**).

It is possible to use language in many different ways. One way is to picture by naming different things and relationships among them in the empirical world. But there are other ways and those other ways do not necessarily try to picture what is empirically the case. Wittgenstein introduced the concept of language games to characterize this new pluralistic approach to meaning. Games have rules and different games have different rules. The rules determining scientific language games do not seem to be the same rules that determine the religious language game. Because religious language does not play by the same rules as scientific games does not mean that it is a meaningless game. It is just a different game.

In the *Investigations* Wittgenstein urged philosophers to give up the idea that words have essences and to begin to investigate the many different ways words are actually used. Before we pronounce a sentence meaningless, we should "look and see" how it is used. The focus of the philosophy of language now shifts from looking at the way language might picture what is the case to the context or "game" in which it is employed.

But, you might want to say: *There is* something all the many different games have in common. They are all games. So there are essences after all. Wittgenstein replied that if we look and see we find "family resemblances" instead of finding something common to all language games. Just as in families, there may be no one trait (blue eyes, let's say) that all the members have in common, so too in language games. Instead of one common or essential trait we find a complex network of overlapping traits, similarities, and differences. This means that the boundaries of our categories become fuzzy. We can no longer say exactly when one activity ceases to be a game of a certain sort and becomes another game (see **J. Z. Smith**).

What is the religious language game? What rules, if any, govern what can be reasonably said or not said? In his *Lectures on Religious Belief*, Wittgenstein disentangled religious talk from factual talk. It is not talk about what is the case even though it may appear so. He pointed out that if we take the religious language game to be the same or nearly the same as the scientific language game fundamental contradictions and unsolvable philosophical problems very soon arise.

Can God create a stone he cannot lift? If God creates moral rules, then is he bound by the same rules? If he is, then he is limited; if he is not, in what sense can we call God good?

Wittgenstein makes the point that denying religious belief does not really contradict anything because religious belief has nothing to do with naming or picturing what is the case or what is not the case. It has to do with how to live and with the meaning we derive from how we live. It is a "form of life," a way of being in the world that we learn and accept or reject just as we do with other ways of living. Belief in the Last Judgment, for example, should not be understood as a belief about what will be the case or not be the case, but as a kind of guiding principle for how we live, especially when we face a crisis like death. Trying to make religious beliefs conform to human reason is, Wittgenstein thought, "ludicrous." He objected, for example, to **Frazer**'s views because he thought **Frazer** mischaracterized and hence misunderstood the "game" that people "played" by telling myths.

Philosophers have regarded Wittgenstein's views on religious belief as a kind of moderate **fideism**. Religious discourse has its own kind of logic that can only be fully appreciated by those who play that particular game. Arguments about the existence or non-existence of God, which are often the staple of philosophers of religion, miss the point. Religious belief is a "passionate commitment" and hence immune from falsification or verification.

If religious belief is immune from proof or disproof, Wittgenstein's ideas about religious belief are not immune from criticism. It might well be that the religious language game is, on the part of those who play it, a "passionate commitment to a system of reference" but it does not follow that it is no more than that. It is hard to imagine someone playing this game and saying there is no reality beyond such a commitment. The passionate commitment believers feel might well be less passionate if the belief that God exists is not part of their reasons for adopting religious discourse.

Wittgenstein's views on language have been immensely influential on the development of the philosophy of religion, as well as on other fields of study. The testimony to their fruitfulness is the development of an immense body of literature illuminating in new ways the often strange and paradoxical manner in which people talk about God, Jesus, the Buddha, the Tao, angels, and much more. Many definitions of religion had tried to articulate the "essence" of religion. Now scholars began to think in terms of non-essential definitions that focus on "family resemblances." This broadened the field, inspiring an examination of worldviews such as totalitarianism that traditionally had not been designated religions (see **Smart**). And the academic study of religion began to pay closer attention to context in its quest to understand the meaning of religious beliefs and practices.

See also: **Asad, Hick, Kierkegaard, van der Leeuw, Smart, Tillich**

Major works

(1958a) *Blue and Brown Books: Preliminary Studies for the Philosophical Investigations*, trans. G. E. M. Anscombe, Oxford: Blackwell.

(1958b) *Philosophical Investigations*, ed. G. E. M. Anscombe and R. Rhees, trans. G. E. M. Anscombe, 2nd ed., Oxford: Blackwell.

(1961)*Tractatus Logico-Philosophicus*, trans. D. F. Pears and B. F. McGuinness, London: Routledge and Kegan Paul.

(1969) *On Certainty*, trans. D. Paul and G. E. M. Anscombe, Oxford: Blackwell.

(1970) *Lectures and Conversations on Aesthetics, Psychology and Religious Belief*, ed. C. Barrett, Oxford: Blackwell.

(1979) *Remarks on Frazer's "Golden Bough"*, ed. R. Rhees, trans. A. C. Miles and R. Rhees, Redford: Brymill.

(1980) *Culture and Value*, ed. G. H. von Wright and H. Nyman, trans. P. Winch, Oxford: Blackwell.

Further reading

Kenny, Anthony. (1973) *Wittgenstein*, London: Penguin.

Malcolm, Norman. (2001) *Ludwig Wittgenstein: A Memoir*, 2nd ed. New York: Oxford University Press.

Phillips, D. Z. (1970) *Faith and Philosophical Enquiry*, London: Routledge and Kegan Paul.

http://plato.stanford.edu/entries/wittgenstein.

GERARDUS VAN DER LEEUW (1890–1950)

[R]eligion implies that man does not simply accept the life that is given to him. In life he seeks power; and if he does not find this, or not to an extent that satisfies him, then he attempts to draw the power, in which he believes, into his own life. He tries to elevate life, to enhance its value, to gain for it some deeper and wider meaning. ... The religious man desires richer, deeper, wider life; he desires power for himself.

(van der Leeuw 1963: 679)

Gerardus van der Leeuw added a footnote to the last line of the above quotation in which he asserted that here, in the quest for power, we can find the "essential unity between religion and culture." This led him to comment, "all culture is religious." Is power and the quest for it the essential key to unlocking the mystery of religion? Is that what religion is all about?

Gerardus van der Leeuw, a Dutch **phenomenologist** of religion, was born and raised in The Hague. He studied theology and the history of religion at the University of Leiden from 1908 to 1913, specializing in Egyptian religion. After studying in Germany, he returned to Holland, where he earned his PhD from Leiden. He became a minister in the Dutch Reformed Church, but his academic interests led him to accept a teaching post at Groningen in 1918, where he taught the history of religion. He did, however, remain active in the Dutch Reformed Church, advocating an "ethical theology" that focused on the value of religion as a "reality of the heart." He became the first president of the International Association for the History of Religion in recognition of his research and publications.

His principal publications contributed to the comparative study of religion and the development of the **phenomenology** of religion. During his career he published several books and many articles on various topics. His *Religion in Essence and Manifestation* (1933) became his most influential contribution to the field of religious studies. The first volume focused on the object of religion (part one) and the subject of religion (part two). In the second volume, van der Leeuw dealt with the reciprocal relationship between subject and object (part three), the world (part four) and forms and founders of religion (part five). In an important "Epilegomena" (supplemental discourse) he provided an account of the **phenomenological** study of religion that dominated the field from about 1925 to the 1970s.

The reader should pay special attention to the words 'essence' and 'manifestation' in the title. The **phenomenology** of religion involves a method of study designed to focus on religious phenomena, that is, the appearance or manifestation of religion. It is empirical insofar as its object of study is the way religion appears in human life. In order to focus on appearance, the scholar employs a procedure called *epoché* or bracketing. To keep the focus on what appears *just as it appears*, all metaphysical issues are set aside. Thus, if we apply the *epoché* to the claim that God or gods reveal some truth, the question of whether there exists such a divine origin, or even if what is revealed is the truth, is set aside or put in brackets. Attention is thereby directed to the *significance* of such a claim for human existence.

If the **phenomenologist** of religion should keep attention on how religion manifests itself in human life, then how can the "essence" of religion ever be discovered? If we mean by essence some metaphysical reality behind appearance, then this could not be revealed by the **phenomenological** method. However, if we mean by "essence" not some metaphysical reality behind appearances, but the essence of religious appearances themselves, then there is the possibility of finding the essence of the manifestation of religion. It is precisely this essence that any adequate theory of religion must discover.

To comprehend the essence of some appearance we must keep in mind that a phenomenon is neither objective nor subjective but a relationship between subject and object. We must also remember that the essence is given in the manifestation. We can get at it by comprehending the structural connections between manifestations. The structure emerges from a reconstruction that shows the "ideal type" (see **Max Weber**). The first step is naming or classification of phenomena into related groups such as demons or angels. Then through an "intense sympathy" scholars must bring into their own subjective life the meaning presented in the phenomena. This makes possible clarification of the meaning by arranging what is given in appearance into types. The goal is to understand the meaning of some religious phenomenon by gaining a "pure objectivity" that results from attending to what appears just as it appears without importing bias, prejudices, or preconceived notions.

If we attend carefully to the many different objects of religion— sacred stones, trees, water, fire, animals, spirits, gods, and much more—we discover that in essence all of these things are manifestations of power. This power is experienced as extraordinary. It elicits awe and fear because power is dangerous. It needs to be controlled by erecting boundaries, separations, and taboos. This renders it sacred by distinguishing it from the profane or the relatively powerless. Even though religions have given a moral interpretation to power, its primary manifestation is amoral. It is power, pure and simple. In time the idea of moral goodness is imported into this power, but we must understand that the power at the heart of all religion can be experienced as either demonic or angelic (see **Otto**).

If we turn our attention to the subject of religion, three distinct regions emerge: the sacred individual, community, and soul. The first category can be understood by a careful analysis of such timeless types as the king, priest, medicine-man/woman, and preacher. Consideration of the community leads to comparative studies of the family, tribe, sect, and church. A **phenomenological** study of the sacred within yields types such as the various forms of the soul, the immortal soul, and the destiny of the soul. Van der Leeuw illustrated each of these types with numerous examples drawn from ancient and modern religions, Asian and European religions, and most of the so-called world religions.

As our focus shifts to the reciprocal relations between object (power) and subject (humans) a **phenomenological** description of sacred celebrations such as sacrifice, purification, festivals, and worship becomes possible along with consideration of mystical experiences, conversion, and rebirth that connect humans to the sacred power. A comparative study of sacred forms yields detailed descriptions of religions of struggle, repose, revival, and love. Likewise a study of founders provides a wealth of information about reformers, teachers, theologians, mediators, and the like. In each case, van der Leeuw sought to uncover and make transparent the essence of the manifestation of all these various types.

Although van der Leeuw's **phenomenology** of religion influenced a generation of scholars seeking to distinguish the study of comparative religions from theology, some objected to his views. Ironically, a persistent criticism by those unsympathetic to his Christianity centered on the theological foundation of his presumably objective and unbiased **phenomenology**. Van der Leeuw was educated as a Christian theologian as well as a historian and he found his theological justification for focusing on the manifestation of religion in the Christian doctrine of the incarnation.

Additional criticisms focused on questions about whether an individual person can truly understand the experiences of others, whether a genuine "science" of religion can ignore natural causes, and van der Leeuw's assumption that there is some kind of essence to religion. Focusing on the meaning of religious manifestations for humans is certainly important. But the natural causes of, let us say, conversion experiences should not be bracketed out of consideration from the start. Since **Wittgenstein**'s critique of the notion of essence and his introduction of the concept of family resemblances, many have found van der Leeuw's essentialist approach inadequate.

These kinds of criticism are important but in spite of their importance there is no denying that van der Leeuw made significant contributions to our understanding of religion and advanced the academic study of religion. He articulated more clearly than others the key ideas of the **phenomenology** of religion.

See also: **Douglas, Eliade, Scholem, Smart, J. Z. Smith**

Major works

(1963) *Religion in Essence and Manifestation*, trans. J. E. Turner, 2 vols, New York: Harper and Row.

(2006) *Sacred and Profane Beauty: The Holy in Art*, trans. David E. Green, New York: Oxford University Press.

Further reading

James, Alfred. (1995) *Interpreting Religion: The Phenomenological Approaches of Pierre Daniel Chantepie de la Saussaye, W. Brede Kristensen, and Gerardus Van Der Leeuw*, Washington, DC: Catholic University of America Press.

Waardenburg, Jacques. (1978) *Reflections on the Study of Religion*, The Hague: Mouton Publishers.

http://en.wikipedia.org/wiki/Phenomenology_of_religion.

GERSHOM SCHOLEM (1897–1982)

> We have seen that mystical religion seeks to transform the God whom it encounters in the peculiar religious consciousness of its own social environment from an object of dogmatic knowledge into a novel and living experience and intuition.
>
> (Scholem 1941: 10)

Gershom Scholem, the leading scholar of Jewish mysticism of his day, indicated in the above passage one of the characteristics of Jewish mysticism as well as one of the marks of theistic mysticism in general. However, he cautioned that there is no such thing as mystical religion in the abstract but only the mysticism of particular religions such as Jewish, Christian, and Muslim. In the historical evolution of a religion, mysticism is a definite trend and is incompatible with other anti-mystical stages of the same religion. His goal was to understand this process, particularly in the case of Judaism.

Gershom was born Gerhard Scholem in Berlin. His father was a printer and was a fierce defender of German nationalism. After a heated political argument, his father banished him from the family home and in 1911 he became a Zionist for political, not religious, reasons. Along with his Zionist friends, he became an ardent supporter of the establishment of a Jewish homeland in Palestine. His home and education had been secular, but he started studying Hebrew and the Talmud after he became involved in Zionism.

He entered the University of Berlin to study mathematics, but decided he did not have the talent to do original work in the field so, after attending several universities, he finished his student days at Munich, where he produced an annotated translation of *The Book of Illumination*, an early work of Jewish mysticism known as the Kabbalah. Although he remained secular, his career was spent studying and writing about Judaism. During his student days he met **Martin Buber** and the philosopher Walter Benjamin. The latter became a close friend and had a lasting influence on his life and thought. In 1922 he left Germany for Palestine and took a position at the National Library and eventually received an appointment to teach at Hebrew University, where he spent his academic career.

Scholem was a scholar's scholar. He spent the early part of his career collecting and carefully analyzing every kabbalistic manuscript he could find. This work provided him with the most complete database on Jewish mysticism that then existed, and his publication of critical essays and reviews began to open up to a wider audience this often strange and misunderstood world of magic, numerology, and mystical enthusiasm. His goal was to try to make sense of the history of Kabbalah from its earliest period to its most recent Hasidic piety.

His most popular work and probably his most influential (*Major Trends in Jewish Mysticism*, 1941) was based on a series of lectures given in the 1930s at the Jewish Institute of Religion in New York. This book was a watershed for kabbalistic studies in particular and Jewish studies in general. It also had a major impact on the wider field of religious studies, especially the study of mystical traditions in the world religions. It revealed for the first time a trajectory to mystical Judaism that made sense of what had been viewed as disparate movements that often seemed unrelated. It also, in its first chapter, provides an early statement of Scholem's ideas concerning the **phenomenology** of mysticism, ideas that he later developed in ways that influenced the study of religion beyond the specialized realm of religious mysticism.

Opinions on Jewish mysticism had fluctuated between hostility and praise and, in Scholem's view, did not advance scholarly knowledge of "the real nature of mystical lore." Previous studies were filled with misunderstandings and lacked adequate knowledge of the sources. In addition, they were often motivated by apologetic concerns because they saw the mysticism of the Kabbalah and Hasidism as a hindrance to the modernization of Judaism. Charlatans entered the field, often, like Aleister Crowley, distorting Jewish mysticism for their own purposes. Scholem indicates his break with previous work by clearly indicating his desire to present a "critical appreciation" of the Jewish mystical tradition.

Although Scholem acknowledged that there is no agreed-upon definition of mysticism, most definitions emphasized that at its heart is an intense, personal, even ecstatic experience of the divine. While this experience is important, it would be a mistake to assume that the whole of what is generally called mysticism is identical with ecstatic, personal experience. Mystical movements are historical and as such need to be understood in their historical and religious context. They constitute definite stages in the history of religion that developed under "certain well-defined conditions."

As long as there is no sharp division between the human and the divine, there will be no mysticism because mysticism seeks to overcome the human and divine abyss. Hence in the first stage of religion, in which natural events and powers are the focus, there is little room for mysticism because humans experience their natural environment as filled with the divine. Spirits and gods are everywhere and the mythology of this early stage reflects this experience. In the creative epoch (second stage) in which the foundations of the major institutionalized religions we know today were established, there is also little room for mysticism because the divine is now removed from nature and experienced as radically different from the natural order. The "Otherness" of God is established and revelation from the divine is required to establish a connection as the forces of nature are demythologized.

Mysticism can now arise not by denying the "Otherness" but by providing ways to overcome the divine/human separation. It strives to reestablish what it claims is a broken unity. In mysticism the "world of mythology," which concentrates on the divine in nature (first stage), and the "world of revelation" (second stage) become united in the "soul of man."

There are other factors that influenced the rise of mystical consciousness. These other factors emerge as mystical movements offer reinterpretations of the doctrines that developed in the second or classical stage. Revelation, for example, is not thought of as a once-for-all-time event, but as an ongoing repetition. The Torah (law revealed in the first five books of Moses) becomes, for the mystic, an ongoing divine activity that can be endlessly mined for new and hidden information. This reflects the fact that the mystical impulse constantly seeks to transform orthodox doctrines into "living experience and intuition." These experiences and reinterpretations are not only shaped by the teachings of particular religious traditions but also by ongoing historical experience. For example, the expulsion of the Jews from Spain in 1492 becomes for the kabbalist a disruption in the divine itself. The hidden meanings discovered by later generations often become more important than the original meaning of scriptural revelation.

Kabbalism shares much in common with other mystical movements, but there are important differences. For example, all mystics struggle with the issue of how human language can express that which is essentially inexpressible, namely the nature of God and the nature of the individual's experience of God. The kabbalists, however, show restraint in describing personal experiences and regard human language more positively than other mystical traditions. Scholem wrote, "Language in its purist form, that is Hebrew, according to the Kabbalists, reflects the fundamental spiritual nature of the world; in other words, it has mystical value. Speech reaches God because it comes from God" (Scholem 1941: 17).

Kabbalah literally means "tradition" and Jewish mysticism, however novel its teachings, has always claimed to be continuing the traditional wisdom revealed to the prophets of old. If people wonder why the teachings of the Kabbalah appeared so different from accepted teachings, the kabbalists reply that it is because they are sharing secret doctrines of the most fundamental truths about the universe and human life. One striking example is the doctrine of creation out of nothing. The kabbalists reinterpreted this traditional teaching, shared by Judaism, Christianity, and Islam, to mean that "nothingness" is a symbol for the infinity of God and hence the truth here concealed is that God created the world out of himself. The traditional teaching is preserved, yet changed in a novel way that continues the mystic desire to establish the unity of the human and the divine. Hence a basic and characteristic value of Judaism, reverence for the tradition, was maintained even as leading kabbalists broke with the tradition.

Scholem's interpretation of Jewish mysticism has faced criticism from those who regard his approach as too **Hegelian**. He divides Jewish history, first into the biblical period, when Judaism struggled to free itself from mythical thought, with some but not complete success (thesis); this is followed by the rabbinic period, in which the rabbis rejected the magic and myth of the previous stage in favor of a rationalized interpretation of the law (antithesis); the Kabbalah enters Jewish history as a reaction against legal and philosophical rationalism, and in an attempt to reestablish the unity between God and the world that informed ancient mythology, albeit creatively reinterpreted in light of the Jewish tradition (synthesis). Critics argue that this dialectical approach to history is "cut and dried" and ignores those aspects of the tradition (e.g. the mythical aspects of rabbinic Judaism) that do not fit into Scholem's overall scheme.

Whatever we may think about Scholem's use of **Hegel**, there is little doubt that his careful scholarship and deep understanding of the sources enabled him to open to a larger audience the fascinating world of Jewish mysticism. In addition, his careful attention to mystical symbolism and language, as well as his use of the comparative method, paved the way for subsequent debates about the relationship between language and mystical experience. Does one first encounter the divine and then borrow language from one's religion to describe it or do the language and symbols of one's religion shape and mold the experience from the start?

See also: **Eliade, van der Leeuw**

Major works

(1941) *Major Trends in Jewish Mysticism*, New York: Schocken Books.
(1949) *Zohar: The Book of Splendor*, New York: Schocken Books.
(1965) *Jewish Gnosticism, Merkabah Mysticism, and Talmudic Tradition*, New York: JTS Press.
(1973) *Sabbatei Sevi: The Mystical Messiah 1626–1676*, Princeton, NJ: Princeton University Press.
(1992) *The Origins of Kabbala*, Princeton, NJ: Princeton University Press.
(1997) *On the Possibility of Jewish Mysticism in Our Time*, Philadelphia, PA: Jewish Publication Society.

Further reading

Biale, David. (1982) *Gershom Scholem: Kabbalah and Counter-History*, Cambridge, MA: Harvard University Press.
Jacobson, Eric. (2003) *Metaphysics of the Profane: The Political Theology of Walter Benjamin and Gershom Scholem*, New York: Columbia University Press.
Wasserstrom, Steven. (1999) *Religion after Religion: Gershom Scholem, Mircea Eliade and Henri Corbin at Eranos*, Princeton, NJ: Princeton University Press.
http://plato.standord.edu/entries/scholem.

GEORGES DUMÉZIL (1898–1986)

> The function of that particular class of legends known as myths is to express dramatically the ideology under which a society lives; not only to hold out to its conscience the values it recognizes and the ideals it pursues from generation to generation, but above all to express its very

being and structure, the elements, the connections, the balances, the tensions that constitute it; to justify the rules and traditional practices without which everything within a society would disintegrate.

(Dumézil 1970a: 3)

Georges Dumézil, a learned and meticulous French scholar of Indo-European mythology, helped to refocus the study of comparative mythology by trying to resolve certain problems that **Max Müller** had been unable to solve concerning the curious and undeniable similarities among Indo-European stories about gods and heroes. His "tripartite" theory, as it came to be called, was elaborated in great detail in over seventy-five books and several hundred articles. As the above quotation indicates, he regarded myths as an expression in dramatic form of an ideology that embodied the values and ideals of society and justified its fundamental practices.

Georges Dumézil was born in Paris and attended the prestigious École normale supérieure. He was drafted into the military during World War I and after his military service resumed his studies at the University of Paris, where he completed his doctoral thesis on comparative Indo-European mythology in 1924. He married Madeleine Legrand in 1925 and began a teaching career at several universities in different parts of the world including Sweden, Turkey, Peru, and the United States. He was appointed to a position created for him at Collège de France where he contributed to a revival of the study of ancient Indo-European culture and religion. Indo-European culture stretched from India to Europe and its languages form the basis of many modern Western languages. Dumézil was convinced that this ancient culture also formed the basis of modern cultures and religions, although his primary interest was in the ancient world.

Religions tell stories, some of which believers regard as particularly sacred. Scholars of religion call these sacred stories myths, although we must hasten to add that the word myth is not here used in the ordinary sense of untrue or fictional story. Myths often survive for generations and enter into the literary traditions of a culture in one form or another. Along with archeological evidence, myths provide valuable clues to cultures and religions long since dead. No theory of religion would be complete without a theory of myth and if we had no myths from ancient cultures our own religious and cultural roots would remain obscure.

Müller's famous "solar mythology" tried to show by often-fanciful etymological studies of the names of gods and heroes in ancient mythology that myths were fundamentally a symbolic portrayal of natural forces such as the moon, storm, thunder, and especially the sun. **Freud** and **Jung** tried to show that myths are symbolic expressions of deep psychic desires and needs. Other scholars, like **J. G. Frazer** and **Jane Harrison** thought that the clue to understanding myths was to uncover how they were connected to ancient rituals often involving themes of death and the renewal of life. Many of these theories of myth had become discredited or at least seriously called into question by the time Dumézil began his work. He realized that a fresh start had to be made, at least insofar as Indo-European mythology was concerned.

At first Dumézil thought that **Frazer**'s focus on the sacrifice of kings and the renewal of the natural order was the best way forward. However, he soon realized that it was inadequate for explaining the diversity of the data. A more fruitful approach could be found in the French sociological school, especially the work of **Durkheim** and his followers. **Durkheim**'s insight that the events and persons that appear in myths represent basic social and cultural realities provided the clue for which he was looking.

The material available from the earliest Indo-European language communities showed that these societies were hierarchically ordered in a tripartite structure. There was a dual sovereignty of king/priest, a warrior class, and a herder/cultivator economic base. Dumézil called these social strata functions because of the role each played in maintaining these early societies. The kings were responsible for the juridical activities of society by making laws and applying them to particular situations. The priests were responsible for the ritual life of the community, whose goal was to maintain the cosmic order and the appropriate relationships between the people and the gods. The third stratum provided sustenance and supported the physical well-being of the community. He claimed, "the central motif of Indo-European ideology [is] the conception according to which the world and society can live only through the harmonious collaboration of the three stratified functions of sovereignty, force, and fecundity" (Dumézil 1970a: 4).

Stories about the gods, heroes, wars, the beginning and end of the world, and much more, reflected in one way or another this tripartite division of functions. Often the strata conflicted. The warriors abused the lower economic strata and the judicial and priestly functions often found themselves in power struggles. Yet the goal of the ideology was to support an ideal of harmonious cooperation as well as justify the role each stratum should play in the overall social drama. The ancient Indo-European myths embodied in symbolic narratives the struggles and resolution of struggles among these three functions as the ancient myths of India showed.

The *Rig-Veda* was composed about 900 BCE and is among the oldest scripture of Hinduism. The myth of the "Primal Man" found in *Rig-Veda* 10.90 provides a clear illustration of Dumézil's ideas. According to this myth, the world and its social order were created out of a cosmic giant who was not only the first male but also a victim of an ancient sacrifice. From his mouth the priests were made, from his arms the warriors, and from his thighs the people. The priests and warriors come into being to rule the people and this social arrangement is rooted in a cosmic order, hence it is presented as the natural order of things; the way things were meant to be. Dumézil and his followers see in myths like this one an expression of an Indo-European ideology that not only embodies a social hierarchy, but the principles of sovereignty, force, and nourishment. The tripartite structure even became reflected in ancient Greek philosophy as Plato's theory of the soul (reason, aspiration, appetite) and society (philosopher-kings, guardians, producers) indicates.

Followers of Dumézil have tried to universalize his insights by uncovering this tripartite division in non-Indo-European cultures. However, Dumézil regarded it as uniquely Indo-European, thereby resisting the temptation to read it into other language groups. Even so, critics have argued that his tripartite theory is "read into" the Indo-European data. Some of the data he used can often be interpreted in other ways. Thus his adoption of the tripartite model can act as a blinder to other possible, and perhaps more fruitful, interpretations.

Although, for a variety of reasons, Dumézil's views have not been widely adopted in Britain and America, especially among anthropological studies of myths, his ideas have made an impact on French **structuralists** like **Claude Lévi-Strauss** and **phenomenologists** like **Mircea Eliade**. It is hard to imagine the contemporary study of comparative mythology without his careful philological and comparative work as a foundation.

See also: **Foucault, J. Z. Smith**

Major works

(1970a) Destiny *of the Warrior*, trans. Alf Hitebeitel, Chicago, IL: University of Chicago Press.
(1970b) *Archaic Roman Religion*, trans. Philip Krapp, Chicago, IL: University of Chicago Press.

(1973a) *Gods of the Ancient Northmen*, ed. Einar Haugen, Berkeley, CA: University of California Press.

(1973b) *From Myth to Fiction: The Saga of Hadingus*, trans. Derek Coltman, Chicago, IL: University of Chicago Press.

(1973c) *The Destiny of the King*, trans. Alf Hitebeitel, Chicago, IL: University of Chicago Press.

(1980) *Camillus: A Study of Indo-European Religion as Roman History*, trans. Annette Aronowicz, Berkeley, CA: University of California Press.

Further reading

Larson, Gerald James, ed. (1974) *Myth in Indo-European Antiquity*, Berkeley, CA: University of California Press.

Littleton, C. Scott. (1982) *The New Comparative Mythology: An Anthropological Assessment of the Theories of Georges Dumézil*, 3rd ed. Berkeley, CA: University of California Press.

http://en.wikipedia.org/wiki/Georges_Dumézil.

E. E. EVANS-PRITCHARD (1902–73)

> The theories of writers about primitive religion have not been sustained by research. During the last century what was presented as theory was generally the supposition that some particular form of religion was the most primitive and that from it developed other forms, ... The form of religion presented by a writer as the most primitive was that which he considered to be the most simple, crude, and irrational; ... Many such origins have been propounded: magic, fetishism, manism, animism, pre-animism, mana, totemism, monotheism, etc. All this was for the most part pure conjecture.
>
> (Evans-Pritchard 1956: 311)

E. E. Evans-Pritchard, an influential British anthropologist famous for his fieldwork in Africa, ended the third volume of his groundbreaking study of the Nuer with the above criticism of previous theories championed by the likes of **Max Müller**, **E. B. Tylor**, and **James Frazer**. The Nuer religion, a "primitive" religion by the standards of the day, impressed him with its refinement, intelligence, and complexity. In light of the data he gathered while living among the Azande and the Nuer in Africa, the simple contrast between primitive religion and modern religion appeared to be little more than prejudices of educated moderns who considered themselves "civilized."

Edward Evans-Pritchard was the son of the Reverend John Evans-Pritchard (Church of England) and Dorothea Edwards. He was educated at Exeter College, Oxford, taking his MA in modern history. In 1923 he began graduate studies in anthropology at the London School of Economics, studying under C. G. Seligman and **B. Malinowski**. At their urging he began fieldwork among the Azande in Africa in 1926 and in 1930 among the Nuer. He married Ioma Gladys Heaton Nicholls in 1939, with whom he had two daughters and three sons. He saw military service (1940–45) in Africa and Syria and became a Roman Catholic convert in 1944. After serving in a variety of academic posts between 1928 and 1945, he became professor of social anthropology and a fellow of All Souls College at Oxford in 1946.

Evans-Pritchard published over 300 articles and several books, three of which became classics in religious studies: *Witchcraft, Oracles, and Magic among the Azande, Nuer Religion*, and *Theories of Primitive Religion*. All three set new standards in the field of ethnography. He regarded **Lévy-Bruhl**'s idea that "primitives" were not mentally deficient but merely thought differently from Europeans as essential to objective anthropological description. He also endorsed **Radcliffe-Brown**'s view that society is an interconnected organic whole, but he was not impressed with **Durkheim**'s "social reductionism." He famously said that it was "Durkheim and not the savage who made society into a god" (Evans-Pritchard 1956: 313).

In his study of witchcraft among the Azande, Evans-Pritchard broke new ground by showing that belief in witches and their activities was not due to any defects in reasoning about what we would call natural causation. They knew very well, for example, that termites eat the supports of granaries and that this causes them to fall. Occasionally some are injured and even killed because people often sit under the granaries to escape the heat. We would say they were in the wrong place at the wrong time and it was bad luck. The Azande would say that it was witchcraft. Witchcraft explains unfortunate events. It explains why, at least to the Azande, these particular people happened to be under that particular granary when it fell. It does not replace the explanation that termites made the granary fall but it supplements it. It is socially useful not only because it explains unfortunate events but also because it provides a system of values that regulate human conduct.

The Azande belief in magic, witchcraft, and oracles is not an irrational belief that flies in the face of evidence, as others have thought. Rather it is a way of explaining *why* certain events are harmful to humans, but it does not explain *how* they happen. The Azande perceive the world just as we do and have empirical knowledge of cause and effect just as we do. But they also have an explanation of unfortunate events that cause harm or injury that we do not have. That explanation is witchcraft. It is a supplemental explanation that is invoked in certain cases (but not all) and it derives from a complex framework of fundamental beliefs. We too have such a framework but ours does not include, or at least for most of us today, a belief in witchcraft.

Among the Nuer the concept of witchcraft plays a minor role. Central to Nuer religion is the idea of *kwoth* or spirit (*kuth* is the plural). Chief among the spirits is *Kwoth nhial* or the "spirit in the sky." Conceptions of this sky spirit are very close to Christian conceptions of God. *Kwoth nhial* is the creator and sustainer of all things. He controls all events on earth and is responsible for the moral order. He unselfishly loves the humans he has created, but humans are small, like tiny ants, in his sight.

The Nuer do not, like the Azande, attribute unfortunate events to witchcraft but to their own behavior. Such events are caused by their own wrongdoing and must be made right before God if their community is to prosper. The pollution caused by wrongdoing or "sin" must be purged. Although there are group sacrifices among the Nuer to mark important occasions such as **rites of passage**, it is personal sacrifice that is the primary means of purging sin. The most valuable possession a Nuer has is an ox and the ox sacrifice plays a major role in the ritual life of the Nuer. Evans-Pritchard describes and analyzes the ox sacrifice in some detail, noting that it is not so much a way of communicating with God, as a gift intended to expiate sin. It is not an exchange. There is no bargaining with God. God does not need the ox but humans need to rid themselves of the pollution caused by their failures to live up to the standards set by God.

Surprisingly, if an ox is not available for whatever reason, something else, even a cucumber, can be sacrificed in its place. How can a cucumber, something of little value, symbolize an ox, something of great value? Evans-Pritchard noted that this datum calls into question other anthropological theories of symbolism. The so-called primitive mind has been largely misunderstood by previous anthropological studies. These studies have been overly literalistic in their approach. The Nuer do not think that a cucumber is literally an ox even though they may say it *is* an ox. A careful analysis of their language in light of their other beliefs shows that "is" is being used metaphorically. Previous studies of the so-called primitive mind as "pre-logical" failed to appreciate the poetic habits of speech that these people employ. They failed to allow for metaphor, multiple meanings of words, and figures of speech, because of their preconceived ideas that such sophistication was somehow "beyond" the capacity of primitive thought and speech.

Previous reports on the Nuer (primarily by Christian missionaries) either claimed they had no religion or that what little religion they had was polytheistic and **totemic**. The Nuer do recognize spirits other than *Kwoth nhial*. There are the spirits "below" (*colwic*) and tribal **totems**. Evans-Pritchard introduced the idea of "social refraction" to explain how these other spirits relate to God, the all-powerful creator spirit in the sky. Just as light is split into different colors by a prism, so the Nuer think that God is "refracted" into different levels of power that apply in different ways to different clans. However, the Nuer also think that their worship of the lower spirits amounts to a worship of the high God, *Kwoth nhial*. God is the eldest of the spirits, the other spirits are "below" like a child is "below" his father, and totemic spirits are the children of those spirits and so on. He noted that the lower down the scale of spirits we go, the nearer we come to the ritualized practices that we in the West normally associate with religion.

There is much more to Evans-Pritchard's description of Nuer society and religion, but it is sufficient to note for our purposes that his narrative paints a picture of a complex religion that is in many ways like "modern" religion. It provides a corrective to the pictures painted by "armchair" anthropologists who relied primarily on missionary reports of "savage" religion and the "primitive mind." They did not do the fieldwork necessary to learn the languages of the natives and live among them. He admonished scholars of religion, "if we wish to seize the essential nature of what we are inquiring into, we have to try to examine the matter from the inside also, to see it as Nuer see it" (Evans-Pritchard 1956: 121–22).

While grand theories of the whole of religion have contributed, in spite of their weaknesses, to our understanding of religion, the primary defect of most theories of primitive religion is that they commit the "If-I-were-a-horse" fallacy. If I were a primitive, they muse, then I would think and act like this. Both psychological and sociological theories are guilty of this kind of fallacious reasoning, as Evans-Pritchard demonstrated in his *Theories of Primitive Religion*. Some of course are better in this or that respect, but Evans-Pritchard thinks scholars have been too hasty to spin grand theories and have not carefully built such theories from the ground up, as it were. We cannot arrive at an abstract theory of religion as a whole without more detailed information on specific religions that takes into account what particular religious beliefs and practices actually mean to the people that practice them. What religion means to "ordinary" people, not to the elite (philosophers and theologians) is what counts.

Evans-Pritchard practiced what he preached. He did not produce, much to the regret of many, any grand theory of religion, primitive or otherwise. He was content to stick with "small" theories, although he hoped that one day anthropology would be in a position to offer a "big" theory of primitive religion. However, his critique of other theories was sometimes overly harsh, and he does not seem to realize that if we are to have any theory of past religion we have little choice but to use well-informed imagination. Likewise, there is no other way to get into the mind of others who believe and practice religions that we do not than to cultivate sympathetic imagination based on the best evidence available.

Whatever his own limitations may have been, there is little doubt that he took careful ethnographic study to a new level. Students of religion who wish to describe religion as it is lived ignore the work of Evans-Pritchard at their peril.

See also: **Asad, Douglas, Geertz, J. Z. Smith, Lévi-Strauss**

Major works

(1937) *Witchcraft, Oracles and Magic among the Azande*, Oxford: Clarendon Press.

(1940) *The Nuer: A Description of the Modes and Livelihood and Political Institutions of a Nilotic People*, Oxford: Clarendon Press.

(1956) *Nuer Religion*, Oxford: Clarendon Press.

(1965) *Theories of Primitive Religion*, Oxford: Clarendon Press.

Further reading

Douglas, Mary. (1980) *Edward Evans-Pritchard*, New York: Viking Press.

Geertz, Clifford. (1988) *Works and Lives: The Anthropologist as Author*, Stanford, CA: Stanford University Press.

Winch, Peter. (1970) "Understanding a Primitive Society," in *Rationality*, ed. Bryan R. Wilson, pp. 78–111, Oxford: Basil Blackwell.

http://en.wikipedia.org/wiki/E._E._Evans-Pritchard.

MIRCEA ELIADE (1907–86)

> [A] religious phenomenon will only be recognized as such if it is grasped at its own level, that is to say, if it is studied *as* something religious. To try to grasp the essence of such a phenomenon by means of

physiology, psychology, sociology, economics, linguistics, art, or any other study is false: it misses the one unique and irreducible element in it—the element of the sacred.

(Mircea Eliade 1963: xiii)

Mircea Eliade, the most influential historian of religions of the last century, signaled in the above quotation his opposition to any and all theories that would explain religion by "reducing" it to non-religious causes such as economics (**Marx**), psychology (**Freud**) or society (**Durkheim**). Religion is *sui generis* ("of its own kind"). But what does it mean to grasp religion "at its own level?" Eliade tried, in numerous books and essays, to show what that means and how to do it.

Mircea Eliade was born in Bucharest, the son of a Romanian army officer. His interests were wide and varied, but he became intrigued by the religions of India and in 1928 went to India to study with Surendranath Dasgupta. A romance with Dasgupta's daughter, about which he later wrote a novel titled *Maitreyi* (in English *Bengal Nights*), led to his expulsion from Dasgupta's home, after which he studied yoga with various teachers. After his return to Romania he wrote his doctoral dissertation (1936) on yoga at the University of Bucharest.

He became involved in the pro-Nazi Romanian Nationalist movement and wrote articles in support of the Legion of the Archangel Michael, a political group that was anti-Semitic, although Eliade was, most likely, more interested in the nationalist thrust of this group. The issue of whether he personally was anti-Semitic is still debated but there is little evidence to support that charge. After World War II he immigrated to Europe, living and teaching in Paris, where he developed some of his key ideas. In 1956 he moved to the United States and became a professor at the University of Chicago. Through his writing and teaching he became a pivotal figure in the development of religious studies in the United States.

In addition to championing the idea that religion is not a dependent but an independent variable in explaining human behavior, Eliade promoted the use of both historical and **phenomenological** methods in the study of religion. Historical methodology focuses on the development of religions in their historical context and **phenomenological** method focuses on comparing patterns or types of religious phenomena such as founders, scriptures, gods, rituals, experiences, myths, and more in an effort to clarify what these mean from a participant's viewpoint.

Central to any theory of religion is definition. In one of his most popular books, *The Sacred and the Profane*, Eliade defined religion in terms of the sacred. A basic feature of religion is the distinction between sacred and profane. The profane is the realm of everyday events and activities. Everyday activities are ordinary, commonplace, and largely insignificant. The sacred is the opposite. It is a realm of extraordinary events that are highly significant, and believed to show a realm of order and perfection in contrast to the disorder and imperfection of the profane. Eliade thought that we could best grasp the sacred/profane distinction by looking at the life of archaic people. He wrote:

> The man of the archaic societies tends to live as much as possible in the sacred or in close proximity to consecrated objects. This tendency is perfectly understandable, because, for primitives as for the man of all pre-modern societies, the *sacred* is equivalent to a *power*, and, in the last analysis to *reality*. ... Sacred power means reality and at the same time enduringness and efficacy.
>
> (Eliade 1961: 12)

Eliade's understanding of the sacred is indebted to the work of **Otto**, **van der Leeuw** and **Durkheim**, but unlike **Durkheim** he denies that the reality behind the sacred is society. The reality of the sacred is unique and unlike anything else. There is nothing "behind" it to which it can be reduced. It is "wholly other" to borrow **Otto**'s terminology. Its authority controls all aspects of life because it shows people how life *ought* to be lived.

It is not surprising that archaic peoples are ever on the lookout for hierophanies or appearances of the sacred in one form or another. Nor is it surprising that the *axis mundi* or connecting link between the world below and the sky above plays a significant role in their myths and rituals. For instance the sacred tree, which is a common and widespread symbol, expresses just such a relationship as it rises from the earth, toward the sky. Sacred mountains are also examples of an *axis mundi*. *Homo religiosus* or religious man longs to live in the sacred even while having to live in the profane. The religious person exhibits a "nostalgia for Paradise" – for that which is perfect and everlasting.

The proof for such nostalgia can be found, according to Eliade, in the symbols and myths of archaic and modern religions. Because the sacred is by definition a unique reality irreducible to anything else, it can only be expressed indirectly. Symbols are a vehicle for revealing the "wholly other" in events and objects that we can grasp. They are based on analogy, and myths combine symbols into a narrative form. A close study of both reveals common patterns much like **Jung**'s archetypes (although Eliade thought **Jung**'s views **reductionistic**). Eliade's *Patterns in Comparative Religion* (1949) explores in detail some of the symbols and myths that Eliade thought showed, in one way or another, the "nostalgia for Paradise." Creation myths, for example, often posit a "beginning" of the cosmos during which a paradise of innocence existed on earth.

Any ordinary thing can be a symbol, from a stone to a river, but to be a symbol it must appeal to the imagination and embody the idea of contradiction. Water, for example, can symbolize both death (chaotic and destructive floods) and new life or rebirth (spring rains). A single symbol can reintegrate contradictory notions just as water, understood as a symbol, brings together the ideas of death and life.

Another characteristic of symbols is their ability to be endlessly linked and associated to create symbolic systems. So the moon can become linked to the notion of femininity, Mother Earth, fertility, cosmic change, water (the tides), and so on. The history of religions focuses on how such symbols and the myths that grow up around them change over time and become replaced or revalorized. It writes the story of the growth and decay of symbols. This story, Eliade claimed, shows the recurring and expanding patterns of symbolic thinking.

In *The Myth of Eternal Return* (1949), Eliade develops the idea of "nostalgia for Paradise" in ways that connect his theory of archaic religion with what some claim is the existential situation in which all people, archaic or modern, find themselves. The desire to go back to the beginning when the world was pristine or, on a personal level, when our own lives were innocent, is a longing to escape the "terror of history" or the fear that there is no greater meaning to life than "one damn thing after another." Archaic religion tried to relieve this terror by developing a cyclical view of time. We can, it assured the religious, return to the purity of the beginning via religious practices. It is a defiant gesture of denial, seen clearly in the Hindu and Buddhist ideas of rebirth.

Something new entered the religious landscape when Judaism, Christianity and Islam replaced, or at least tried to replace, a cyclical view of time with a linear view. However, if time is a line from the start to the end of time, what comfort can be found in that? The comfort comes from the claim that this line has a meaning or purpose. It claims that the sacred can be found within history as well as outside history. A time will come, at the end of history, when the sacred will be fully restored. This is the first revolution against archaic religion because it asserts that time itself can be sacred. But this revolution gives way to a second revolution—modern historicism. The modern secular world denies meaning can be found in time *and* outside of time. Archaic religion sacralized nature and historical religions of revelation desacralized nature, placing the divine "outside" of nature. Nevertheless, historical religions sacralized time. Modern historicism denies that either nature or time is sacred.

Are moderns then left with despair over whether anything can make life worthwhile? Secularism in whatever form it takes, from fascism to communism to atheistic humanism, claims that humans can create their own meaning. They are captains of their own soul. But is this sort of meaning and purpose any better than that offered by archaic religion or the Abrahamic faiths? Eliade had serious doubts.

In order to avoid misunderstandings, we must add that these phases of religious development Eliade outlined should not be understood in any evolutionary sense. He was not outlining progressive stages. He did not think that, religiously speaking, human existence is necessarily getting better. We should add that he did not want to leave his readers with the impression that archaic religion is dead and gone. The past persists in one form or another in disguised modern versions. The "nostalgia for Paradise" is still around in our religious hopes and fears about the end of time and in our secular movies, fiction, and popular culture.

Criticisms of Eliade's methods and his claims about religion have been growing in recent years. Some critics have argued that his historical method is superficial. He ignored the historical context of many myths and symbols. He was primarily interested in similarities but largely ignored differences. Others have argued that his key analytic concepts are fuzzy. Particularly unclear is his notion of the sacred. What precisely is it? Some critics have argued that he has a hidden agenda, to promote a kind of Christian supernaturalism.

Perhaps his weakness can also be seen as a strength. He boldly asserted the independence of religious behavior and denies that religion can be fully understood once we have uncovered its non-religious causes. Economics may make the world go round but so too does religion. Does this mean that there is a supernatural reality hidden from view but ultimately guiding what transpires in the world? Eliade never made clear his own personal views, and we should beware of conflating religious causation with supernatural causation. But it is difficult to deny that religious motives appear to play an important role in human behavior.

See also: **Douglas, Dumézil, Geertz, van Gennep, Gross, Radhakrishnan, Schleiermacher, Scholem, Smart, J. Z. Smith, Tillich, Turner**

Major works

(1959) *The Myth of the Eternal Return: Cosmos and History*, trans. Willard R. Trask, New York: Harper and Row.

(1961) *The Sacred and the Profane: The Nature of Religion*, trans. Willard R. Trask, New York: Harper and Row.

(1963) *Patterns in Comparative Religion*, trans. Rosemary Sheed, New York: The World Publishing Company.

(1969) *Images and Symbols: Studies in Religious Symbolism*, trans. Philip Mairet, New York: Sheed and Ward.

(1978) *A History of Religious Ideas: From the Stone Age to the Eleusinian Mysteries*, Vol. 1, trans. Willard R. Trask, Chicago, IL: University of Chicago Press.

(1982) *A History of Religious Ideas: From Gautama Buddha to the Triumph of Christianity*, Vol. 2, trans. Willard R. Trask, Chicago, IL: University of Chicago Press.

Further reading

Cave, David. (1993) *Mircea Eliade's Vision for a New Humanism*, New York: Oxford University Press.

Dudley, Gilford, III. (1977) *Religion on Trial: Mircea Eliade and His Critics*, Philadelphia, PA: Temple University Press.

Olson, Carl. (1992) *The Theology and Philosophy of Eliade: A Search for the Centre*, New York: St. Martin's Press.

Rennie, Bryan. (1996) *Reconstructing Eliade: Making Sense of Religion*, New York: State University of New York Press.

http://www.westminster.edu/staff/brennie/eliade/mebio.htm.

CLAUDE LÉVI-STRAUSS (1908–2009)

> We have to resign ourselves to the fact that the myths tell us nothing instructive about the order of the world, the nature of reality or the origin and destiny of mankind. We cannot expect them to flatter any metaphysical thirst, or to breathe new life into exhausted ideologies. On the other hand, they teach us a great deal about the societies from which they originate … and most importantly they make it possible to discover certain operational modes of the human mind.
>
> (Lévi-Strauss 1981: 639)

Claude Lévi-Strauss has been called the father of modern anthropology and was an influential leader in a movement known as structuralism. Unlike functionalists such as **Durkheim** and **Radcliffe-Brown** who thought the key to understanding religion was found in identifying how it satisfied social needs, Lévi-Strauss focused attention on the logical structure of myths and what they reveal about the "operational modes of the human mind." What exactly is that logical structure, how can we discover it, and what is its significance for understanding not only religion but also the workings of the human mind?

Lévi-Strauss was born in Brussels, where his father was working as a painter. The family later moved to Paris, where he grew up. He studied both law and philosophy at the Sorbonne but eventually made his career as an ethnographer, a field in which his first wife, Dina Dreyfus Lévi-Strauss, was trained. Between 1935 and 1939 he lived in Brazil, conducted research among the natives, and taught sociology at the University of São Paulo.

During World War II he moved to the United States in order to escape the Nazi persecution of Jews and taught at The New School for Social Research in New York. In 1948 he returned to France and assumed a chair in social anthropology at the Collège de France. He became a leading intellectual in France, was honored by many universities, and in 1973 was elected a member of the prestigious Académe Française.

In his influential work, *Triste Tropiques*, which was based on his research in Brazil, he argued that Western civilization should not be considered any better than other civilizations, however different it may be. The fundamental features of the human mind were the same everywhere even though the cultural institutions and religions varied from place to place. He elaborated these ideas in *The Savage Mind*, where he set forth his theories of culture, mind, history, and social change. The impact of the book was immense and widespread.

Much of Lévi-Strauss's research focused on myths. He maintained that myths show the central contradictions of a social system as well as attempts to resolve those contradictions. They also contain concrete systems of classification that not only reveal the reasons for the beliefs and practices of any given society, but also offer clues to the way the human mind operates in trying to grasp reality.

Religion lives in its myths and rituals. When we look at the myths of different religions and of different cultures we cannot help but be struck by the similarity of the stories even though the narratives are fantastic and on the surface seem unpredictable. Birds and snakes talk, animals act like humans, people change into animals and animals into people. What is going on here? The paradox of myth that Lévi-Strauss wanted to solve was to account for the contingency of content *and* the similarity of myths from different times and places. He addressed this problem in many books but Chapter Eleven of his *Structural Anthropology* provides one of his clearer explanations.

The key to solving the paradox can be found in the linguistic theories of Ferdinand de Saussure. On the surface languages are very different. Yet they are also similar. Careful analysis shows there is a structure that can generate these similarities. If we think of myths as a kind of language or a system of communication, then we should be able to discover the universal laws that generate the similarities just as linguists can find the universal laws of language. How can this be done?

The linguist breaks down language into constituent parts (phonemes, morphemes, and sememes) and then looks at how they are related. If we think of myths as a type of language, then we can analyze them into their constituent units as well. Lévi-Strauss names these units mythemes. Just as the linguist must focus on how the constituent linguistic units are related in order to understand language, so the student of myth must understand the relations among the mythemes to unravel the meaning of myths.

After careful analysis and comparison of many different myths from around the world, Lévi-Strauss concluded that myths always progress from the awareness of oppositions and move toward their resolution. So the logical structure of myths can be boiled down to three terms, two opposite terms and a mediating term that solves the opposition. Clearly shades of **Hegel**'s dialectic of thesis, antithesis, and synthesis live on in Lévi-Strauss's thoughts.

The clearest illustration of this can be found in his analysis of the trickster figure in North American native mythology. The trickster in these stories is often portrayed as a raven or coyote and is an ambivalent character. It can be a force for good or bad. It can be helpful or a hindrance, it can flaunt cultural standards of right and wrong and support such standards. How are we to understand such a figure?

Lévi-Strauss argued that the trickster figure is a mediating figure. It brings together life and death. How he gets there is somewhat complex. Life is analogous to agriculture, which is concerned with producing life, while death is analogous to hunting, which produces death. Herbivores (plant eaters) and beasts of prey (meat eaters) are associated with agriculture and hunting respectfully. Both coyotes and ravens eat carrion and are scavengers. Thus they are like both beasts of prey that eat meat and herbivores that do not catch their food. In other words, coyotes and ravens share characteristics of both beasts of prey and herbivores, thereby mediating agriculture and hunting, and finally life and death. If this reading of trickster myths is correct, then it should be no surprise that the trickster figure is ambivalent. He is tricky.

Lévi-Strauss maintained that the mind of the "uncivilized savage" is not inferior to the "civilized mind" as other anthropologists had argued. They did so, he thought, in order to support both a theory of evolution and the superiority of colonial cultures (see **Asad**). However, there are differences. In *The Savage Mind* he contrasts the "bricoleur" or handyman who works with his hands using whatever materials and tools are available and the "engineer" who plans projects from start to finish and designs or creates whatever tools may be required to accomplish a project. The universe of the bricoleur is "closed" in the sense that she is often forced to make do with what is at hand and the universe of the engineer is "open" in the sense that she can create new materials and tools to accomplish her goals. Both are skilled, logical, and intelligent but they must deal with different environments. The bricoleur is like what we call the "savage mind" and the engineer is like what we call the civilized mind.

Magic, which we often associate with the "savage mind," is not a forerunner of science, but a complete and integrated method for gaining knowledge. It differs from science insofar as it postulates an all-embracing determinism. Magic, in short, is the science of the concrete because it deals with immediate events. Science is abstract and deals with events beyond immediate experience.

Just as we have misunderstood magic, so too have we misunderstood **totemism**. **Totemism** is best understood as a system of classification, not as some sort of religious institution. It is a concrete and metaphorical way of organizing experience. Its logic is one of binary oppositions. Thus one clan or tribe is able to distinguish itself from another by the presence of certain features (distinctive beliefs, myths, rituals, marriage rules, and so on) or their absence. The **totem** sums these up in a type of code. To say one's **totem** is the bear and not the deer, for example, is to speak volumes to others who understand the code. **Totems** send messages, but those who are not part of the culture are only vaguely aware of how to read them.

Lévi-Strauss was an astute critic of the views of other scholars, but he also attracted his share of criticism. His structural method of analysis often appears forced, as if he is superimposing a preconceived idea on the evidence to make it say what he wants it to say. For example, both coyotes and ravens have many characteristics that might be emphasized to explain why these animals were used in trickster myths. Both can be tricky and deceptive in different ways and it may be these other aspects that led to their role in myths, not the ones Lévi-Strauss selects. Further, not all tricksters are ravens or coyotes. Some are spiders. And why is the bear that both hunts and scavenges not selected to represent trickster? Lévi-Strauss's focus on structure, while valuable, can lead to overlooking other important features such as the aesthetics of the narrative or its political usefulness for some group in society. According to his critics, he consistently ignores the cultural contexts of the myths he studies. There is more to a good story than its structure.

Even though we have entered an age of "post-structuralism," no one can doubt that Lévi-Strauss was a crucial figure in developing and promoting structural analysis. His work is studied across a wide range of disciplines and echoes of his methods can be found in philosophy and literary studies, as well as anthropology. It is now common for students to try to "uncover" *both* the function and the structure of religious phenomena. He developed no grand theory of religion, but he did show religious mythology and ritual were more than just the products of wild, unfettered imagining. They have a meaning and a structure that reflects the ways that humans try to make sense their world.

See also: **Boyer, Dumézil, Evans-Pritchard, Malinowski, J. Z. Smith**

Major works

(1963a) *Totemism*, trans. Rodney Needham, Boston, MA: Beacon Press.

(1963b) *Structural Anthropology*, trans. Claire Jacobson and Brooke Grundfest Schoepf. New York: Basic Books.

(1966) *The Savage Mind*, trans. George Weidenfeld, Chicago, IL: University of Chicago Press.

(1969) *The Raw and The Cooked*, trans. John and Doreen Weightman, New York: Harper and Row.

(1970) *Tristes Tropiques*, trans. John Russell, New York: Atheneum.

(1976) *Structural Anthropology*, Vol. II, trans. Monique Layton, New York: Basic Books.

(1981) *The Naked Man: Introduction to the Science of Mythology: 4*, trans. John and Doreen Weightman, New York: Harper and Row.

Further reading

Pace, David. (1983) *Claude Lévi-Strauss: The Bearer of Ashes*, Boston, MA: Routledge and Kegan Paul.

Wiseman, Boris, ed. (2009) *The Cambridge Companion to Lévi-Strauss*, New York: Cambridge University Press.

http://www.guardian.co.uk/science/2009/nov/03/claude-levi-strauss-obituary.

WILFRED CANTWELL SMITH (1916–2000)

> Neither religion in general nor any one of the religions, I will contend, is in itself an intelligible entity, a valid object of inquiry or of concern either for the scholar or for the man of faith.
>
> (Smith 1964: 16)

This claim appears to announce the demise of the academic study of religion (see **Asad, J. Z. Smith**). It is a scholarly pursuit that has no real object and a religious pursuit that should be of no concern to "the man of faith." The statement comes from the introduction to Cantwell Smith's most influential book, *The Meaning and End of Religion*. What exactly did he mean by this claim and what are its implications for the study of religion?

Wilfred Cantwell Smith was a distinguished historian of religion specializing in Islam, as well as a theologian and ordained minister in the United Church of Canada. He was born to Victor Arnold Smith and Sarah Cory Cantwell in Toronto, where he studied oriental languages at the University of Toronto, graduating with honors in 1938. He married Muriel MacKenzie Struthers, who subsequently aided him in his research. He earned his PhD at Princeton University and established the Institute of Islamic Studies at McGill University, where he taught. In 1964 he became director of the Center for the Study of World Religions at Harvard University. He held several academic appointments, received numerous academic honors, and in 2000 was inducted into the prestigious Order of Canada.

Smith's book *Islam in Modern History* discussed the conflict between contending forces in Islamic nations and competing visions of the future of Islam. He described the conflict between modernizers who support the separation of mosque and state, and traditionalists who support a theocratic state. He did not venture to predict the future outcome of these conflicts, but he did note that Islam contains a spiritual insight that can be useful. The absolute ban on all forms of idolatry and the insistence on the absolute transcendence of God imply that God is more important than all institutions, including religious and political institutions (see **Tillich**). Smith ventured the hope that the creative future of Islam lies with those whose concern for the institutions of their religion is subordinate to their concern for responding to the transcendent divine that they believe stands behind their religion.

His study of Islam and other religions, as well as his travels in the Middle East, made him sensitive to the need to respect the religious traditions of others, the sincerity of other people's faith, and the need for open and honest dialogue. This led him to promote inter-religious dialogue and argue that all religions are historically interconnected in complex ways. He championed a "theory of continuous creation" rather than a "big-bang" theory of religion (see *Towards a World Theology*, 1981). Religions are not created once and for all time by some alleged founder, but are and have been continuously changing in response to changing conditions.

The Meaning and End of Religion, from which our opening quotation comes, begins by noting that the concept religion as well as the singular "a religion" are disputed concepts with no clear and agreed-upon definition among scholars. This fact led Cantwell Smith to suggest that perhaps we have been asking the wrong question when we inquire into the "nature" of religion. We should drop the use of the concept and replace it with something more useful because it refers to nothing that is concretely real. It is an abstraction that has become reified, an abstract idea that has been mistaken for a concrete thing.

A careful historical survey of how the concept religion has been used reveals four distinct but interrelated meanings. First, it has been and is used to name personal piety (e.g. "Jane is very religious"), second, people use it to refer a system of beliefs and practices, third people think of this system as having a history and naming a particular community as in "the world religions" (e.g. Hinduism), and finally the concept has been and is used in a generic sense to refer to religion in general. These different uses indicate not only the ambiguity of the concept, but often mask or blend two very different meanings. For example, sometimes the names for different religions blend ideal and historical meanings, as "Christianity" does when it is used to name a historical tradition and to name some ideal as in "true Christianity."

Most of the so-called world religions are not self-named. Often hostile outsiders gave them their names and the members of the named community only gradually accepted these names. Islam, however, is an exception. It claims that the name "Islam" was given by Allah (God) himself. It is a divine, not a human, name and there-fore is sacred. After a careful description of how the word "Islam" has been used, Smith concluded, "that [Islam] has been in some ways from the first the most reified of all man's living religious movements, that it has at its birth and throughout been subject to massive reifying pressures; and yet like all the others it began (was proclaimed in the Qur'an) as a ringing personal summons to men and women to have faith in God ... " (Smith 1964: 107). Part of the pressure toward reification was the apologetic need to defend itself against its detractors.

If outsiders have named most religions and if the names are reifications, then they are inadequate for conveying the personal faith of real believers. The participants of what we call religions are concerned with transcendence while the observers are concerned with the religion. Hence the names are misleading, even more the attempts to conceptualize them is a contradiction in terms because there is more to any person's faith than concepts can capture.

If the concept of religion is inadequate and should be dropped, what did Smith propose we use in its place? He argued that we should use two concepts: cumulative tradition and personal faith. By cumulative tradition he meant "the entire mass of overt objective data that constitute the historical deposit, as it were, of the past religious life of the community in question ... " (Smith 1964: 141). This historical deposit would include, among many other things, institutions, moral codes, myths, doctrines, scriptures, temples, and artistic expression. Personal faith, the second element, refers to the inner spiritual experience of any person responding to what he or she believes to be an encounter with transcendent reality. The first element accounts for both the historical and concrete manifestations of what we call religions and are available for outsiders to study and describe. It is the objective element. The second element (the inner personal faith of participants) outsiders cannot adequately describe because it is subjective (see **Kierkegaard**). These objective and subjective elements are, Smith believed, more accurate terms to use when we talk and think about what we usually call religion.

Critics have challenged Smith's outsider/insider dichotomy and accused him of championing a kind of ecumenical inclusiveness that wrongly assumes religious goals are the same for all. It is all good and well to talk about the transcendence that stands behind the outward manifestations of religion, but this idea is itself an abstraction. Transcendence is a concept that different religions interpret in different ways. The scholar should not ignore these differences in the hope of showing that personal faith is more important than other features of what we call religion. This not only betrays a kind of Protestant bias, but also tries to protect "personal faith" from scholarly theories by placing it "off limits" to the prying eyes of outside observers.

While there has been sympathy among scholars for Smith's criticism of the term religion and his proposal for thinking instead in terms of cumulative tradition and personal faith, Smith's proposal for abandoning the use of the term religion and religions has not taken root. Yet his insistence on religious tolerance and respect for the faith of others has found wide acceptance and few would question that inter-religious dialogue is beneficial to understanding the spiritual longings and aspirations of humans. Many have welcomed his strong support for viewing religious studies as a humanistic discipline while at the same time insisting that disciplines more oriented to scientific approaches also make important contributions to our understanding.

See also: **Hick, James**

Major works

(1957) *Islam in Modern History*, Princeton, NJ: Princeton University Press.
(1964) *The Meaning and End of Religion*, New York: The New American Library.
(1976) *Religious Diversity: Essays*, ed. Willard G. Oxtoby, New York: HarperCollins.
(1977) *Belief and History*, Charlottesville, VA: University Press of Virginia.
(1981) *Towards A World Theology: Faith and the Comparative History of Religion*, Philadelphia, PA: The Westminster Press.

Further reading

Asad, Talal. (2001) "Reading a Modern Classic: W. C. Smith's The Meaning and End of Religion," *History of Religion* 40: 205–22.
Robert D. Baird, ed. (1975) *Methodological Issues in Religious Studies*, Chico, CA: New Horizons Press.
Whaling, Frank, ed. (1986) *The World's Religious Traditions: Current Perspectives in Religious Studies: Essays in Honour of Wilfred Cantwell Smith*, New York: The Crossroad Publishing Company.
http://en.wikipedia.org/wiki/Wilfred_Cantwell_Smith.

VICTOR TURNER (1920–83)

Liminal entities are neither here nor there; they are betwixt and between the positions assigned and arrayed by law, custom, convention, and ceremonial. As such, their ambiguous and indeterminate attributes are expressed by a rich variety of symbols in the many societies that ritualize

> social and cultural transitions. Thus, liminality is frequently likened to death, to being in the womb, to invisibility, to darkness, to bisexuality, to the wilderness, and to an eclipse of the sun or moon.
>
> (Turner 1969: 95)

Victor Witter Turner, one of the most influential cultural anthropologists of the last century, developed the idea of **liminality** in order to describe a wide variety of cultural phenomena, including religious rituals that marked transitional phases in personal and cultural development. What exactly is the **liminal** and why is it important for understanding religion?

Victor Turner was born in Scotland. His mother was an actress who inspired his lifelong interest in drama and his father was an engineer. He entered University College, London to pursue his interest in classics but World War II interrupted his studies. He served as a noncombatant and during the war married Edith Turner, who collaborated with him in his later research. After the war he returned to University College to finish a degree in anthropology, pursuing an interest he had developed during the war and one he pursued in graduate studies at Manchester University. He did field work studying the Ndembu tribe of Zambia and worked at the Rhodes-Livingston Institute. After completing his PhD in 1955 he accepted a number of academic appointments in the United States, eventually spending most of his academic career at the University of Virginia.

In his dissertation (*Schism and Continuity in African Society*, 1957), Turner used the term "social dramas" to describe the public eruption of inevitable social conflict and its resolution. He developed this idea by analyzing the phases of social dramas – breach, crisis, redressive action, and reintegration. Breach refers to the beginnings of disharmonic processes in a society, which develops into a crisis as the divisions between parties in conflict deepen and widen. Redressive actions of various kinds (mediation, arbitration, legal) are designed to facilitate an eventual reintegration into the social order of the parties in conflict.

Turner recognized that symbols played an important role in social processes and he developed a general theory of symbols, especially the role symbols played in religious and secular rituals (see *The Forest of Symbols: Aspects of Ndembu Ritual*, 1967). He noted that one symbol could stand for many things, what he called "multivocality." Symbols also unify and condense different and often disparate meanings.

So, for example, the symbol water can stand for both new life and destruction of life. In addition, symbolic meanings tend to polarize by clustering around ideological poles (moral, political, and social meanings) and orectic (sensory, affective) poles.

These characteristics of symbols indicate that anthropologists and scholars of religion must pay attention to different kinds of symbolic meaning. Turner identified three levels of meaning: exegetical, operational, and positional. Exegetical meaning is the indigenous meaning, that is, what the symbols mean to the people who use them. Operational meaning can be determined by observing what is done with symbols. This requires paying attention to the social context such as the characteristics of the group using the symbols as well as the groups that are excluded from its use. For example, in a ritual context one must determine what is done with water, who does it, and who is prohibited from using it in some way specific to the ritual. Positional meaning refers to the meaning some symbol has by virtue of its relationship to other symbols. To determine this one needs to engage in comparative studies. For example, if water in a certain symbol system is juxtaposed to symbols associated with death, this reinforces its positional meaning as supportive of life and vice versa.

Turner was particularly interested in ritual processes. He thought of rituals as sort of mini-dramas involving a stereotypical sequence of actions. Rituals should be thought of by analogy with dramatic performances that involve role-playing, rhetorical speech, an audience, knowledge and acceptance of a shared set of rules governing the ritual and its climax. In a religious context, ritual performances were intended to influence supernatural forces, although other types of ritual, such as political rituals, can have different goals. He distinguished between rituals that elevated one's social status (e.g. initiation, marriage, graduation) and rituals that lowered one's social status, what he called rituals of status reversal (e.g. excommunication, carnival). The former are usually classified as **rites of passage** and the latter are cyclical or calendrical rites.

Turner was particularly interested in **rites of passage** and was strongly influenced by **Arnold van Gennep**'s analysis of such rites into the phases of separation, transition, and reaggregation. He went beyond **van Gennep**'s analysis, however, by focusing on the period of transition, which he called **liminality**. A clear example of such a rite is puberty rituals found in many different pre-industrial societies. Groups of individuals are separated from others in the tribe, isolated and instructed in important matters such as the myths and taboos of the tribe, then reincorporated into the tribe. They leave as children and return as adults.

During the period of isolation "they are betwixt and between" social roles. In this ambiguous situation, *"communitas"* develops among the initiates, that is, a deep sense of equality and comradeship. Persons or groups in a **liminal** state have several characteristics including the stripping away of pre- and post-liminal attributes, limbo status in a process of transition, and submissiveness while being inscribed with new knowledge. If pre- and post-liminal states are structured (e.g. norms, rules, roles), the **liminal** state is anti-structure.

Turner generalized his ideas concerning **liminality** and *communitas* beyond the context of **rites of passage** to religious, cultural, and social movements. He thought the structure/anti-structure dialectic of **rites of passage** could be seen in millenarian and utopian movements as well as movements of social rebellion such as the hippies of the 1960s and political populist movements of one sort or another. These sorts of movements exhibit the "high/low" polarization of the **liminal** phase. What is highly valued in the structured society is given a low valuation and what is given a low valuation in the structured society is given a high valuation among such groups. They are phenomena in transition. For example, such movements often espouse a new set of sexual values, either preaching sexual continence or sexual indulgence, both of which are at odds with the dominant social order. Sex is either highly valued (e.g. free love) or undervalued (e.g. celibacy).

Turner argued that there are characteristics common to **liminal** groups. They fall in the interstices of social structure, usually occupy the lowest levels of society, and live on the margins of the dominant society. This led him to conclude that *communitas* develops in the absence of normal social structure. He cited **Martin Buber**'s claim that *communitas* (what **Buber** calls community) happens spontaneously when an I–Thou relationship occurs. **Buber**'s insight led Turner to distinguish among spontaneous (existential), normative, and ideological *communitas*. The spontaneous type cannot be adequately expressed in a structural form and is unpredictable. The normative type arises when people in spontaneous *communitas* feel the need, over time, to organize resources and develop some form of social control. Ideological *communitas* applies primarily to utopian movements that seek ways to spell out the social conditions (such as sharing all property in common) that allow spontaneous *communitas* to flourish.

Turner emphasized what he called the "dialectic" of social processes as alternating between structure and *communitas*. When one of these processes becomes exaggerated the opposite is provoked. Overemphasis on control, social rigidity, and structure triggers anti-structural movements and vice versa. Social wisdom is finding the appropriate balance between the two because genuine society requires both. People need the freedom, spontaneity, pleasure, and that "magical" feeling of endless power characteristic of *communitas* and they need the order, rules, and security that social institutions and structures can provide. What Turner termed the **liminoid** is a state that can be found in modern societies and other societies throughout history along with the need for order and social stability (see **Nietzsche**'s Apollonian and Dioynsian).

Critics of Turner's ideas have questioned whether the idea of **liminality** can be usefully stretched to cover as many situations as Turner claims. There is a tendency, many have thought, to over-generalize to the point where his concepts become so vague as to be almost useless. Some have challenged his central notion of *communitas*, claiming his description is idealized, while others have found his treatment of pilgrimage rituals as **liminal** and hence not part of ordinary daily life just plain wrong.

There is little doubt that Turner's views on ritual as performance have proved useful in a variety of fields, including literature, communication theory, political science, and drama. Some claim he broke new theoretical ground by viewing ritual as a social process with a dramatic structure, and his ideas inspired a new area of research called ritual studies. Although he developed no comprehensive theory of religion, his work drew attention to the importance of ritual action, an often-neglected dimension of religion that is as important, perhaps even more important, than belief when it comes to understanding religion.

See also: **Douglas, Eliade, Tillich**

Major works

(1957) *Schism and Continuity in an African Society: As Study of Ndembu Village Life*, Manchester: Manchester University Press.

(1961) *Ndembu Divination: Its Symbolism and Techniques*, Manchester: Manchester University Press.

(1967) *The Forest of Symbols: Aspects of Ndembu Ritual*, Ithaca, NY: Cornell University Press.

(1968) *The Drums of Affliction: A Study of Religious Processes among the Ndembu of Zambia*, Oxford: Clarendon.

(1969) *The Ritual Process: Structure and Anti-Structure*, Chicago, IL: Aldine.

(1974) *Dramas, Fields, and Metaphors: Symbolic Action in Human Society*, Ithaca, NY: Cornell University Press.

(1978) *Images and Pilgrimage in Christian Cultures: Anthropological Approaches*, with Edith Turner, New York: Columbia University Press.

(1982) *From Ritual to Theatre: The Human Seriousness of Play*, New York: PAJ Publications.

Further reading

Ashley, Kathleen M., ed. (1990) *Victor Turner and the Construction of Cultural Criticism: Between Literature and Anthropology*, Bloomington, IN: Indiana University Press.

Eade, John and Michael J. Sallnow (1991) *Contesting the Sacred: The Anthropology of Christian Pilgrimage*, New York: Routledge.

Grimes, Ronald L. (1982) *Beginnings in Ritual Studies*, Lanham, MD: University Press of America.

http://www.Indiana.edu/~wanthro/turner.htm.

MARY DOUGLAS (1921–2007)

> For it is a mistake to suppose that there can be religion which is all interior, with no rules, no liturgy, no external signs of inward states. As with society, so with religion, external form is the condition of its existence. ... As a social animal, man is a ritual animal. If ritual is suppressed in one form it crops up in others, more strongly the more intense the social interaction. ... It is not too much to say that ritual is more to society than words are to thought. For it is very possible to know something and then find words for it. But it is impossible to have social relations without symbolic acts.
>
> (Douglas 1966: 62)

Mary Douglas, an influential anthropologist and theorist of culture and religion, here states a theme that runs throughout her two major books dealing with religion: *Purity and Danger* and *Natural Symbols*. Humans are social beings who are bound together by symbolic acts that are embodied in the rituals of everyday life and religion. Contrary to the claims of theorists like **Otto**, religion is as much a matter of observable ritual acts, as it is spiritual experiences of the sacred. However, can religion only exist if there are "external signs of inward states"? What does it mean to say that humans are ritual animals and symbolic acts are essential for social relations?

Margaret Mary Tew was born in Italy as her parents were on their way to Burma, where her father worked for the British government.

She was raised a devout Catholic and remained in that faith throughout her life. After education at a convent school, she studied at St. Anne's College, Oxford. She did her graduate work with **Evans-Pritchard** and adopted his view that anthropological theories based on the notion that religions evolve from simple to complex were misguided. Like **Evans-Pritchard** she rejected a sharp distinction between "primitive" and "modern" peoples, holding that humans are fundamentally similar even though their cultures, religions, and social organizations may differ in drastic ways.

She did fieldwork with the Lele people in Africa and many of her ideas were drawn from her fieldwork data. She completed her doctorate in the 1950s and married James Douglas, with whom she had three children. She taught anthropology in both England and the United States. Her reputation and published work led to an appointment as Avalon Professor of the Humanities at Northwestern University. In 2006, a year before her death, she became Dame Commander of the Order of the British Empire.

Douglas was impressed by **Durkheim**'s insight that the categories which humans use to classify their experiences of the world arise from their social experiences. People develop categories of thought in order to solve problems that arise as they try to organize experiences into a meaningful system. However, people do not construe their world in any way they wish. There are institutional and social constraints on what can be thought and hence what can be valued.

The categories people develop lead to classification systems, including religious systems. Systems of classification have two features that Douglas found particularly significant. First, they generate anomalies and ambiguity because no matter how complex the categories, there are things that just do not fit neatly into them or appear to fit in more than one category. Second, they draw boundaries that separate things into one class or another. Douglas found the existence of anomalies a key to understanding cultural and religious ideas of purity/pollution, clean/unclean, acceptable/unacceptable, and the like. She also discovered that the way boundaries are drawn and their relative strength or weakness is a key to understanding symbol systems.

Central to religion is the idea of what is sacred and what is profane, as **Durkheim** had remarked. Douglas noted that the sacred referred to what was set apart and separated from the profane. She also noted that it was set apart because it was both precious and dangerous. The sacred was ambiguous. It was something that was both a benefit to humans and also dangerous. It fit into more than one category and hence was not completely controllable by social institutions and human thought.

Douglas saw a link between power and danger. Humans seek to create order by their classification systems, but they do not totally reject disorder because they recognize the potential for change that it contains. The potency of disorder is recognized in ritual activity. Energy to command spirits, special powers to heal, to change weather conditions, comes from those who, for a time, leave rational control behind as they enter ecstatic states generated by ritually induced trances and frenzies.

Danger resides in the transitional states because one enters the realm of the indefinable. Rituals, such as **rites of passage**, try to control this danger by ensuring a manageable process of change. They seek to both break down, at least temporally, the categories of accepted behavior and then restore them. Hence, Douglas concluded, "beliefs which attribute spiritual power to individuals are never neutral or free of the dominant patterns of social structure" (Douglas 1966: 112).

Neither, we might add, are dietary codes and ideas about polluting substances such as feces and blood. If we carefully examine the way different groups define impurity, we find that these definitions function to maintain the social order. The impure and the polluting are things that do not completely conform to their class. They violate the classification system. Scholars have often tried to explain dietary codes such as those found in Leviticus in the Hebrew Bible as expressions of an early concern with hygiene and disease. Douglas argued that this was not the case based on a comparative analysis of the sorts of animals and plants humans in different societies declared unclean. What is the case is that unclean animals and polluting substances do not conform fully to their class. For example, pork is unclean for Jews and Muslims and it is forbidden as food because pigs are cloven-hoofed but not ruminant. As Douglas puts it, "Hybrids and other confusions are abominated" (Douglas 1966: 53). The claim that the divine abhors something is a way of saying it is dangerous to the order of the group because it confuses, mixes, or otherwise disturbs the classification system that provides order.

Natural Symbols is primarily a defense of the importance of ritual for social life. The natural symbol to which Douglas referred is the physical body. The body has boundaries that demarcate what is inside from what is outside. Further, it orders what is inside (the parts of the body) by placing them in relation to each other. If we think of human organizations as social bodies, then understanding their boundaries should help us understand a whole variety of social behaviors and shared ideas.

Douglas calls social bodies a group and their internal parts a grid. This leads to what others have dubbed the "group/grid" model or theory. The group boundaries separate one group from another. These boundaries range from strong (preventing penetration and mixing) to weak. Likewise grids, the rules regulating how one part of the group stands in relation to another part, range from strong to weak. This framework leads to four correlations: strong group and grid, strong group and weak grid, weak group and strong grid, weak group and grid.

If a group has strong boundaries, we can predict there will be pressure to conform to its norms along with a strong sense of group identity. If a group is weak, we can expect little pressure to conform and a weak sense of distinctive identity. The dominant symbols of a society are a clue to the strength and weakness of group and grid. These symbols will change as the attitude toward group and grid boundaries changes. For example, the traditional *caste* system of Hinduism reflects strong grid with clear definitions of identity, and once it is replaced by a *class* system and the grid weakens, the definitions of identity will become less clear or change entirely. In Christian cultures the change from a strong distinction between sinners and saved to a weak distinction leads to fuzzier boundaries concerning who is a Christian and who is not.

Douglas and her followers have used the group/grid model to analyze religious features of various societies. For example, in societies with a strong group/grid, magic entails a belief in the power of symbols to effect change, and the society is strongly ritualistic. In societies with a weak group/grid, magic is usually rejected as ineffective and there is often an anti-ritualistic attitude with high value placed on spontaneity.

While many scholars have found Douglas's ideas useful, others have been skeptical of their value. The group/grid model is confusing, her critics argue, and its usefulness depends on subjective and hence often disputed interpretations of cultural and religious symbols. Should group and grid be understood as variables and if so which is the dependent variable and which the independent? Some claim her ideas conceal a social determinism of human thought, although Douglas has disputed that. Douglas has been accused of allowing her strong and conservative Catholic faith to prejudice her scholarship because her writing appears to reflect a nostalgia for the days when Western society had a strong group/grid with clearly defined lines of authority.

While her ideas and methods went out of fashion for a time, some now claim that they need to be revisited and reapplied in new ways.

They may contain a coherent direction for future study after more recent theories have been found wanting. Searching for anomalies in cultural classification systems has proved valuable and her group/grid model, although problematic, may contain the seeds for a more objective comparative method.

See also: **Eliade, van Gennep, van der Leeuw, Turner**

Major works

(1963) *The Lele of the Kasai*, London: International African Institute.

(1966) *Purity and Danger: An Analysis of the Concepts of Pollution and Taboo*, New York: Frederick A. Praeger.

(1982) *Essays in the Sociology of Perception*, London: Routledge and Kegan Paul.

(1983) *Natural Symbols: Explorations in Cosmology*, New York: Pantheon Books.

(1988) *Missing Persons: A Critique of Personhood in the Social Sciences*, with S. Ney, Berkeley, CA: University of California Press.

(1993) *In the Wilderness: The Doctrine of Defilement in the Book of Numbers*, Oxford: Oxford University Press.

(1994) *Risk and Blame: Essays in Cultural Theory*, London: Routledge.

(1999) *Leviticus as Literature*, Oxford: Oxford University Press.

Further reading

Bergesen, Albert. (1984) "The Cultural Anthropology of Mary Douglas," in *Cultural Analysis: The Work of Peter L. Berger, Mary Douglas, Michel Foucault, and Jürgen Habermas*, Boston: Routledge and Kegan Paul.

Fardon, Richard. (1999) *Mary Douglas: An Intellectual Biography*, London Routledge.

Heap, S. Hargreaves and A. Ross, eds. (1992) *Understanding the Enterprise Culture: Themes in the Work of Mary Douglas*, Edinburgh: Edinburgh University Press.

http://www.alanmacfarlane.com/ancestors/douglas.htm.

JOHN HICK (1922–)

There are many general interpretations of religion. These have usually been either naturalistic, treating religion as a purely human phenomenon or, if religious, have been developed within the confines of a particular confessional conviction which construes all other traditions in its own terms. The one type of theory that has seldom been attempted is a religious but not confessional interpretation of religion in its plurality of forms; and it is this that I shall be trying to offer here.

(Hick 1989: 1)

John Harwood Hick, a philosopher of religion, here states his goal in his influential and controversial book *An Interpretation of Religion*. He develops his religious interpretation in five densely argued sections, starting with **phenomenological** considerations and ending with a discussion of the problem of conflicting truth claims. But what does he mean by a religious interpretation that is not confessional? Is such a thing even possible?

John Hick was born in Yorkshire, England to Mark and Aileen Hick. He had originally intended to study law but after service in World War II in a non-combat capacity (he is a pacifist) he became interested in philosophy and completed his education at the University of Edinburgh in that field. After he graduated from Edinburgh, he pursued a doctorate at Oxford University. Following the completion of his doctorate, Hick served as a pastor to a Presbyterian church, and in 1953 he married Joan Hazel Bowers.

After leaving the ministry, Hick held a series of teaching posts in the philosophy of religion and theology. In 1967 he was appointed to the H. G. Wood Chair of Philosophy at Birmingham University. Birmingham was a city of diverse religion and culture, and Hick was disturbed by the bigotry the Christian churches showed toward other faiths. His own concern to develop a viable theory of religious pluralism arose from these experiences. In 1980, Hick accepted an appointment to the Danforth Chair in the Philosophy of Religion at Claremont Graduate School in Claremont, California, from which he has now retired.

Hick has written many books dealing with a wide variety of topics, ranging from the incarnation of Christ to the problem of evil. In each of his books he has offered novel and often unorthodox (he was twice brought up on heresy charges) interpretations of traditional Christian teachings. For example, he argued that the doctrine of the incarnation is a myth that should be interpreted metaphorically. It means that Jesus was a human being that was open and responsive to God's love and reflected that divine love in his own life. However, he was not unique because others have also reflected such love; hence Christian claims to exclusiveness cannot be sustained. With respect to the problem of evil (how can a perfectly powerful and loving God allow evil), Hick developed a "soul-making" **theodicy** in which he argued that humans were created good but not perfect. The suffering they encounter in life is meant to help them develop morally, a journey that continues after death.

Hick is also famous for his theory of "eschatological verification," which claims that religious language about non-empirical realities was meaningful because in principle it could be confirmed after death. He developed this idea in response to the claim of some philosophers that only those statements that were in principle verifiable or falsifiable were meaningful. Talk about God or other alleged supernatural realities was meaningless if it lay beyond the possibility of verification or falsification.

Rather than focusing on the more traditional Christian theological themes that Hick addressed, it is better to discuss his views on religion in general in order to get a clear picture of how Hick develops his argument for religious pluralism. Religious pluralism refers to a position centering on the claim that there are many different paths to salvation and no single path has a monopoly on religious truth.

Hick believes that today a revolution in thinking about religions comparable to the Copernican revolution in astronomy in the sixteenth century is taking place. The Ptolemaic view of the earth as the center of the universe dominated scientific and theological thinking until Copernicus's heliocentric theory replaced it. "Ptolemaic" thinking about religion, Hick argues, holds that the teachings of one of the world's religions are at the core of religious truth. Which one someone thinks is at the center depends on the religion to which that person belongs. So Christianity (if one is a Christian) or Islam (if one is a Muslim), and so on, is the "true center" of the universe of faiths. Just as Ptolemaic astronomy was geocentric, so Ptolemaic religion is ethnocentric. The accident of birth mostly determines which religion if any we think of as the true one. The new revolutionary thinking about religion is beginning to recognize a new center around which all religions revolve. Hick calls that center the Real.

What is the Real? Hick relies on a modified version of **Kant's** distinction between **noumena** (things-in-themselves) and **phenomena** (things-as-they-appear) to explain his idea of the Real. He distinguishes between the Real-in-itself that, like **noumena**, is beyond human apprehension, and the Real-as-it-appears that, like **phenomena,** can be apprehended.

With this distinction established, Hick formulates what he calls the pluralistic hypothesis. The Real-in-itself is always present but when it appears to human consciousness (Real-as-it-appears) we speak of religious experience. It is these historically and culturally conditioned experiences that give rise to different concepts of the Real. Hence the

Real has different names. In some traditions it is named Brahman, in others the Dao, in still others Allah, or God. Each religious tradition generates its own names and concepts of the Real. Like **Schleiermacher**, Hick grounds religion in religious experience, but unlike **Schleiermacher** he takes a wider perspective and emphasizes the importance of historical and cultural context.

Hick thinks that most of these different conceptions can be reduced to two main types. One type thinks of the Real in personal terms. Like humans it is conscious, has a will, and cares about people. The other type interprets the Real in impersonal terms. It is called the Absolute, the Principle, the Infinite, the Eternal, and so on. Hick contends that, even though these two types appear to be very different, indeed even opposites, they are not mutually exclusive. Rather, he maintains, they should be thought of as complementary.

Hick recognizes that the task of demonstrating the complementarity of the personal and impersonal concepts of the Real is not easy, but he is encouraged by the fact that all the different religions, whether they conceive the Real as personal or as impersonal, have developed traditions that promote human spiritual and moral transformation. The spiritual transformation Hick points to is the "transformation of human existence from self-centredness to Reality-centredness" (Hick 1989: 300). The moral transformation refers to the attempt on the part of many different religions to improve the ethical quality of human life and society. He writes, "the ethical principles of the great traditions express essentially the same ideal of love, compassion, forgiveness" (Hick 1989: 336).

When Hick turns to the thorny problem of assessing conflicting religious truth-claims, he translates his ideas of spiritual and moral transformation into soteriological (having to do with salvation) and ethical criteria. We can judge, at least to some extent, a religion's truth and authenticity by how successful it is in promoting spirituality and morality. We need to realize that difference does not necessarily imply incompatibility and we need to distinguish conflict about significant core claims from conflict about minor historical details. In the final analysis, Hick argues, the "truth or validity or authenticity of [differing] manifestations of [ultimate Reality] lies in their soteriological effectiveness" (Hick 1989: 373).

Hick's argument for the viability of the pluralistic hypothesis concludes on a positive note:

> My conclusion, then, is that the differences between the root concepts and experiences of the different religions, their different

and often conflicting historical and trans-historical beliefs, their incommensurable mythologies, and the diverse and ramifying belief-systems into which all these are built, are compatible with the pluralistic hypothesis that the great world traditions constitute different conceptions and perceptions of, and responses to, the Real from within the different cultural ways of being human.

(Hick 1989: 375–76)

However attractive Hick's ideas may be, they have not escaped criticism. Some have found his **theodicy** insufficiently sensitive to the brutal reality of evil and suffering in human life. Others have found his argument for the pluralistic hypothesis too rationalistic, based on unproved assumptions such as the existence of the Real, developed on a almost vacuous level of abstraction, and not sufficiently sensitive to the real differences among the world's religious traditions. Others have found Hick's version of pluralism a significant and positive attempt to not only understand religion but also to interpret it in ways that promote tolerance and cooperation among the different traditions. Perhaps its most attractive feature is its religious but non-confessional attempt to promote religious tolerance.

See also: **James, Otto, Radhakrishnan, W. C. Smith, Wittgenstein**

Major works

(1957) *Faith and Knowledge*, New York: Cornell University Press.
(1966) *Evil and the God of Love*, New York: Harper and Row.
(1976) *Death and Eternal Life*, New York: Harper and Row.
(1977) *The Myth of God Incarnate*, ed. J. Hick, London: SCM Press.
(1985) *Problems of Religious Pluralism*, New York: Macmillan.
(1989) *An Interpretation of Religion: Human Responses to the Transcendent*, New Haven: Yale University Press.
(1993) *The Metaphor of God Incarnate*, London: SCM Press.
(2002) *John Hick: An Autobiography*, Oxford: Oneworld Publications.

Further reading

D'Costa, Gavin. (1986) *Theology and Religious Pluralism: The Challenge of Other Religions*, Oxford: Basil Blackwell.
Dean, Thomas. (1995) *Religious Pluralism and Truth: Essays on Cross-Cultural Philosophy of Religion*, Albany, NY: State University of New York Press.

Sharma, A. ed. (1992) *God, Truth and Reality: Essays in Honour of John Hick*, Basingstoke: Macmillan.
http://people.bu.edu/wwildman/WeirdWildWeb/courses/mwt/dictionary/m wt_themes_875_hick.htm.

RENÉ GIRARD (1923–)

> Violence and the sacred are inseparable.
>
> (Girard 1979: 19)

This claim is just one small, but significant part, of René Girard's bold and controversial theory explaining the origins of violence, religion, culture, and more. At first glance it seems paradoxical if not outright false. We normally associate the sacred with non-violence. Religions can support violent acts on occasion. But we tend to assume that such occasions have little to do with the nature of religion itself and more to do with political and economic factors. Girard wants us to rethink the association between the sacred and violence. He wants to understand how they are inextricably bound together.

Born in historic Avignon, France on Christmas day, René Noël Théophile Girard grew up fascinated with history and in 1943 moved to Paris to study medieval history. In 1947 he entered graduate school at Indiana University, receiving his PhD in 1950. He taught language, literature, and history at a number of universities before becoming a professor at Stanford University. He retired in 1995 after publishing a number of books dealing with literature, mimetic desire, violence and religion. In 2005 he was elected to the prestigious Académie Française.

Contrary to what we normally think, desire is not a spontaneous emotion aroused by the attractiveness of some object. After a careful reading of great literature (Cervantes, Dostoevsky, and so on) Girard discovered what he calls mimetic desire. We *learn* to desire some object by imitating the desire some other has for the object. This inevitably creates competition for the object and hence rivalry among those who desire it. According to Girard, this "acquisitive mimesis" is a core human characteristic.

The desire to acquire something that someone else desires soon leads to conflict, which triggers a change in focus. The parties no longer focus on the object but on competing with each other for the object. They become "doubles," as each mirrors the other's desire, thereby becoming models for one another as well as obstacles for each other if both cannot obtain the object. As the object of the original desire recedes in importance and as the competition increases in intensity, violence will eventually erupt. Now winning or losing the object of desire has become transformed into defeating one's "enemy."

We can make this less abstract by thinking of two children playing. One spots a ball the other has not seen or has ignored. The first child goes for the ball to play with it. The second child suddenly wants the ball too because the actions of the first child reveal that it is indeed an object worthy of desire. Children playing quietly together have now become rivals and find themselves in competition for the ball. As the competition intensifies, and no one powerful enough to stop it is present, physical fighting will likely erupt.

If we imagine a time before cultural institutions or other mechanisms for arresting violence existed, then we can see why violence can potentially intensify without end because it is itself mimetic and thus contagious. It is like an infectious disease because one act of violence arouses more violence in retaliation. Once I attack my enemy thinking I can stop the violence, those who support my enemy will attack me. If they harm or eliminate me, those who support me will attack them. Each side feels justified because each side believes it is righting a wrong. Revenge breeds revenge and each victory spawns new opponents. "Vengeance professes to be an act of reprisal, and every reprisal calls for another reprisal" (Girard 1979: 14). Remember the Hatfields and McCoys?

Unchecked, the cycle of revenge can threaten the existence of the whole community as violence spreads like a plague. But how can it be stopped? If only violence can put an end to violence, then, in the absence of mutually agreed-upon alternatives, the only solution is to find a victim who has no way of striking back. A scapegoat is needed.

A scapegoat, when violence is enacted on it, can reunite a community by providing it with a common enemy. The scapegoat becomes, in people's minds, the "cause" of all the violence in the community (its disintegration into warring factions and its blood feuds). The rage of the community can be vented on the scapegoat, who is usually selected from marginal members of the community (the disabled, social misfits, minority religions, and the like) so it is powerless to strike back. However, Girard insists, the designation of the victim is arbitrary in the sense that actual guilt for some crime against the community is not necessary for the selection of the victim. An imagined crime is enough.

If the selection process is arbitrary, it is also hidden to the agents who select and sacrifice or harm in other ways the scapegoat. They do not know the victim for what he or she is, a victim randomly selected from the powerless who bears no guilt for the crimes the community imagines the victim has perpetrated. The witch-hunts throughout history are good examples of the way the truth is obscured because the witch is imagined to be guilty of all kinds of horrible crimes when in fact the witch is only a hapless victim on which the community has focused its own violence.

After the sacrifice of the scapegoat, peace and harmony return to the community, if only temporarily. Paradoxically, the scapegoat is thought to be responsible for all the troubles and violence in the community and, at the same time the solution to that violence. It is elevated to a sacred status and valorized because its sacrifice returns social order and peace. In some archaic societies the scapegoat was deified.

To sacrifice something is to make it sacred. This process of sacralization is a distorted representation of the process of victimization. The sacred at the heart of religion is essentially linked to violence. So too is culture and social order. The social order is an unintended consequence of the self-regulating mechanism of violence in which violence visited on the scapegoat can itself bring a temporary end to violence. The myths, rituals, and rules that grow up around the sacrifice and its periodic repetition in community rites and celebrations eventually lead to ordinances and laws for the acquisition of the objects that first became the object of desire deflected into rivalry and violence. Even language, which is at the very heart of culture, arises from the process of sacrificing the scapegoat because the scapegoat is a *representation* of something else, a symbol if you will of what is wrong and a substitute for what is really wrong; human violence. Symbolic representation is what makes language possible and it is also essential to the victimization of the scapegoat.

Girard's theory of the link between violence and the sacred faces a formidable challenge when we turn our attention to the Judeo-Christian tradition. If his theory is correct, a religion that takes the part of the victim and sides with the scapegoats of society should not exist. Yet it does. How is it possible for a religion to preach love, peace, and non-violence if the very origin of the notion of the sacred originates in violence?

Girard argues for a novel interpretation of scripture in his book *Things Hidden since the Foundation of the World*. The Bible, he argues, systematically exposes the real mechanism of violence that people hide from themselves. The scapegoat victim is *not* the cause of the violence that is destroying the community; the community itself, or more precisely mimetic desire that starts the process, is what leads to violence. The Biblical exposé begins the long process of the desacralization of nature (the thunderstorm is not a god) and the secularization of society as the priests required for the scapegoat sacrifice, indeed, as bloody sacrifice itself, ceases to be necessary to control violence.

This reinterpretation leads to a rejection of the atonement theory of Christ's crucifixion. God did not require his son to die for our sins. Christ died as a scapegoat, an innocent victim of the long process of victimization that shapes human history. The symbolism is clear. He is as innocent as a lamb. The death of Christ should not be understood as a sacrifice, but as a revelation of the innocence of the victims of community violence and of a God of love who sides with the victims of this world.

Girard moves from the arena of social science and literary interpretation to the arena of theology with the claim that this unveiling of the process of victimage and violence, of what has been hidden and necessarily hidden, could only come via revelation. Revelation is necessary because the mechanism of violence requires that its real cause be hidden.

With this turn of the argument, Girard appears to abandon any pretense of a social scientific theory that can generate testable hypotheses. However, Girard argues that social science can only develop when the sacred no longer grips human thinking about the origin and legitimacy of the social order. If something is sacred in its origins and divine in its justification, then to question it is a sacrilege. But the Bible does just that and by so doing unleashes a process that eventually gives rise to a thoroughly secular understanding of society and culture.

Girard develops his views by careful analysis of literary, mythological, and ethnographic sources. He piles examples on top of examples, from ancient and more recent societies, leading the reader down a path that twists and turns but in the end seems to provide supportive evidence. Along the way he criticizes other theories of the origin of violence, of ritual, of language, of religion, and of culture, showing how his own view can explain what the other theories leave unexplained.

Parts of Girard's theory can be tested and have been confirmed by psychological experiments showing that mimetic desire is a real phenomenon. Humans learn by modeling and they not only copy the ideas and behaviors of others, they also imitate their desires. But what follows from the fact that acquisitive mimesis influences human behavior? The critics step in at this point and try to show that Girard has not only misinterpreted some of his sources (for example the Bible), he has failed to prove that the origin of the sacred is inseparable from violence. His theory breaks down on the same rocks that other theories of the origin of religion have broken down. We simply no longer have access to the evidence concerning the origins of religion, language, and society. We also have no way to empirically verify claims about divine revelation.

Girard's views have generated more than controversy, they have also launched serious research programs in many fields. His writings have proved a rich resource in the attempt to solve numerous problems associated with understanding religion, culture, and literature. The impact has been immense but how long it will continue to generate new insights and stimulate new research remains to be seen.

See also: **Boyer, Burkert, Derrida, Foucault, J. Z. Smith**

Major works

(1965) *Deceit, Desire, and the Novel*, trans. Yvonne Freccero, Baltimore, MD: Johns Hopkins University Press.

(1979) *Violence and the Sacred*, trans. Patrick Gregory, Baltimore, MD: Johns Hopkins University Press.

(1986) *The Scapegoat*, trans. Yvonne Freccero, Baltimore, MD: Johns Hopkins University Press.

(1987) *Things Hidden since the Foundation of the World*, with Stephen Bann and Michael Metteer, Stanford, CA: Stanford University Press.

Further reading

Dumouchel, Paul, ed. (1988) *Violence and Truth: On the Work of René Girard*, Stanford, CA: Stanford University Press.

Fleming, Chris. (2004) *Violence and Mimesis*, Cambridge: Polity.

Hamerton-Kelly, Robert, ed. (1988) *Violent Origins: Walter Burkert, Rene Girard, and Jonathan Z. Smith on Ritual Killing and Cultural Formation*, Stanford, CA: Stanford University Press.

Williams, James G., ed. (1996) *The Girard Reader*, New York: Crossroads.

http://www.jeramyL.org/papers /girard.html.

CLIFFORD GEERTZ (1926–2006)

[A] religion is: (1) *a system of symbols which acts to* (2) *establish powerful, pervasive, and long-lasting moods and motivations in men by* (3) *formulating conceptions of a general order of existence and* (4) *clothing these conceptions with such an aura of factuality that* (5) *the moods and motivations seem uniquely realistic.*

(Geertz 1973: 90)

This famous and widely discussed definition of religion was first published by the noted and influential anthropologist Clifford Geertz in 1966 and republished in his award-winning *The Interpretation of Cultures* in 1973. It embodies, in condensed form, key ideas found in many theories that focus on what religion does and how it does it. Definitions are not complete theories and Geertz was no friend of grand theories that go far beyond the evidence, but he was a friend, as we shall see, of "thick" description (an ideal he adapted from the philosopher Gilbert Ryle) and what he called interpretative anthropology.

Clifford Geertz was born in San Francisco, California and attended Antioch College in Ohio, earning a degree in philosophy in 1950. He entered Harvard University to do graduate study in anthropology and received his PhD in 1956. While doing graduate work, he spent, along with his wife Hildred, two years on the island of Java in Indonesia doing fieldwork. After receiving his doctorate, he did fieldwork in Bali and later went to Morocco in North Africa in order to gather more information on Islamic culture for purposes of comparison. After teaching at the University of California, Berkeley and the University of Chicago (1960–70), he was invited to join the Institute for Advanced Study at Princeton University, where he remained for the rest of his career.

Geertz published articles and books that caught the attention of scholars both within and outside the field of anthropology. In addition to his acclaimed *The Interpretation of Cultures*, his 1983 book *Local Knowledge* championed a new direction in anthropological study that focused on detailed descriptions of cultures that included the intentions of the actors and on interpreting the systems of meaning (culture) within which humans live, work, and die.

A key idea of interpretative anthropology is that humans do not simply respond to their "raw" natural environments, they respond to the *meanings* their environments (natural, social, cultural) have for them, and they also create those meanings by developing complex symbol systems. It follows that to understand human behavior we must understand (interpret) the meanings humans attribute to their experience. Symbols are the key to those meanings and so some have referred to Geertz's approach as "symbolic anthropology." To provide a thick description is to make as clear as possible to others the link between the intention of actors and their behavior in its historical and cultural context.

Talcott Parsons, one of Geertz's teachers at Harvard, was strongly influenced by **Weber** and introduced his students to **Weber**'s idea of *Verstehen* (understanding). Parsons developed a view at odds with **Durkheim**'s **reduction** of the sacred to society. Parsons thought that there were three primary components to human groups: individual persons, social systems, and cultural systems. Of these, the last was of decisive importance and could be found in an objective system of symbols that included a whole array of items: artifacts, music, dance, gestures, science, ideology, language, and much more. Religion was one component of culture. It was an extremely significant part, however, because it embodied the values of a culture that shaped, consciously or unconsciously, the meaning humans construct as they try to make sense of their experiences. From Geertz's point of view, humans are animals who live their lives "suspended in a web of significance" and it is a web that humans themselves have spun.

Although Geertz was the first to admit that we should approach all generalizations with a healthy skepticism, his definition of religion, quoted above, deserves closer attention because it reflects many of his key notions about religions. The very first element ("*a system of symbols which acts*") signals his approach to cultural anthropology. Symbol systems contain just about anything that conveys meaning. Although members of a culture internalize the meanings of the symbols they use, meanings are not totally subjective or private. Symbols convey meaning to others that can be understood. Because symbols function as a means of communication, meaning is public (objective) as well as private (subjective). Hence the anthropologist can grasp the meaning and, more importantly, describe the meaning that members of a culture grasp.

There is a double aspect to symbols. They are both models *for* and models *of*. A sacred symbol, such as a saint, provides models *for* others to follow but also represents (models *of*) an idealized way of life. The saint is but one small part of a complex of interrelated and mutually reinforcing symbols for conducting one's life and directing one's thought. Non-symbolic systems, such as genes, serve as models *for* the development of some living organism but they do not function as models *of* and hence are non-symbolic in the sense that Geertz used that term. In other words, they are not cultural entities.

What systems of sacred symbols do is "(2) *establish powerful, pervasive, and long-lasting moods and motivations in men* ... " This means that religious symbol systems create dispositions in worshippers (motivations) and stimulate certain feelings (moods), which compared to many other momentary feelings are relatively long-lasting. Dispositions or motivations are things like tendencies, propensities, habits, proneness and the like. Moods of the religious sort are things like piety, reverence, solemnity, exuberance, and the like. Motivations have vectorial qualities that indicate a direction or course of action that has an endpoint or consummation. Moods are scalar. They vary in intensity but they are not directed towards any goal or course of action.

Sacred symbols establish moods and motivations "(3) *by formulating conceptions of a general order of existence* ... " All symbols can create motives and moods; what is distinctive about religion is the means for doing this. It revolves around providing a "general order of existence" or a worldview that claims to offer an ultimate explanation of the world and human experience. There are moments in life when what *is* crashes into what *ought to be*—facing unbearable suffering, unacceptable injustice, the mystery of life–death. These are times when humans turn to explanations that offer the comfort of some transcendent truth. **Paul Tillich** refers to these times as limit situations and Geertz described them as points when chaos threatens because humans seem "at the limits of [their] analytic capacities, the limits of [their] powers of endurance, and the limits of [their] moral insight" (Geertz 1973: 100). The main interest of religion is not with everyday routines—sports and games, fashions and fads in music or clothes—but in articulating through a system of symbols a meaning of ultimate significance that provides assurance when meaninglessness threatens to overwhelm (see **Berger**).

Humans, Geertz pointed out, depend on symbol systems "with a dependence so great as to be decisive for [their] creatural viability and, as a result, [their] sensitivity to even the remotest indication that they may prove unable to cope with one or another aspect of experience raises within [them] the gravest sort of anxiety" (Geertz 1973: 99). This is because the plasticity of human nature is such that humans would be incomplete without the assistance of cultural symbols. They cannot rely on their instinctual nature alone in order to get on in the world. The value of religion is that it provides one kind of system of symbols that contributes to human viability.

In addition to formulating a general order of existence, religion clothes "*(4) these conceptions with such an aura of factuality that (5) the moods and motivations seem uniquely realistic.*" Sacred symbols claim to connect humans to what is "really real" and what matters most in human life. If we focus on religious rituals, we can see how religious conceptions are bathed in an "aura of factuality" and how the moods and motivations that religious symbols evoke are made to seem "uniquely realistic." Ritual is a symbolic activity and it synthesizes in physical action the ethos of a people—"the tone, character, and quality of their life, its moral and aesthetic style and mood" (Geertz 1973: 89). At the same time, ritual synthesizes a people's worldview—"the picture they have of the way things in sheer actuality are, their most comprehensive ideas of order" (Geertz 1973: 89). In ritual actions, ethos and worldview mutually reinforce each other so a kind of fusion between ethos and worldview occurs. Rituals confirm religious worldviews by causing people to have the moods and motivations appropriate to their worldview. When this happens, it seems impossible to doubt the truth of the symbols. Religious beliefs and practices render a particular ethos reasonable, making it seem like common sense to people of a particular culture.

My summary of some of Geertz's key ideas is abstract. One should turn to his writings on specific religions, such as *The Religion of Java* and *Islam Observed*, for studies that put flesh on these definitional bones. However, we must, in the space remaining, turn our attention to some of the criticism of Geertz's ideas.

One line of criticism centers on Geertz's claim that his interpretative anthropology is a science while remaining particularistic in his orientation, wedded to thick description, and suspicious of generalization. Science depends on generalization from particulars and is not content to remain on a purely interpretative level. Hence some have argued that Geertz cannot have it both ways. He cannot claim that interpretative anthropology is a science and avoid generalizing. In fact, in spite of his claims, he does generalize, as his definition of religion indicates.

Geertz claimed that ethos and worldview are equally important, yet his writings on specific religions focused more on ethos than worldview. In his *Islam Observed*, he compared Islam in Indonesia and Morocco, carefully pointing out the differences in ethos between the two. Yet he says little about how their respective worldviews differ. If ethos and worldview mutually interact, as he claimed, then one would expect that difference to show up in their worldviews. However, Geertz curiously neglected any detailed discussion of such differences.

Talal Asad has argued that while Geertz's definition has pretension of being a universal definition it is too heavily influenced by the Christian tradition to be of much use. There are not only problems with his understanding of symbol, but also he ignores the role that power plays in creating religious "truth."

Although Geertz's views are open to criticism, they are widely admired and immensely influential. He, along with the likes of **Eliade** and **Evans-Pritchard**, provided a welcome counter to the **"reductionisms"** of **Freud**, **Durkheim**, and **Marx**. Even though he was personally agnostic, he recognized the significance of religion for giving meaning and purpose to human life.

See also: **Bellah, Douglas, Smart, Turner**

Major works

(1960) *The Religion of Java*, Glencoe, IL: The Free Press.

(1968) *Islam Observed*, Chicago, IL: University of Chicago Press.

(1973) *The Interpretation of Cultures: Selected Essays*, New York: Basic Books.

(1983) *Local Knowledge: Further Essays in Interpretative Anthropology*, New York: Basic Books.

(2000) *Available Light: Anthropological Reflections on Philosophical Topics*, Princeton, NJ: Princeton University Press.

Further reading

Inglis, Fred. (2000) *Clifford Geertz: Culture, Custom and Ethics*, Cambridge: Polity Press.

Rice, Kenneth A. (1980) *Geertz and Culture*, Ann Arbor, MI: University of Michigan Press.

http://en.wikipedia.org/wiki/Clifford_Geertz.

MICHEL FOUCAULT (1926–84)

> Everyone, every Christian, has the duty to know who he is, what is happening in him. He has to know the faults he may have committed: he has to know the temptations to which he is exposed. And, moreover, everyone in Christianity is obligated to say these things to other people, to tell these things to other people, and hence, to bear witness against himself.
>
> (Foucault 1997b: 202)

Michel Foucault, a French philosopher, historian, social critic, and one of the most influential thinkers of the last century, spoke these words in a lecture delivered at Dartmouth College in 1980. What is the significance of this obligation to confess one's faults to oneself and others? What does it imply for the development of modern ideas about the self that one has a duty to care for the self and that this care involves bearing witness *against* one's own self?

Paul-Michel Foucault was born in Poitiers, France. His father was a surgeon and hoped his son would follow in his footsteps but Michel's interest in the history of ideas and institutions took him in a different direction. He entered the École normale supérieure in 1946 where he studied **Hegel** and **Marx**, among others, and came under the influence of **Dumézil**'s early structuralist (see **Structuralism**) approach to mythology. He became Professor of the History of Systems of Thought at the prestigious Collége de France in 1969, but throughout his career, he taught at many different universities (Uppsala, Warsaw, Hamburg, Berkeley) and gave numerous public lectures. He published influential books and articles on a wide variety of topics such as madness, prisons, the clinic, and sexuality. Some of his lectures and portions of his books discuss religion, but he developed no general theory of religion. Even so his analysis of the relationship between knowledge and power, along with his analytical methods of "archaeology" and "genealogy," had a deep impact on what he called "the human sciences" (the social sciences and humanities) including religious studies.

The study of knowledge (epistemology) had been a philosophical concern from the early days of Greek philosophy. **Immanuel Kant** introduced a critique of knowledge that sought to reveal its limits by showing its necessary conditions. This project, **Kant** thought, would further the goals of the **Enlightenment** project of liberating humans from the tyranny of superstition. Although Foucault also sought to liberate human thought from domination, he showed that much of what passes for knowledge, especially in the human sciences, actually leads to ever more complex, expansive, and subtle forms of domination, thereby limiting both human thought and action.

The techniques of power and domination are dependent upon getting people to believe certain things are true. The human sciences, especially in the modern era, while hailed as new "scientific knowledge" that frees people from the mythologies of the past, actually extend power and domination by objectifying the human subject via scientific inquiry. It does this by engaging in "dividing practices." Madness and sanity, criminal deviancy and law-abiding citizen, abnormal and normal are some of the categories through which knowledge or "discourse formations" produced by the human sciences exercise power over thought, practice, and the creation of institutions such as clinics and prisons.

His first major book, *Madness and Civilization*, is a detailed study of the development of the modern concept of "mental illness" in Europe and illustrates the dividing practices of the human sciences.

Although many hailed the advances made by modern psychiatry as the liberation of the "mad" from brutality and the ignorance of previous ages, Foucault's research questioned whether the transformation of the "mad" into the "mentally ill" was a progressive step toward human liberation. The evidence, Foucault argued, actually showed that the discourse couched in the scientific neutrality of medicine was a cover story for the imposition of conventional bourgeois morality on those who did not conform to middle-class definitions of "sanity."

In *The Birth of the Clinic* he undertook a critique of modern clinical medicine by showing how teaching hospitals dehumanize patients by treating them as *objects* of a "scientific discourse." Hence they establish boundaries to the treatment of and thinking about health and disease. Likewise, in *Discipline and Punish*, he showed how the development of less severe forms of criminal punishment (imprisonment rather than killing and torture) nevertheless punished people judged to be deviant by assuming almost total control of their lives. He argued that prisons became a model for control by instituting techniques of observation, examination, and evaluation throughout society in hospitals, factories, and schools. The goals of knowledge and the goals of power converge in treatment of the insane, the sick, and the criminal insofar as they require turning humans into objects.

Foucault characterized *Madness and Civilization* as an "archaeological" study. It was an intellectual excavation of successive layers of different discourses and their "games of truth" that controlled thought about madness from the seventeenth through the nineteenth centuries. This method was important because it dug beneath the conscious level to uncover the rules and procedures that control human thinking.

In *Discipline and Punish*, Foucault employed a "genealogical" method, consciously adapted from **Nietzsche**, to explain the transitions from one level of thinking to another. It showed that, contrary to **Hegel**'s idea of a grand scheme of history progressing to ever higher levels of reason and truth, historical changes were contingent, often caused by chance events. There was no necessary and inevitable progress in any given domain of thought.

In the last years of his life, Foucault turned his attention to ethics or what he called the "care of the self." He focused primarily on changing ideas of sexuality, not only because this allowed him to focus on the self but also because it allowed him to contrast Greek and Roman culture with Christian culture.

In his lecture on "Christianity and Confession," from which I quoted at the outset, Foucault focused on "techniques of the self" that play a major role in the genealogy of modern ideas about the self.

His problem was to discover how the interpretative analysis of self (what he called the "**hermeneutics** of the self") was formed in modern Western societies. The **hermeneutics** of the self was practiced in Greek and Roman societies, whose philosophies tried to devise techniques such as self-examination in order to create an ideal unity of what one wills to do and what one ought to do. Christianity built on these techniques but its goal was quite different. The goal of self-examination in Christianity was to decipher a hidden truth.

Christianity imposes two different "obligations of truth." The first is to believe the truth (creeds, dogmas, church teachings, the Bible) and the second is the duty to know your self (faults, secret desires, temptations) *and* to confess this knowledge of self to others. In orthodox Christianity these two obligations are linked, but not identical as in some religions such as Buddhism. Christian salvation is dependent on fulfilling both obligations whereas in Buddhism awakening derives from knowing the truth about one's self, which is nearly identical to knowing the truth of the Buddha's teachings.

If we focus on the second obligation in Christianity, the duty to know one's faults and to publicly confess them, it is helpful to examine them in two different institutions—penitential rites and monastic life. Penitential rites in early Christianity were not the same as the sacrament of penance that developed later. In the first centuries of Christianity penance is not an act, but a status. A crucial element of this penitential status was to manifest the truth about oneself. The punishments and austerities imposed were designed to destroy the effects of the confessed sin and restore the purity and innocence given by baptism. Paradoxically, restoring purity required showing to others that in reality one was "dirty, defiled, sullied" (Foucault 1997b: 209).

Two basic elements of Christian spirituality, obedience and contemplation, influenced the rites of confession that developed in Christian monasteries. In Greek and Roman Stoicism, the student obeyed a spiritual adviser in order to gain mastery of the self. The Christian monk obeyed a spiritual director in order to attain the supreme good of the monastic life, contemplation of the divine.

Part of the practice of contemplation involved examining one's thoughts. This examination was necessary because the Devil can be found lurking within thoughts. Someone else was thought to dwell in one's soul, someone evil and unclean. How could thoughts be examined and the Devil within exposed?

Confession was the key. Satan cannot stand the light of day, so to honestly and openly make public one's hidden thoughts was the mechanism by which the evil within could be expunged. Verbalization constitutes a way of sorting out thoughts and examining them. Hence it performs an interpretative function, frees the soul from Satan's rule, and opens it to obedience to the law of God. If Satan dwells in the soul, this movement toward God is at the same time a renunciation of the self.

Foucault thought these developments mark the "first time in history that thoughts are considered as possible objects for analysis" (Foucault 1997b: 220). Foucault also thought that Christianity introduced to Western thought the idea that truth and sacrifice are closely connected. Truth about ourselves comes with a price because, according to Christianity, we "have to sacrifice the self in order to discover the truth about ourselves, and we have to discover the truth about ourselves in order to sacrifice ourself [sic.]" (Foucault 1997b: 226).

Although Foucault did not systematically develop an archeological and genealogical history of religion, many scholars (see **Asad**) applied his ideas and methods to the study of religion, thereby revealing the connections between claims to religious knowledge and the resulting domination of people's beliefs and practices. However, Foucault did draw connections between Christian "technologies of the self" and the rise of the human sciences. He asserted:

> From the eighteenth century to the present, the techniques of verbalization have been reinserted in a different context by the so-called human sciences in order to use them without renunciation of the self but to constitute, positively, a new self. To use these techniques without renouncing oneself constitutes a decisive break.
>
> (Foucault 1988b: 49)

Perhaps two of the most serious criticisms leveled against Foucault are the charges of cultural determinism and relativism. Uncovering the mechanisms that influence human thought and values beneath the level of conscious agency appears to imply that human agency has little power to fight domination. And revealing how "games of truth" with respect to madness, medicine, criminality, and sexuality have changed raises serious questions about whether there is any such thing as truth apart from the values that happen to dominate particular historical periods. He has denied these charges by asserting that, however limited it may be, humans do have the freedom to promote justice. Further, he indicated that his work was never intended to deny the idea of objective truth but only to bring to the light of day the historical forces that have shaped the knowledge claims in the human sciences.

See also: **Derrida, Girard, Gross**

Major works

(1965) *Madness and Civilization*, trans. Richard Howard, New York: Pantheon.

(1972) *The Archaeology of Knowledge*, trans. A. Sheridan Smith, New York: Harper and Row.

(1973a) *The Order of Things: The Archaeology of the Human Sciences*, New York: Vintage.

(1973b) *The Birth of the Clinic*, trans. A. Sheridan Smith, New York: Pantheon.

(1977) *Discipline and Punish*, trans. Alan Sheridan, New York: Pantheon.

(1988a–90) *History of Sexuality*, 3 vols. *Introduction, The Uses of Pleasure*, and *Care of the Self*, trans. Robert Hurley, New York: Vintage.

(1988b) *Technologies of the Self*, ed. Luther Martin et al., Amherst, MA: University of Massachusetts Press.

(1997a–99a) *Essential Works of Foucault, 1954–1984*, 3 vols., ed. Paul Rabinow, New York: The New Press.

(1997b) *The Politics of Truth*, ed. Sylvère Lodtringer and Lysa Hochroth, New York: Semiotext(e).

(1999b) *Religion and Culture*, ed. Jeremy R. Carrette, New York: Routledge.

Further reading

Arary, Janet and Kevin B. Anderson, ed. (2005) *Foucault and the Iranian Revolution: Gender and the Seductions of Islamism*, Chicago, IL: University of Chicago Press.

Carrette, Jeremy R. (2000) *Foucault and Religion: Spiritual Corporality and Political Spirituality*, New York: Routledge.

Racevskis, Karlis, ed. (1999) *Critical Essays on Michel Foucault*, New York: G. K. Hall.

http://en.wikipedia.org/wiki/Michel_Foucault.

NINIAN SMART (1927–2001)

By dialectical phenomenology I mean more particularly the relationship between *different dimensions* of religion and worldviews. In general we can say about any system or scheme that one element in it is in principle affected by all others.

(Smart 1996b: 7)

Roderick Ninian Smart, philosopher, **phenomenologist**, and scholar of comparative religions, wrote the above in order to tell his readers that he regarded religion as one kind of worldview that functions like an organism with mutually interconnected parts or, as he preferred, "dimensions." There are secular worldviews, such as nationalism and various political ideologies (for example **Marxism** and Fascism), as well as religious worldviews. Smart urged students of religion to expand their focus to include secular worldviews and to engage in what he called "worldview analysis."

Ninian Smart's father, William Marshall Smart, was an astronomer at the University of Cambridge, where Ninian was born. Both parents were Scottish and Smart attended the Glasgow Academy before joining the military in 1945. He lived and traveled in Ceylon (now Sri Lanka) as a member of the British Army Intelligence Corps and became interested in Buddhism. After leaving the military he resumed his education at Oxford University, majoring in classics and philosophy. He held a number of academic posts after graduating, finally assuming a joint appointment at the Lancaster University in England and the University of California, Santa Barbara.

Among his many accomplishments, he founded the first department of religious studies in England and became a leader in promoting the development of departments of religious studies in both England and America. In the mid-1960s, when the academic study of religion as we think of it today was developing, Smart decisively shaped the present-day study of religion in secular universities with his insistence that cross-cultural and comparative studies should be at the core of the emerging field. His textbooks, *The Religious Experience* and *The World's Religions*, introduced countless students to the academic study of religion.

Smart's contributions to the field went far beyond writing useful textbooks. He is primarily noted for developing a methodology for the study of religion that he termed dialectical **phenomenology**. Smart hoped to find a middle way between the **reductionisms** of people like **Freud** and **Marx** and theologically biased theories such as **Otto**'s views. With scholars like **Eliade** and **Geertz**, he held that religion was an autonomous force that could not be entirely reduced to psychological, social, political, or economic factors. He argued that the **phenomenological** method, with its bracketing of belief in the existence of supernatural powers (a kind of methodological agnosticism) and its insistence on the use of empathy to enter into the "experiences and intentions of religious participants," was the best way to avoid both **reductionism** and advocacy.

Religions are global phenomena and their academic study should be cross-cultural, comparative, and neutral in the sense that no single tradition should be given priority or used as a norm for judging other traditions. We must be careful to distinguish between descriptive and normative uses of such names as Christianity, Islam, Buddhism, and the like. We must also constantly remind ourselves that the traditions we call the "world religions" are plural. Each can be divided into numerous subgroups and movements, such as Protestantism and Roman Catholicism, and within these further distinctions can be drawn. The history of religions is littered with millions of strains, trends, movements, groups of one sort or another and often each claims to be the "true" version of the religious worldview named on the macro level as this or that world religion.

Smart defended comparative studies against those who argue neutrality is not possible because we are all influenced by the values of our culture and necessarily see others through our own cultural lenses. He argued that comparative studies often raise important issues for different religions and worldviews to consider and can serve as a counterpoise to cultural tribalism. For example, what Buddhists say about meditation can be useful for Christians to consider when they think about what it means to pray. Cultural and ideological prejudices can be overcome if we pay careful attention to the dynamic nature of traditions, the context in which certain ideas develop, and use a dialectical **phenomenology** that recognizes the interaction among the various dimensions of worldviews, be they secular or religious.

What are the dimensions of both secular and religious worldviews? Smart identified seven dimensions (in some publications six): the ritual or practical, the philosophical or doctrinal, the mythic or narrative, the experiential or emotional, the ethical or legal, the organizational or social, the material or artistic. He provided two names for each dimension (for example ritual or practical) because he felt it helped to elucidate them. He also provided examples. For instance, he suggested "worship, meditation, pilgrimage, sacrifice, sacramental rites and healing activities" as illustrations of what he meant by the ritual or practical dimension and chapels, cathedrals, temples, mosques, icons, and statuary as examples of the material or artistic dimension.

Smart noted that diverse traditions put different weights on the various dimensions. So one tradition or part of one tradition may develop elaborate rituals and emphasize the importance of formal worship, while another tradition or part of another tradition may de-emphasize rituals and focus more on the experiential or emotional dimension. We see exactly this within Christianity in the contrast between Russian Orthodoxy and the Society of Friends (Quakers).

He illustrated the dynamic or dialectical nature of these dimensions with several examples drawn from Christianity mentioning how the creation of monasticism (organizational/social) led to the creation of monasteries (organizational/social and material/artistic), which in turn favored the cultivation of mysticism and hence the absorptions of Neo-Platonist ideas (doctrinal/philosophical) into Christianity.

In his more developed discussion of the various dimensions, Smart offered further distinctions, thereby providing more refined categories for the analysis of worldviews, whether secular or religious. He offered, for example, what he called the "two-pole theory" of religious experience. He borrowed **Otto**'s idea of a numinous experience to describe one pole and characterized the other pole as mystical/contemplative. In the numinous experience an awe-inspiring Divine Other who escapes all categorization overwhelms the individual. In the mystical experience of the non-dual type, there is no "Other" to overwhelm the individual. The subject/object dualism of normal, everyday consciousness is transcended in the mystical experience.

Smart increased the utility of his analysis by offering further refinements. Theoretically, religious experiences might be exclusively of the numinous or the contemplative type, or some combination of these two poles in which one pole or the other is dominant or both are equal. This complexity will correspond to complexity in the doctrinal/philosophical dimension that simultaneously claims that God cannot be described yet offers a whole list of attributes (all-knowing, all-merciful, all-loving, and so on).

So far I have been concentrating on Smart's book *Dimensions of the Sacred*, which is quite appropriately focused on sacred worldviews (religions). In his book *Worldviews*, he offered more examples of his dialectical **phenomenology** from secular worldviews. For instance, he identified secular humanism as a modern worldview and pointed out that its emphasis on freedom from religious authority often goes hand and hand with a generally liberal outlook (doctrinal/philosophical dimension) and democratic institutions (organizational/social dimension). He also noted how secular worldviews could interact with religious ones. Existentialism is a philosophy often associated with secular humanism, but Smart noted how it has interacted with Christianity in such thinkers as **Kierkegaard**.

Smart influenced a whole generation of students, many of whom went on to start up or work in departments of religious studies in secular universities. Many found the categories he developed useful ways to organize and classify aspects of religion for easier comprehension in the classroom. His dimensions were useful descriptors. Others found them less useful, complaining that they were too vague and general to be of much help in research and were often misleading. His claim to have found a middle way between naturalistic **reductionism** and theological advocacy has been questioned on the grounds that the supernatural explanations that are given by the believer and placed in "brackets" by the **phenomenologist** nevertheless stand in conflict with naturalistic explanations.

The work of Ninian Smart is no doubt open to criticism, but it has also advanced the academic study of religion. His tireless work in promoting its significance for a well-educated public and his publications that made it accessible to a wider audience have been useful contributions.

See also: **van der Leeuw, J. Z. Smith, Wittgenstein**

Major works

(1958) *Reasons and Faith: An Investigation of Religious Discourse, Christian and Non-Christian*, London: Routledge and Kegan Paul.

(1964) *Doctrine and Argument in Indian Philosophy*, Sydney: Allen and Unwin.

(1969) *Philosophers and Religious Truth*, 2nd ed., London: SCM Press.

(1973a) *The Phenomenon of Religion*, New York: Herder and Herder.

(1973b) *The Science of Religion and the Sociology of Knowledge: Some Methodological Questions*, Princeton, NJ: Princeton University Press.

(1981) *Beyond Ideology: Religion and the Future of Western Civilization*, San Francisco: Harper and Row.

(1996a) *The Religious Experience*, 5th ed., Upper Saddle River, NJ: Prentice Hall.

(1996b) *Dimensions of the Sacred: An Anatomy of the World's Beliefs*, Berkeley, CA: University of California Press.

(1998) *The World's Religions*, 2nd ed. Cambridge: Cambridge University Press.

(2000) *Worldviews: Crosscultural Explorations of Human Beliefs*, 3rd ed., Upper Saddle River, NJ: Prentice Hall.

Further reading

Burris, John P. ed. (1997) *Reflections in the Mirror of Religion*, New York: St. Martin's Press.

Kuruvachira, Jose. (2004) *Religious Experience; Buddhist, Christian, and Hindu: A Critical Study of Ninian Smart's Philosophical Interpretation of the Numinous and the Mystical*, New York: Intercultural Publications.

Masefield, Peter and Donald Wiebe, eds. (1995) *Aspects of Religion: Essays in Honour of Ninian Smart*, New York: Peter Lang.

http://www.scottlondon.com/interviews/smart.html.

ROBERT BELLAH (1927–)

> Behind the civil religion at every point lie Biblical archetypes: Exodus, Chosen People, Promised Land, New Jerusalem, Sacrificial Death and Rebirth. But it is also genuinely American and genuinely new. It has its own prophets and its own martyrs, its own sacred events and sacred places, its own solemn rituals and symbols. It is concerned that America be a society as perfectly in accord with the will of God as men can make it, and a light to all the nations.
>
> (Bellah 1967: 18)

With these words Robert N. Bellah, a sociologist of religion, brought to a close his seminal and controversial essay on "Civil Religion in America." Arguments about whether civil religion exists, what it is, and whether Bellah had put his finger on something new and of importance erupted almost immediately. What exactly is "civil religion," does the United States have one, and how does it relate to the churches, synagogues, temples, and mosques that dot the American landscape?

Robert Neelly Bellah was born in Altus, Oklahoma. After his father's death, he moved with his mother to Los Angeles, California. He graduated from Los Angeles High School in 1945 and went to Harvard University for both his BA (1950) and PhD (1955). He studied with Talcott Parsons, who introduced him to the work of **Weber**. While in college he joined the American Communist Party. This involvement led the then dean, McGeorge Bundy, under the influence of the McCarthy anti-communist witch-hunts, to threaten to withdraw his fellowship if he refused to provide the names of other students. He did not provide the names.

After graduation, Bellah taught at Harvard and in 1967 became the Ford Professor of Sociology at the University of California, Berkeley. He is currently the Elliot Professor of Sociology Emeritus. In 2000 he received the United States National Humanities Medal. His dissertation, *Tokugawa Religion*, was published in 1957, and he is the author of several books and numerous essays. He is best known for his publications on civil religion, the evolution of religion, and communitarian ethics (*Habits of the Heart*, *The Good Society*). The latter celebrates working for the common good and critiques the excessive individualism of American culture.

The term civil religion comes from the political philosopher Jean-Jacques Rousseau (1712–78) who in his book *The Social Contract* discussed the "creed" of a civil religion as affirming God's existence, the afterlife, rewards and punishments for virtue and vice, and the practice of religious tolerance. The idea seems to go back to the Roman notion of *religare*, meaning "to bind," which refers to the power of religion to knit together Roman citizens into a religious and moral community. The strong influence of **Durkheim** on Bellah's concept of civil religion should not go unnoticed.

Bellah points out that every American president in his inaugural address, as well as the "founding fathers" of the American republic, invokes the name of God. It is used in the *Declaration of Independence* (but not in the *Constitution*), in the pledge to the flag, on the presidential seal, and on money. Although many citizens associate this God with the Judeo-Christian tradition, it is not the specific God of any particular religion. However, this non-specific God is not simply God in general. It is a God who has taken a special interest in the American nation and its destiny. The founding fathers and early preachers often drew an analogy between America and Israel. Europe was Egypt and America the promise land. Americans were the new chosen people and had a collective task to carry out God's will by exemplifying to all nations the ideals of democracy, justice, and freedom.

The God of civil religion is a God of law, order, freedom, and human rights. He (it is assumed this god is a he) secures, creates, and upholds the rights of freedom and the pursuit of happiness. Every American president swears an oath to the American people and to God, because God is the divine source of those "inalienable rights" that make the sovereignty of the people the legitimate basis of democratic government.

The scriptures of this civil religion are the *Declaration of Independence* and the *Constitution*. They are the final court of appeal in all matters political and legal. Like sacred documents, scholars carefully study them, and learned experts reinterpret them in light of changing circumstances.

In addition to sacred scriptures, this civil religion has a founder. He is George Washington, the "Father of the Country," who, like Moses, led the new, divinely blessed democracy out of tyranny.

If Washington is the Moses figure of American civil religion, then Abraham Lincoln is its savior figure. In leading the country through a bloody civil war he added a new theme to the providential theme of American civil religion established at its beginning. It was the theme of death, sacrifice, and rebirth. Lincoln himself became a symbolic Christ figure when many began to interpret his assassination as a sacrificial shedding of blood along with the thousands of soldiers who died in the conflict that gave birth to a new *united* nation.

In addition to sacred documents, founders, and saviors, the civil religion of America has its sacred spaces, such as Arlington National Cemetery, sites of battles long since fought, and the monuments of the United States Capitol. Many American citizens make pilgrimages to these sites at least once in their lifetime, pause to remember with a sense of reverence what happened in the past, and what these sacred spaces represent today. There are sacred rituals as well, such as Memorial Day, Thanksgiving, and the Fourth of July. Thanksgiving Day functions to integrate "the family into American civil religion" and Memorial Day serves to "integrate the local community into the national cult" (Bellah 1967: 11).

Bellah points out that since American civil religion has never been militantly secular, it was and is able to borrow selectively from specific religious traditions so that most Americans see no conflict with their personal religious commitments and their commitments to the civil religion (of which most are largely unaware) of the nation. This is particularly true in a time of war, when religious themes mingle with patriotic themes in order to bind the people together in a collective endeavor requiring the sacrifice of their sons, daughters, and treasure. It is also at times of war when the civil religion is used to justify actions that often conflict with its moral ideals. For example, the analogy with Israel was used to justify the genocidal treatment of American natives and the conviction that America has a special role to play in spreading democracy has been used to justify the invasion of other nations.

Bellah's description of civil religion has a deeper purpose than simply drawing analogies between civil religion and the Judeo-Christian tradition. He emphasizes that American civil religion "at its best is a genuine apprehension of universal and transcendent religious reality as seen in or, one could almost say, as revealed through the experience of the American people" (Bellah 1967: 12). This emphasis on a higher power is the prophetic and potentially revolutionary aspect of American civil religion and without "awareness that our nation stands under higher judgment, the tradition of the civil religion would be dangerous indeed" (Bellah 1967: 17).

Since publishing the article on civil religion in 1967, Bellah has continued to return to its themes in other writings, lamenting the fact that the promise of civil religion to bind the nation together into a unified community of moral purpose is in danger of being broken. In *Habits of the Heart*, he writes that the American nation today has "committed what to the republican founders of our nation was the cardinal sin: we have put our own good, as individuals, as groups, as a nation, ahead of the common good" (Bellah 1985: 285).

In his essay "Religious Evolution" (see *Beyond Belief*), Bellah takes up a topic that had been neglected by scholars of religion after the early evolutionary theories of anthropologists like **Tylor** and **Frazer** were discredited. Bellah distances himself from the older views by asserting that he does not assume evolution is inevitable, progressive, or necessarily follows a single course of development. He explicitly denies that "religious man" evolves, but does argue that "religion as a symbol system" does. By religion he means, echoing **Tillich** and **Geertz**, "a set of symbolic forms and acts that relate man to the ultimate conditions of his existence" (Bellah 1970: 21). He defines evolution as a "process of increasing differentiation and complexity of organization" that results in a greater capacity to adapt to the environment and creates the possibility of greater autonomy or freedom relative to the environment.

Bellah identifies five stages of development: primitive, archaic, historic, early modern, and modern. Each of these stages is described with respect to their religious symbol systems, practices, organization, and social implications. For example, both primitive and archaic religions have symbol systems that express a monistic worldview while religions in both the historic and early modern stages have dualistic symbol systems resulting in a sharp distinction between this world and the supernatural. In modern religions the dualistic worldview is "broken" and is replaced by a "multiplex" symbol system that allows humans to become "self-consciously symbolic" and this affords greater freedom for both individuals and society relative to environing conditions.

Perhaps the most strident criticism of Bellah's notion of civil religion is the denial that it really exists. There is, these critics say, no overarching belief system in American society. There may have been something like it in the early formative years of the republic, but American society has become so secularized and so many different religious, quasi-religious, and anti-religious voices now clamor for attention that we can no longer claim it exists. On an empirical level sociologists have found difficultly testing the hypothesis of a civil religion because of the absence of any precise definition. Some define it as a folk religion, others as religious nationalism, and still others see it as a version of a kind of Protestant civic piety.

Bellah's theory of religious evolution has not had wide influence. Critics have found it oversimplified and downright misleading. The analytic categories Bellah uses, critics claim, are ill-defined and of little use in research. They obscure more than they illuminate.

Bellah has responded to his critics and continued to refine his ideas in subsequent publications. While the controversies over civil religion have died down, the renewed debates about the proper relationship between church and state and the rise of religious nationalism on the right have recently refocused attention on Bellah's ideas. A testimony to his influence is that most textbooks on the sociology of religion contain some discussion of civil religion.

See also: **J. Z. Smith**

Major works

(1957) *Tokugawa Religion: The Values of Pre-Industrial Japan*, Glencoe, IL: The Free Press.

(1967) "Civil Religion in America," *Daedalus* 96(1): 1–21.

(1970) *Beyond Belief: Essays on Religion in a Post-Traditional World*, New York: Harper and Row.

(1982) *Varieties of Civil Religion*, with Philip E. Hammond, San Francisco, CA: Harper and Row.

(1985) *Habits of the Heart: Individualism and Commitment in American Life*, with Richard Madsen, William M. Sullivan, Ann Swidler, Steven M. Tipton, Berkeley, CA: University of California Press.

(1992a) *The Broken Covenant: American Civil Religion in Time of Trial*, 2nd ed., Chicago, IL: University of Chicago Press.

(1992b) *The Good Society*, with Richard Madsen, Steven M. Tipton, William M. Sullivan, New York: Vintage.

Further reading

Fenn, Richard K. (1976) "Bellah and the New Orthodoxy," *Sociological Analysis* 37: 160–66.

Gehrig, Gail. (1979) *American Civil Religion: An Assessment*, Society for the Scientific Study of Religion, Monograph Series No. 3.

http://www.pbs.org/moyers/journal/archives/bellahwoi_flash.html.

PETER BERGER (1929–)

> Every human society is, in the last resort, men banded together in the face of death. The power of religion depends, in the last resort, upon the credibility of the banners it puts in the hands of men as they stand before death, or more accurately, as they walk, inevitably, toward it.
>
> (Berger 1967: 51)

Peter L. Berger, a sociologist of religion and a Christian theologian, here indicates what he sees to be the role and power of religion in human society. The task is to find out what exactly these banners are, and how they are deployed. He gives some hints when he says, "religion is the audacious attempt to conceive of the entire universe as being humanly significant" and when he defines religion as "the establishment, through human activity, of an all-embracing sacred order, that is, of a sacred cosmos that will be capable of maintaining itself in the ever-present face of chaos" (Berger 1967: 28, 51). We need to explore what he means by a "sacred cosmos" and how humans create it.

Peter Ludwig Berger was born in Vienna, the son of a business-man. He completed his secondary education in England and immi-grated to the United States in 1946. He enrolled in what was then Wagner Memorial Lutheran College in New York with the intention of entering the ministry. However, he abandoned those plans and entered the New School for Social Research, where he earned his PhD in 1954. Although an undergraduate major in philosophy, he focused much of his graduate work on sociology. After teaching at various universities, including Rutgers University, he became University Professor of Sociology and Theology at Boston University. He is presently Professor Emeritus of Religion, Sociology and Theology as well as director of the Institute on Culture, Religion, and World Affairs at Boston University.

Berger is a prolific writer, having published over twenty books and nearly a hundred articles on a variety of topics. Many of his books (*The Precarious Vision*, *The Noise of Solemn Assemblies*, *A Rumor of Angels*) have become popular with general audiences and generated considerable controversy. His book *The Social Construction of Reality* (written with Thomas Luckmann) established his reputation in the field of sociology as an advocate for **phenomenological** sociology and *The Sacred Canopy* made a significant contribution to the sociology of religion. Both books reveal the influences of **Hegel**, **Marx**, **Durkheim**, **Weber**, and Alfred Schutz, among others. Schutz's attempt to provide a philosophical foundation for the social sciences was a substantive influence on Berger's ideas concerning the sociology of religion.

In *Social Construction*, Berger contends that consciousness is both intentional, in the sense that it is directed toward something, and social, in the sense that it arises in interaction with others. He argues that humans create various spheres of reality in an attempt to make sense of their experiences. One such sphere is the reality of "everyday life." Within that sphere humans have developed "typificatory schemes" in apprehending and interacting with others. In other words, humans apprehend others as a "type" (English, Asian, American, and so on). Social structure is an essential feature of everyday life because it is "the sum total of these typifications and of the recurrent patterns of interaction" they establish (Berger/Luckmann 1966: 33).

When Berger turns his attention to religion, he uses a metaphor, the sacred canopy, to characterize his general theory of religion. This metaphor compels us to ask what this canopy is, how is it made, how is it maintained, and what it does. His theory provides answers to these questions and is based on the premise that society is dialectical (see **Hegel**) in the sense that it is constructed by humans who in turn interact with what they have constructed.

How is the social world constructed? There are three interrelated processes that Berger calls externalization, objectivation, and internalization. Humans must project (externalize) society because unlike other animals they are not completely determined by their instincts. They are, if you will, unfinished, hence some kind of social order is necessary to "finish" them. Objectivation refers to the externalized product, which Berger characterizes as a *nomos* or a system of rules that provides descriptive and prescriptive (normative) meaning. Internalization refers to the third phase of the dialectic in which the projected social order (*nomos*) is taken back into human consciousness through the processes of socialization. Central to internalization is language because becoming socialized (integrated into a society) takes place via learning a language.

Berger contrasts *nomos* (social order) with *cosmos* (natural order). Religion attempts to "cosmetize" (make natural) a given nomos (created by humans) by declaring it a sacred cosmos. It claims, for example, that gods have created for humans a cosmic order and a nomic order. The divine gives both and hence both are "natural"— the way things are supposed to be. However, social worlds are precarious because experiences of anomy (e. g. madness, ecstasy, natural catastrophes, death) and pluralism (encounters with different social worlds) can and do occur.

The nomic canopy can spring leaks, therefore it must be maintained. Socialization is one way to maintain a society and another way is to legitimize it by explaining and justifying its existence. Historically, religion is the most widespread and effective means of legitimation because it hides the human origin of society, provides "plausibility structures" by giving a semblance of inevitability and durability to the social order, motivates people to face marginal situations such as war, and through ritual clothes human activities with cosmic significance.

If religion is to justify a social order, it must provide an effective **theodicy** that explains why evil things happen to good people. There are different kinds of **theodicies**, ranging from the nonrational to the rational, but one thing they all have in common is the necessity to surrender to a power greater than human power in order to obtain the pleasure of overcoming the anomy of evil. Hence there is a masochistic element present in all **theodicy**.

Promoting a masochistic attitude is not the most serious danger of religion. Religion promotes alienation (**Feuerbach**), false consciousness (**Marx**) and bad faith (Jean-Paul Sartre). It does this by hiding the human origin of society, thereby replacing choice with a fictitious necessity. Hence religion promotes a deeply conservative attitude about social structures that can slow or prevent needed change. Nevertheless, Berger sees a positive contribution deriving from the prophetic Judeo-Christian tradition that criticizes the social order by relativizing it. Only God is divine, not human societies (see **Tillich**).

Berger has been particularly concerned with understanding the process of secularization. He defines it as the "process by which sectors of society and culture are removed from the domination of religious institutions and symbols" (Berger 1967: 107). Ironically, this process has religious roots in the prophetic critique of organized religion found in the Bible and the Protestant Reformation. As modern societies become more secularized, religious pluralism increases, leading to increased secularization. Religion becomes a matter of private choice and becomes subject to "free-market" pressures as increasingly diverse religious groups compete with one another for funds and followers. This competition generates a "credibility crisis" that changes religion as different groups try to tailor their products to the tastes of consumers and seek to be "relevant" to this or that cultural trend. As secularization increases, religion increasingly fails to legitimate the social order.

The proclamation of the death of religion popular in the 1960s and 1970s seems premature. Religion appears to be on a rebound on a global scale. Berger addresses this problem by admitting that early sociological predictions about the demise of religion were mistaken and by arguing that secularization has changed religion itself. Religion persists and is reviving, but it is a highly secularized type of religion in which the "gospel of prosperity" begins to replace the gospel proclaimed by Jesus.

Berger himself is a Christian believer, not an atheist, but he argues that to protect the objective and scientific nature of sociology a kind of "methodological atheism" (probably "agnosticism" is a better term) must be employed. Sociology cannot soar beyond the sacred canopy to tell us what is "really" out there. It can, however, help us understand how and why humans behave as they do under the cover of the canopy they erect. Just because religious beliefs are relative to culture and society does not mean that some of those beliefs are correct or incorrect. The way we *think* about the divine may be relative, but it does not follow that the divine itself is relative.

Perhaps one of the most pervasive criticisms of Berger's theory is that it generates few empirically testable hypotheses and is focused mostly on Western religions. There has been some empirical work done using the idea of plausibility structures but it is not clear how many of his key concepts, such as the sacred canopy, could be operationalized. This is not surprising since Berger's style of sociology is less concerned with the quantification techniques and statistics favored by many sociologists today and more concerned with issues of value and meaning. Perhaps this is why his influence is greater in the more humanistic wing of religious studies.

Berger has also been accused of inconsistency. His "methodological atheism" seems to fall by the wayside in his later work such as *A Rumor of Angels*. Apparently "rumors" do find their way through the canopy that blocks the human view of the "beyond."

Berger's concern with the role religion plays in creating meaning and purpose in human life has contributed to making sense of religion by locating it in a broader social context. His ideas have illuminated the appeal of new religious movements in a secular age, and he has contributed to keeping the influence of the European tradition stemming from **Durkheim** and **Weber** alive in religious studies.

See also: **Asad, Derrida, Geertz**

Major works

(1961a) *The Noise of Solemn Assemblies: Christian Commitment and the Religious Establishment in America*, Garden City, NY: Doubleday.

(1961b) *The Precarious Vision: A Sociologist Looks at Social Fictions and the Christian Faith*, Garden City, NY: Doubleday.

(1963) *Invitation to Sociology: A Humanistic Perspective*, Garden City, NY: Doubleday.

(1966) *The Social Construction of Reality: A Treatise in the Sociology of Knowledge* (with Thomas Luckmann), Garden City, NY: Doubleday.

(1967) *The Sacred Canopy: Elements of a Sociological Theory of Religion*, Garden City, NY: Doubleday.

(1969) *A Rumor of Angels: Modern Society and the Rediscovery of the Supernatural*, Garden City, NY: Doubleday.

(1981) *Sociology Reinterpreted: An Essay on Method and Vocation* (with Hansfred Kellner), Garden City, NY: Doubleday.

Further reading

Hunter, James Davison. (1984) "The Phenomenology of Peter L. Berger," in Robert Wuthnow, et al. *Cultural Analysis*, Boston, MA: Routledge and Kegan Paul, 21–76.

Hunter, James Davison and Stephen C. Ainlay, ed. (1986) *Making Sense of Modern Times: Peter L. Berger and the Vision of Interpretive Sociology*, London: Routledge and Kegan Paul.

http://pewforum.org/events/?EventID=172.

JACQUES DERRIDA (1930–2004)

> Of what should one take particular note in trying to formalize, in a concise manner, the axiom of the two sources around each of the two "logics" if you like, or each of the two distinct "resources" of what in the West goes by the Latinate name, "religion"? Let us remember the hypothesis of these two sources: on the one hand, the fiduciary-*ity* of confidence, trustworthiness < *fiabilité* > or of trust < *fiance* > (belief, faith, credit and so on), and on the other, the unscathed-*ness* of the unscathed (the safe and sound, the immune, the holy, the sacred, *heilig*).
>
> (Derrida 2002: 93)

Jacques Derrida, an Algerian/French philosopher and one of the most influential thinkers of recent times, immediately comments that two things need to be stressed. First, these "resources" presuppose each other and, second, both render "possible, but not necessary, something like a religion" in the sense of an institution with its dogmas, authority, and faithful community. Derrida is notoriously difficult to read and the above passage gives a hint of the strangeness of his prose and the density of his writing. Patience is required.

Jacques Derrida was born in Algeria (a French colony at the time) into a Sephardic Jewish family. He suffered, along with other Jews, under the anti-Semitic "Jewish laws" the Vichy regime enacted. On his second try (1952), he passed the rigorous entrance exam in philosophy and began his studies at the prestigious École normale supérieure in Paris. He taught in both France and the United States and was one of the founders (in 1982) of the Collège Internationale de Philosophies in Paris. Although he wrote very little on religion, his work has had a profound impact on those in the field of religious studies who favor humanist, theological, and feminist (see **Rita Gross**) approaches to understanding religion.

In 1967 Derrida published three groundbreaking books: *Writing and Difference*, *Speech and Phenomena*, and *Of Grammatology*. All three books mention deconstruction in passing, but this concept caught on with his readers and, much to his surprise, he became famous as the "father of deconstructionism." This is ironic because all so-called -isms are the target of what he called "deconstruction," a word inspired by the philosophy of Martin Heidegger.

Derrida thought of deconstruction as a way of "inheriting tradition." For Derrida, to inherit an intellectual tradition is not simply to receive a gift from the past and remain faithful to it, but also to accept an obligation to criticize it, thereby opening it up to its future. Deconstruction reveals paradoxes, contradictions (*aporia* in Greek) in the Western intellectual tradition. It focuses attention (in its first phase) on binary oppositions and the hierarchical way in which these oppositions are arranged, making one of them more central than the other. The marginalized concept is thereby devalued. For example, the idea of mind (thought, reason) emerges in the tradition as more important than body (senses, emotion). The result is the valorization of the mind and the devaluation of the body. Enormous and far-reaching consequences flow from this, largely unconscious, value system.

Derrida was particularly interested in what he called logocentrism. Logos is a Greek word meaning word or reason and the intellectual tradition, stemming from Plato, associated it with speech, thereby creating a binary and hierarchical opposition between speech and writing. Logocentricism, Derrida argued, is dependent on phono-centrism, which means, "hearing-oneself-speak." The Western philosophical and religious tradition is based on a phonocentric idealization of the voice. When we speak to ourselves, we assume that our inner voice and mind are united in a kind of "self-presence" and that meaning is private and immediately present to consciousness. This idealization of voice and mind sets up, Derrida claimed, a system of binary oppositions such as interior/exterior, mind/body, spirit/ matter, rationality/emotion. In each case, the first term of the opposition is given more value than the second. Thus in both the philosophic and religious tradition the interior life, mind, spirit, and reason are more valued than their supposed opposites.

The second phase of deconstruction is to reverse the oppositions, thereby making the marginalized the center. Thus, for example, the body can be valorized and the mind marginalized. This leads directly to the third phase in which the inherited oppositions that inform our thinking, shape our language, values, and culture, are destabilized. We come to see that one is not "better" than the other and hence the center does not hold. This allows us to realize that historical and cultural circumstances have shaped what we take to be reality or the way things are. We can now understand that things could be different. This liberates our thinking and practices to reshape the tradition. For example, logos or reason was identified with males, thereby degrading females as "phallogocentrism" came to shape human society in the form of patriarchy. Deconstruction exposes this history, destabilizes it, and opens it up to change.

Deconstruction also shows us that the very possibility of realizing concepts in time and space is dependent, paradoxically, on their impossibility. For example, justice can only become possible in a conditioned and imperfect way. But justice itself, ideal or perfect justice, is impossible because unconditioned. Yet the very attempt to realize justice and make it possible depends on this "impossibility" of justice. All human attempts to institute justice face this *aporia*.

Derrida coined the term differ-*a*-nce in an attempt to recover the importance of the other—the different, the strange, the unlike, the marginalized—that phonocentrism has masked by privileging interiority. "Differ-*a*-nce" combines the verb "to differ" with the verb "to defer." It refers to that which is both dissimilar or distinct and delayed or postponed. A phonocentric scheme is based on the self/other distinction combined with the privileging of the self. Under its influence we are accustomed to thinking of the self as primary and the other-than-self as secondary. Derrida's concept of differ-*a*-nce suggests that there is something more primordial than self-presence, indeed that "hearing-oneself-speak" is not the primary or "originary" act but is itself "grounded in" a differ-*a*-nce that announces the "self" is secondary, not primary, and is always deferred, never complete, never fully possessed.

This brief account of Derrida's views on deconstruction, logocentricism, phonocentricism, possibility/impossibility, and differ-*a*-nce is only a small part of the story. Our concern, however, is with religion and so we must turn our attention to what he had to say about it. His most sustained discussion of religion is in the essay "Faith and Knowledge: Two Sources of 'Religion' at the Limits of Reason Alone," first published in French in 1996 (English, 1998) and the lead essay in his book *Acts of Religion* as well as a volume he edited titled *Religion*. The opening quotation comes from this essay and provides one of at least three different descriptions of the "two sources." The subtitle is important. It recalls Henri Bergson's *Two Sources of Religion and Morality*, and **Kant**'s *Religion within the Bounds of Reason Alone*. **Kant** distinguished between the "religion of cult" with its emphasis on sacramental supernaturalism and "moral religion." For **Kant** the "religion of cult" is *beyond* the limits of reason but moral religion is *within* the limits. Derrida wanted to overcome this binary opposition between reason and religion by rethinking religion *at the limits* of reason.

Near the beginning of the essay, Derrida indicated that he wished to talk about what can be made of the "return of the religious" in our day, a return that often takes the form of fundamentalisms that endorse and justify violence. This is one form of the *aporia* or problematic of religion but in its most abstract form it is the question about *"revealability"* and whether this is *"more originary than revelation ... and hence independent of all religion"* (Derrida 2002: 54). His deconstruction of religion uncovers a "duplicity of the origin," which he characterized as the messianic and *chora* (*khora*). The messianic refers to *"the opening to the future or the coming of the other as the advent of justice"* (Derrida 2002: 56). This is *"messianicity without messianism"* in that it is prior to any specific prophecies such as those found in Judaism and Christianity. It is a *"general structure of experience"* and is linked to the desire for "possible/impossible" justice. The ideal of unconditional justice always remains elusive, something that we hope will come, but we cannot control its coming. It is always something in the future.

Chora, a word used by Plato to indicate what is beyond Being, refers to the "nothing" out of which the cosmos comes. However, even calling it nothing, according to Derrida's use of Plato's term, is misleading because it is prior to all oppositions including the oppositions of being and nothingness, sensible and intelligible, religion and irreligion. Even though it is called *chora*, it is unnamable because all names conceal oppositions and distinctions. The "beyondness" of *chora* prompts Derrida to characterize it as a desert that our thinking cannot penetrate.

The theme of the "two sources" returns when Derrida speaks of religion as a convergence of two experiences—of belief and of the sacred. As the opening quotation indicates, "belief" is shorthand for a host of related meanings such as confidence, trust, and faith while "sacred" is a truncated way of indicating the unscathed, safe, immune, holy, and related concepts. The drive to believe and the drive to remain unscathed or pure indicates that religion, as we think of it, is "allergic to contamination" and yet it, like other institutions, suffers from "auto-immunity." An autoimmune condition is one in which an organism turns its own immune defenses against itself. For example, religion today is dependent upon science and technology to spread its message and carry out its acts of violence, yet it is at war with science and technology because it views them as a threat.

This autoimmune condition appears in a religious "double postulation." On the one hand it preaches respect for life, and on the other hand it calls for the sacrifice of life. How can we make sense of this *aporia*? We must see that "life has absolute value [for religion] only if it is worth *more than* life." In other words, life is to be respected "only in so far as it bears witness, in some manner, to the infinite transcendence of that which is worth more than it ... " (Derrida 2002: 87).

Derrida is not without his critics. Perhaps the most persistent criticism is that his writing often appears to be little more than wordplay and free association that masks superficial analysis with a seeming profundity. What, for example, does deconstruction boil down to? It is not, critics maintain, anything more than the attempt to uncover contradictions and inconsistencies in the writings of others. This is what scholars normally do and to mask it with obscure language about discovering the "impossible" as the very "possibility" of some concept does not further the critical cause, or the cause of clarity for that matter.

However, scholars of religion have found Derrida's ideas useful, particularly in uncovering contradictions in previous theoretical enterprises such as the attempt to find the historical origin of religion, revealing the insidious distortions of the marriage of religion and patriarchy, and the space it opens for a/theological thinking after the "death of God" (**Nietzsche**).

See also: **Burkert, Foucault, Girard, J. Z. Smith**

Major works

(1973) *Speech and Phenomena*, trans. David B. Allison, Evanston, IL: Northwestern University Press.

(1974) *Of Grammatology*, trans. Gayatri Spivak, Baltimore, MA: The Johns Hopkins University Press.

(1978) *Writing and Difference*, trans. Alan Bass, Chicago, IL: University of Chicago Press.

(1998) *Religion*, ed. Jacques Derrida and Gianni Vattimo, Stanford, CA: Stanford University Press.

(2002) *Acts of Religion*, ed. Gil Anidjar, London: Routledge.

(2003) *Philosophy in the Time of Terror: Dialogues with Jürgen Habermas and Jacques Derrida*, ed. Geovanna Borradori, Chicago, IL: University of Chicago Press.

Further reading

Caputo, John D. (1999) *The Prayers and Tears of Jacques Derrida*, Bloomington, IN: Indiana University Press.

Hägglund, Martin. (2008) *Radical Atheism: Derrida and the Time of Life*, Stanford, CA: Stanford University Press.

McCance, Dawne. (2009) *Derrida on Religion: Thinker of Differance*, London: Equinox.

http://www.iep.utm.edu/derrida.

WALTER BURKERT (1931–)

> I propose the existence of biological patterns of actions, reactions, and feelings activated and elaborated through ritual practice and verbalized teachings, with anxiety playing a foremost role. Religion offers solutions to various critical situations recurring in individual lives. Through manifold forms and functions of ritual behavior and cultural interpretations, religion can still be seen to inhabit the deep vales of the landscape of life.
>
> (Burkert 1996: 177)

Why has religion survived, indeed flourished, during the long course of human evolution? Is there a "religious gene" that aids humans in adaptation to the environment or is something else at work? Religion costs a lot of valuable resources. It is expensive and there seem to be no obvious survival benefits that result from sacrificing resources to unseen and imagined higher powers. Walter Burkert, a historian of ancient Greek religion, sets out to answer this and associated questions in his groundbreaking book *Creation of the Sacred*.

Walter Burkert was born in Bavaria and studied classical philology, history, and philosophy at the Universities of Munich and Erlangen, where he earned his doctorate in 1955. He married Maria Bosch in 1957 and taught at various universities in Europe and the United States, gaining a reputation for scholarly excellence. Among his numerous honors was an invitation to present the Gifford Lectures (published as *Creation of the Sacred*) at St. Andrews University (1989) and the award of the Balzan Prize for Study of the Ancient World (1990). His books on *Greek Religion* and *Ancient Mystery Cults* are noted for their erudition and careful scholarship. He is a celebrated specialist who is not afraid to theorize.

Burkert broke new ground in his use of biological data and evolutionary theory to understand ancient religious rituals and beliefs. He characterized himself in the English Preface to his influential book *Homo Necans* ("Man the Killer") as "a philologist who starts from ancient Greek texts and attempts to find biological, psychological and sociological explanations for religious phenomena ... " (Burkert 1983: xix). He drew on the work of **Jane Harrison** and Konrad Lorenz (*On Aggression*) to develop the idea that "blood and violence lurk fascinatingly at the very heart of religion" (Burkert 1983: 2).

Although **Freud**'s theory of a "primal murder" has been largely rejected, his insight that there is a deep connection between violence and the sacred finds echoes in the work of **René Girard** and in Burkert's own study of sacrificial rituals in the ancient world. Burkert argues that hunting for food has had a deep and lasting influence on human evolution and culture. It was decisive for the development of culture, including religion, because early hominoids needed to kill in order to get food, yet lost the biological equipment (large teeth, claws, great strength and speed) of their primate cousins. This led to the invention of new and improved weapons, promoted social solidarity because cooperation for the hunt was necessary, required initiation (**rites of passage**) of boys into manhood by emphasizing the traits necessary for being a good hunter (courage, reliability, endurance), and reinforced a division of labor between "men's work" and "women's work."

Religious sacrifice has its roots in the killing and consuming of game. It constitutes, for ancient people, the basic experience of the sacred because animal sacrifice became a "necessary" activity in order to ensure game and protect the hunters. Practically everywhere our ancestors looked there were altars on which sacrifices were being offered. A study of the details of sacrificial rites in different cultures shows, Burkert argues, the interrelationship of hunting, killing game, and the sacrifice of animals to the unseen "powers" that were thought to control the success or failure of getting food. "Only *homo necans* can become *homo sapiens*" (Burkert 1983: 212).

The subtitle for Burkert's book, *Creation of the Sacred*, from which our opening quotation comes, is *Tracks of Biology in Early Religions*. This subtitle is significant because in this book he expands on the material developed in *Homo Necans* and argues that a careful study of religious rites and myths shows how they reflect biological behaviors intended to lessen the fear and anxiety associated with life. In short, religion has survived even though it appears to have no practical benefit because it does have a hidden benefit. Hunters must learn to control their anxieties prompted by the dangers and uncertainties of the hunt in order to be successful. Religion promotes human survival by helping humans cope with a threatening and dangerous world. It indirectly helps them get food and thereby survive.

The seriousness of religion resides in the fact that it is linked to the fear of death (see **Berger**). The "fictitious worlds" that religions create deal with that fear and its anxiety by reassuring humans that the gods are ultimately in charge. Moreover, in a world without established legal structures, the gods may well have come into existence in order to guarantee oaths and thereby diminish the chances of being deceived. They serve to mitigate the human capacity to lie and therefore are called upon to witness oaths and other human transactions. Religion is, from this point of view, an expression of optimism in the face of danger.

The claim of sociobiology that genes and culture coevolve cannot be verified in the case of religion. Nevertheless, we should not separate culture from biology when trying to make sense of religion and its survival because biology can illuminate some puzzling features of religion. Religious sacrifice, for example, appears to be a useless waste of resources. The smoke from burnt offerings is not going to prevent a disaster, no matter how loudly humans plead or how many oxen they kill. However, a search for animal instances of sacrifice shows that they will often sacrifice something of value, even a part of themselves, in order to save themselves. So a fox gnaws off its paw to escape a trap. This *pars pro toto* ("give up a part to save the whole") makes rational sense, but it is not obvious that this is what is going on in human sacrifice. However, in scapegoat sacrifices it is believed that one dies so many can live. This relieves anxiety in the community just like herd animals calm down when a predator kills one of their number, thereby allowing the others to escape.

Schleiermacher thought the origin of religion was in the feeling of absolute dependence. Among animals, especially the higher primates, we find a complex system of rank in which those of inferior rank submit to the control of those of higher rank (think of silverback gorillas). The dominance of the stronger not only increases the safety of the whole but also makes solidarity possible. Religions develop systems of rank and authority with the strongest (the gods) at the top, thereby creating communal solidarity.

Systems of social rank require submission rituals. The weaker bows to the stronger in order to stop aggression. In religion humans bow to the divine in veneration and show their submission in many ways. One way is to employ strategies of praise that exalt the divine. This is the other pole of humiliation. Praise stabilizes systems of rank and power, offering a sense of safety to those of inferior rank. Burkert calls attention to what he calls the "double tier of power." Subjects submit to rulers and rulers submit to the gods, thereby confirming the ruler's position of earthly power and securing a dominant role. The ruler ceases to be alone at the top of the social pyramid, deflecting the potential aggression of those of lower rank.

An important feature of religion is gifting. It is a universal feature of human civilization and can be found among the higher primates as well. Gifting is based on the principle *do ut des* ("I give in order that you shall give"). A gift comes with strings attached—the expectation of reciprocity. This behavior reinforces a sense of community and social connectedness. So sacrifices to the gods are made in the expectation of some kind of return and an exchange connection is established between the human community and the divine.

But it is clear that the gift (often food) never gets to the gods. The gift is destroyed, recycled, or transformed into durable monuments. Also, the gods often do not respond, or seem to respond in negative ways. Yet sacrifices continue. Why? A clue can be found in the fact that sometimes gifts are tributes seeking to keep the god, demons, or the dead away. Perhaps the meaning of gifting in a sacrificial context is to acknowledge a higher power, and if that power can do harm then some relief from the anxiety of threat is gained. Burkert writes, "One might indeed be tempted to say that every form of religion is, among other things, an organization to elicit gifts" (Burkert 1996: 145).

There are many other features of religion that Burkert analyzes in his attempt to reveal "biological tracks." We should note, however, that Burkert acknowledges that his argument is basically an argument from analogy. There are analogies but not homologies between religious practices and biological patterns. These analogies are strong enough, Burkert thinks, to show how religion can contribute to human survival even though it may seem, at first glance, useless from an evolutionary point of view.

Critics of Burkert have, as might be expected, accused him of **reductionism**. If, the argument goes, scholars like **Schleiermacher** reduced religion to feeling, or like **Freud** reduced it to sexuality, or like **Durkheim** reduced it to society, then Burkert has reduced it to biology. Other critics have argued that his research base is too narrow. He knows an enormous amount about ancient religions in the Mediterranean world, but what about the Asian, African, and American material? Do the same "tracks" appear in these other areas?

Burkert acknowledges his limitations in dealing with the vast material relating to religion around the globe, but he has, he thinks, opened up an important area of research opportunities. He shifted the focus of study of ancient religions since the time of **Frazer** from agriculture to hunting. Biological explanations of religious behavior open a new direction for understanding religion and Burkert's work has pointed the way.

See also: **Derrida**

Major works

(1979) *Structure and History in Greek Mythology and Ritual*, Berkeley, CA: University of California Press.

(1983) *Homo Necans: The Anthropology of Ancient Greek Sacrificial Ritual and Myth*, trans. Peter Bing, Berkeley, CA: University of California Press.

(1985) *Greek Religion*, trans. John Raffan, Cambridge, MA: Harvard University Press.

(1987) *Ancient Mystery Cults*, Cambridge, MA: Harvard University Press.

(1996) *Creation of the Sacred: Tracks of Biology in Early Religions*, Cambridge, MA: Harvard University Press.

(2001) *Savage Energies: Lessons of Myth and Ritual in Ancient Greece*, trans. Peter Bing, Chicago, IL: University of Chicago Press.

Further reading

Atran, Scott. (2002) *In Gods We Trust: The Evolutionary Landscape of Religion*, Oxford: Oxford University Press.

Feierman, Jay R. (2009) *The Biology of Religious Behavior: The Evolutionary Origins of Faith and Religion*, New York: Praeger.

Hamerton-Kelly, Robert, ed. (1988) *Violent Origins: Walter Burkert, Rene Girard, and Jonathan Z. Smith on Ritual Killings and Cultural Formation*, Stanford, CA: Stanford University Press.

Wilson, David Sloan (2002) *Darwin's Cathedral: Evolution, Religion, and the Nature of Society*, Chicago, IL: University of Chicago Press.

http://ase.tufts.edu/cogstud/papers/burkert.htm.

TALAL ASAD (1932–)

> My argument is that there cannot be a universal definition of religion, not only because its constituent elements and relationships are historically specific, but because that definition is itself the historical product of discursive processes.
>
> (Asad 1993: 29)

This claim by Talal Asad, Distinguished Professor of Anthropology at the City University of New York, if true, would appear to undermine any possibility of a viable universal theory of religion because such theories depend on some kind of universal definition. Thus Asad's definitional skepticism calls into question the very possibility of generalizing about all religions and the search for essential attributes that can be used to distinguish religion from other matters such as politics or economics. However, skepticism can be useful, because it stimulates thought, uncovers weaknesses, and deepens understanding of the problems religious studies must face if it is to promote better insights into what we usually call "religion."

Talal Asad was born in Saudi Arabia and his early years were spent in Pakistan and India. His father was a Jewish convert to Islam and was deeply involved in the new government of Pakistan, becoming its representative to the United Nations in 1952. Talal Asad studied in England and was awarded his PhD by the University of Oxford in 1968. He immigrated to America in 1989 and has been a visiting professor at a number of universities, both in the United States and abroad. He is the author of many books and articles, two of which will be our main focus, *Genealogies of Religion* and *Formations of the Secular*. Asad utilizes the genealogical analysis developed by **Nietzsche** and **Foucault** to unpack the historical processes that have led to the construction of the concepts "religion" and "secular" along with the role they have played in the formation of modern nation-states and European colonialism.

Building on **Wittgenstein**'s idea of language-games and **Foucault**'s notion of discursive formations, Asad points out that language-games embody ideological perspectives because they are not merely historical, but also political. Hence ideology influences theoretical understanding. For example, many anthropologists fail to take into account the unequal power relations between the West and the Third World, writing as if their views of Africa or Asia were ideologically neutral. But inequalities of power enter into the very act of "cultural translation" whereby the Third World is represented in European and American culture.

The lead essay in *Genealogies* critically unpacks **Clifford Geertz**'s definition of religion as a system of symbols. Asad begins by arguing that **Geertz**'s understanding of symbol, an essential feature of his definition, is confused. Sometimes he treats symbols as aspects of reality and at other times as *representations* of reality. Further, **Geertz**'s discussion of symbols and the role they play in religion is too simple. It largely ignores the role that power plays in creating religious "truth."

According to Asad, **Geertz** confuses two kinds of discourse; the sort of discourse used *in* religious practice and the discourse used to speak *about* practice. This results in paying insufficient attention to the "authorizing processes" by which religion is created. What gets labeled "religion" in any given society is determined by other discourses in that society. Discourse about religion has a history and that history determines how the concept of religion gets applied.

Geertz's definition has limited value because it rests, in part, on Christian ideas of religion as essentially a matter of belief and on the development of the notion of "natural religion" in the early modern period of Western culture (see **Kant**). The development of the construct "natural religion" is a crucial step in the formation of the modern notion of religion because it identifies three elements—beliefs, practices, and ethics—that many scholars, including **Geertz**, have come to believe are essential elements. Of these three elements, beliefs have emerged as the primary focus in many modern studies. Further, beliefs are treated as a "state of mind," which reflects the Protestant Christian emphasis on faith.

What is the content of symbols, be they expressed in beliefs, practices or ethics, that is specifically religious? They vary widely, but **Geertz** characterizes religious symbols as "*formulating conceptions of a general order of existence.*" In other words, they make claims about the whole cosmos and this is what distinguishes them from other kinds of symbol systems such as science, politics, and aesthetics. But there is a shift in emphasis, according to Asad, as **Geertz** develops his ideas; a shift from claiming that religious symbols must make specific claims about the cosmos as a whole to the idea that they express a perspective that reflects a positive attitude. This "modest" view of religious beliefs as a "positive perspective" is a product of post-**Enlightenment** secular society that allows only a limited psychological space in which religion can operate.

Geertz's attempt to distinguish religious symbols from other kinds of symbols results in separating them from the "form of life" in which they dwell. The crucial question is what discourse authorizes such symbols and that question cannot be answered without considering the nonreligious symbols which are part of their historical context. All of the problems that plague **Geertz**'s definition, according to Asad, stem from **Geertz**'s attempt to provide a universal definition of religion that abstracts religion from particular historical and social situations, thereby ignoring the authorizing discourses that give it power. One hears here echoes of **W. C. Smith**'s critique of the scholarly use of the term "religion" and the problems it poses.

In *Formations of the Secular*, Asad discusses modern theories of religion that often focus on the processes of secularization. He notes that many regard secularization as a distinctive feature of modern societies that distinguishes them from traditional societies (see **Berger**). The so-called secularization thesis takes different forms, but José Casanova has identified three elements found in most versions and considers the first and third essential. The three elements are (1) the separation of religion and politics resulting from the increasing differentiations of social spaces that characterize modernity, (2) the privatization of religion, and (3) the declining social significance of religious belief and institutions. This thesis is, Asad remarks, both descriptive and normative. He points out that many have argued the secularization thesis ought to be abandoned because there has developed a resurgence of religion in recent years in both secular and traditional societies. Others defend the thesis, at least in a modified form, by arguing that this resurgence marks the deprivatization of religion as it moves from the private to the public sphere. However, this element (2 above) is not essential to the thesis because the crucial issue is *how* deprivatization occurs. If religion enters the public arena in a way consistent with the basic requirements of modernity, such as democratic government, then it is consistent with modern secularized societies and not seen as a problem. It becomes an issue only when it is at odds with the values of secularized societies.

Asad argues that both the supporters and critics of the secularization thesis have not paid sufficient attention to the concepts "secular" and "religion." In developing this idea, he explores three important questions. First, because the experience of religion in the "private" sphere (home or school) influences peoples' reactions (positive or negative) to religious/political debates in the public sphere, a crucial question becomes how do different conceptions of religion form the ability of listeners to these debates to be publicly responsive? Can they engage in free and open debate about matters they hold dear or not? If they cannot, then the deprivatization of religion is not compatible with the values of modern society.

Second, can the entry of religious adherents to the public sphere leave the "preexisting discursive structure intact"? A religion that enters the public sphere "on its own terms" may well threaten the authority of existing institutions and ideas. If its position is uncompromising, then it is difficult to see how it can leave the "preexisting discursive structure intact" because that structure is built on a willingness to compromise on at least some matters in order to promote the "greater good."

Third, Asad asks why secularists fear the intrusion of religion into public life when they support the right, characteristic of modern values, to speak and listen freely and recognize that in modern societies the political "increasingly penetrates the personal." A partial explanation may be that secular societies value the right of individuals to "freely" form their religious identity but *only if* it is of a certain type. There may be subtle and not so subtle forms of coercion to conform to the prevailing secular ethos if the religious identity and values they bring to the public sphere do not conform to a "certain type." The controversy in France over the dress of Muslim women is a case in point.

Asad next turns his attention to two important questions, (1) "Should nationalism be understood as secularized religion ... or should Islamism be regarded as nationalism" and (2) is it not paradoxical to claim that nationalism is secular and at the same time to argue that it can produce a kind of nationalistic secular religion (Asad: 2003: 187/195)? Consideration of the various responses to the first question leads Asad to question the consistency of the sharp separation between religion and the secular that proponents of the secularization thesis often employ. In his discussion of the second question, Asad argues that Islamism's concern with state power is not the result of its commitments to nationalism but to the "modern nation-state's enforced claim to constitute legitimate social identities" (Asad 2003: 200). In other words, it is not a nationalistic desire that fuels Islamism's antagonism but a rejection of the social values the modern nation-state seeks to impose on Islamic radicals.

Asad concludes his discussion of secularization by claiming that if the secularization thesis seems to be increasingly untenable it is not due to the fact that in the modern secular world we encounter a religious resurgence but "because the categories of 'politics' and 'religion' turn out to implicate each other more profoundly than we thought, a discovery that has accompanied our growing understanding of the powers of the modern nation-state" (Asad 2003: 200).

Critics of Asad have not only raised questions about his specific interpretations of the ideas of others, such as **Geertz** and Casanova, but also questioned his use of the genealogical method. It is certainly important to trace the genealogy of particular concepts but does the fact that an idea has a history invalidate it? If that is the case then all human ideas have no hope of ever being true because every idea has a history and a social/cultural location (including Asad's). Asad appears to have committed the "genetic fallacy" which claims that the truth of an idea is invalidated by where it came from and how it developed.

Asad and others who use the genealogical method would respond that the usefulness of knowing the historical development and social location of ideas does not necessarily invalidate them, but provides a useful cautionary flag to those who would use notions like religion and the secular naively, assuming that they are unproblematic. It also calls attention to the inconsistencies in concepts that get used in political and social debates without attention to the necessary qualifications and limitations. This is not without value, since the liberal and secular nation-state, while decrying the violence of others, engages in its own violence in the name of what it considers a righteous cause. Asad challenges the student of religion to use a more culturally contextualized approach, paying particular attention to authorizing systems of discourse and power.

See also: **Evans–Pritchard, James, Lévi–Strauss, J. Z. Smith, Tylor**

Major works

(1970) *The Kababish Arabs: Power, Authority and Consent in a Nomadic Tribe*, New York: Praeger.

(1973) Talal Asad, ed. *Anthropology and the Colonial Encounter*, New York: Humanities Press.

(1993) *Genealogies of Religion: Discipline and Reasons of Power in Christianity and Islam*, Baltimore, MA: Johns Hopkins University Press.

(2003) *Formations of the Secular: Christianity, Islam, and Modernity,* Stanford, CA: Stanford University Press.

(2007) *On Suicide Bombing,* New York: Columbia University Press.

Further reading

Scott, David and Charles Hirschkind, ed. (2006) *Powers of the Secular Modern: Talal Asad and His Interlocutors,* Stanford, CA: Stanford University Press.
http://www.youtube.com/watch?v=kfAGnxKfwOg.

JONATHAN Z. SMITH (1939–)

> [W]hile there is a staggering amount of data, of phenomena, of human experiences and expressions that might be characterized in one culture or another, by one criterion or another, as religious—*there is no data for religion.* Religion is solely the creation of the scholar's study. It is created for the scholar's analytic purposes by his imaginative acts of comparison and generalization.
>
> (Smith 1982: xi)

Historian of religion Jonathan Z. Smith makes this arresting, almost shocking assertion in the Introduction to his widely read book *Imagining Religion.* It appears to make the study of religion a purely subjective enterprise. How can there be a "staggering amount of data" that people label as "religious" but no data for religion? Is religion a useless generalization with little or no grounding in fact? Is it a fiction of the imagination?

Jonathan Z. Smith was born in New York City and developed an early interest in botany, a study he planned to pursue. However, after entering Haverford College in 1956 he decided to major in philosophy. He went to Yale University for graduate study in religion where he wrote his PhD dissertation on **Frazer**'s *The Golden Bough.* After teaching at Dartmouth College and the University of California in Santa Barbara, he accepted an appointment at the University of Chicago and in 1982 became the Robert O. Anderson Distinguished Service Professor of the Humanities.

An early and lasting influence resulted from his encounter with the ideas of the philosopher Ernst Cassirer. Cassirer "sealed" Smith's allegiance to neo-Kantianism (see **Kant**), an allegiance that was confirmed by the work of **Durkheim** and reinforced by the structuralism of **Lévi-Strauss**. The claim that the category religion is a product of the scholar's imagination has a definite **Kantian** ring because it underscores the role that theoretical imagination plays in making sense of data that people call, for one reason or another, religious.

Cassirer taught Smith to take myths and symbols seriously. Contrary to **Romantic** views of religious symbols that see them as expression of emotions, symbols should be approached as a "mode of thought." People think *in* and *through* symbols, be they religious or mathematical. They are ways in which humans try to solve problems that arise in the course of living. Because human language is made up of symbols, the study of humans must begin with thinking about language as a way of creating, not just reflecting, the world. Myths or symbolic narratives must be presumed to be rational. To label them as irrational nonsense is an imperialistic move to denigrate others whom we deem to be "unlike" us.

According to his own account, Smith also learned from Cassirer to regard the data provided by ethnographies not as a collection of exotica but as ordinary data that requires constructive inquiry. Cassirer did philosophy by thinking within the history of ideas, not against it, and Smith came to adopt an "ethic of careful reading" that took due care with contextualizing the material but without abandoning suspicion and criticism. Smith himself probably did more than anyone to dismantle the **"phenomenological** paradigm" constructed by **Mircea Eliade** and yet showed respect for his work, especially **Eliade**'s search for patterns.

One way to highlight the key ideas in Smith's work is to examine what he has identified as his "persistent preoccupations" (see the first chapter of *Relating Religion*). He discusses five: (1) reversal and rebellion, locative/utopian; (2) situation, incongruity, and thought; (3) taxonomy and comparison; (4) culture, difference, and thought; and (5) redescription, translation, and generalization. We shall briefly examine each in turn.

Reversal and rebellion refers to a religious pattern that is always available as an alternative to the dominant religious picture of the world and appears at certain times in history. **Eliade** had argued that archaic cultures had a deep faith in an ordered cosmos that was expressed in religious celebrations of the creation of that order, and reinforced, through myth, rituals, and ethical norms, a deep sense of the human responsibility for maintaining and renewing the cosmic order created "in the beginning" by the gods. Smith points out that this is only part of the story because in some cultures the created order the gods ordained is experienced to be chaotic and evil. In response to this experience (which usually occurred at times of political and cultural stress) the desire to escape the creation by making contact with a better reality beyond this world arises. Rather than rituals designed to renew the order created by the gods, rituals of escape to another realm become a religious preoccupation. Smith called the first pattern identified by **Eliade** "locative" because it emphasizes renewing and maintaining one's place and the second (rebellion and reversal) "utopian" because it seeks escape to a "no place" on this earth.

Smith cautioned against using this dichotomy (locative/utopian) in an evolutionary context. He did not intend to argue that so-called primitive and archaic cultures were locative and modern cultures were utopian. Both the locative and the utopian forms of religion are "existential possibilities" for humans at any point in history.

The second preoccupation (situation, incongruity, and thought) begins with the premise that "incongruity gives rise to thought." A close examination of the evidence for the locative map of the world raises the suspicion that it should not be generalized into a universal pattern, as **Eliade** had done, but that it amounts to a self-serving ideology designed to promote conformity and obedience to priests and kings. The locative/utopian maps of the world appear as one of many different ways humans have devised to make sense of their experiences. A third way, which Smith characterizes as the "joke," neither denies nor flees from the disjunction between experience and ideology but shows that situational incongruity can be lived with by treating it with a humor that both preserves the incongruity and exposes it. Trickster figures, found in many myths, play "jokes" on people, often by creating items of value in incongruous and outrageous ways such as by defecating parts of the cosmos.

The third persistent preoccupation of Smith's scholarly labors focuses on taxonomy and comparison. Smith's early interest in botany sparked an interest in systems of classification (taxonomies). Smith realized that religious studies could gain greater sophistication in its taxonomic and comparative work by paying attention to the advances made in botanical classification. He proposed that *monothetic* classification systems based on one alleged "essential feature" should be replaced by *polythetic* taxonomies that are based on many different traits none of which may be unique. For example, essential (substantive) definitions for the class "religion" have failed to gain consensus among scholars in the field. A polythetic approach, which Smith advocates, abandons the claim that there is a unique trait, and proceeds by listing and describing a number of different traits that cultural phenomena have, which allow scholars to classify them as religion (see **Wittgenstein**).

Although Smith himself offers no formal definition of religion, he describes a number of characteristics associated with religion. He writes:

> Religion is the quest, within the bounds of the human, historical condition, for the power to manipulate and negotiate ones "situation" so as to have "space" in which to meaningfully dwell. ... Religion is a distinctive mode of human creativity, a creativity which both discovers limits and creates limits for humane existence. What we study when we study religion is the variety of attempts to map, construct and inhabit such positions of power through the use of myths, rituals and experiences of transformation.
>
> (Smith 1978: 291)

One important method scholars use when they study this "distinctive mode of human creativity" we call religion is the method of comparison. Comparative methods have gotten a bad reputation among religious scholars because they often privilege one member of the comparison. For example, when scholars influenced by the Christian tradition (an inescapable influence in most Western cultures) have compared Christianity or some aspect of it to "other" religions (for example Islam), the "other" religions have appeared in a less favorable light.

Comparison is, Smith argues, unavoidable because it is a basic feature of thinking and essential to building taxonomies. However, poor comparisons are avoidable. The enterprise of comparison at its best is the result of thinking in a disciplined way, requiring the acknowledgement of difference and the recognition that comparison involves three or more terms with a structure such as "r resembles s more than t with respect to some trait." A critical survey of different kinds of comparison leads Smith to insist that analogy is the best model for understanding comparative thinking.

Smith uses a cluster of words ("culture, difference, and thought") to name his fourth persistent preoccupation. He views culture as an attempt to reduce the unlimited possibilities present in nature to a manageable level. In the course of creating culture by way of reduction, differences are necessarily created (human/not human, we/they, like us/not like us, and so on) and sometimes these differences are overcome. Difference is always relative, never absolute, and frequently involves a "hierarchy of prestige" that labels as "other" those too much like us for comfort (see **Derrida**). Otherness, like difference, is a relative category because it is a term of interaction. Hence views of the "other" always involve a political element. Otherness occasions some of our most difficult intellectual, political, and moral issues.

"Redescription, translation and generalization" describe in condensed form Smith's fifth persistent concern. The study of religion involves contextual description, comparison, redescription, rectification (of our categories of imagining) and, the most difficult of all, explanation. The latter is occasioned by the surprise of bringing the "unknown into relations to the known." This process involves translation, which can never be perfect, and generalizations that are selective and thus admit of exceptions. For these reasons no explanation is ever complete.

This brief account of Smith's persistent preoccupations would not be complete without mentioning his constant concern to show that, contrary to the claims of many, religion is *not* based on a disclosure that gives rise to a particular experience usually called "the sacred" (see **Otto**, **Eliade**, **Schleiermacher**). It is instead the "relentless human activity of thinking through a 'situation'" of incongruity, in order to reassure us that human existence matters (Smith 2004: 32).

Critics have seized on Smith's claim that religion is a product of the scholar's imagination. This undermines, they claim, any possibility of objective verification because hypotheses can only be checked against what is "imagined" by the very people who have created the hypotheses in the first place. Defenders have pointed out that just because something is imagined in the human mind does not imply that it does not exist outside the imagination.

Critics have also claimed that his approach is too intellectual and distorts the richness of religion by reducing it to a way of thinking, even though Smith has said, "Theory is not life, but I know with perfect surety that it is liveliness" (Smith 2004: 32). Nevertheless, many have found his ideas useful and his contribution to the field of religious studies immense. He moved it, supporters claim, in a new and better direction after **Eliade**.

See also: **Asad, Bellah, Dumézil, Evans-Pritchard, van Gennep, Girard, van der Leeuw, Müller, Radcliffe-Brown, Smart, W. C. Smith, Troeltsch**

Major works

(1978) *Map is Not Territory: Studies in the History of Religion*, Leiden: E. J. Brill.

(1982) *Imagining Religion: From Babylon to Jonestown*, Chicago, IL: University of Chicago Press.

(1987) *To Take Place: Toward Theory in Ritual,* Chicago, IL: University of Chicago Press.

(1990) *Drudgery Divine: On the Comparison of Early Christianities and the Religions of Late Antiquity,* Chicago, IL: University of Chicago Press.

(2004) *Relating Religion: Essays in the Study of Religion,* Chicago, IL: University of Chicago Press.

Further reading

Braun, Willi and Russell T. McCutcheon, eds. (2008) *Introducing Religion: Essays in Honor of Jonathan Z. Smith,* London: Equinox.
http://www.chicagomaroon.com/2008/6/2/full-j-z-smith-interview.

RITA GROSS (1943–)

> [A]n androgynous account of religion must ... include descriptions of women's lives and consciousness, [and] of their own experience of the religious context in which they live. Such accounts must also include the cultural stereotypes and norms made about women or femininity in any religious context, especially investigating the consonance or discontinuity between those norms and people's actual lives. Finally such accounts must describe the female personalities populating the mythological universe fully and accurately, without androcentric projections, expectations, or stereotypes.
>
> (Gross 1996: 80)

According to Rita Gross, Professor Emerita of Comparative Religions at the University of Wisconsin, Eau Claire, the descriptive task of any adequate theory of religion must include the three elements outlined above. We need to examine what she means by androgynous, androcentrism, and how this descriptive task is related to the normative obligation to criticize the oppression of women present in different religions.

Rita M. Gross was born in Rhinelander, Wisconsin. After graduating from high school she attended the University of Wisconsin, Milwaukee. She studied comparative religions at the University of Chicago and wrote her PhD dissertation on the role of women in Aboriginal Australian religions.

After practicing Judaism for nearly a decade, she converted to Buddhism and began the practice of meditation along with an intense study of Asian religions. She edited with Nancy Falk a groundbreaking book on women in the world religions, *Unspoken Worlds: Women's Religious Lives in Non-Western Cultures*, and has published books on Buddhism (see below). For our purposes I will focus on her book *Feminism and Religion* from which the opening quotation comes.

Gross insists that to avoid Eurocentrism, it is important to study feminism in the context of comparative religions, not just within the context of a particular Western religious tradition. She argues that within this broader setting it is vital to make a distinction between descriptive and normative approaches. The former seeks to gather, interpret, describe, and compare the data objectively and the latter addresses the concerns feminists have to critique patriarchy and reconstruct a spirituality that incorporates feminist values. She argues that it is possible to understand a religious tradition without adhering to it and that, from a purely descriptive standpoint, the truth or falsity of religious beliefs is irrelevant to the scholar.

Definitions of religion that focus on how religion functions in human lives serve the academic study of religion well because there are no religious beliefs that are held universally. Thus she favors definitions inspired by **Tillich** and **Eliade** that focus on religion as an expression of "ultimate concern" and center on the idea of the sacred. Crucial to understanding any particular religion is its worldview or beliefs about the nature of reality.

However, is it really possible to understand a worldview that may be radically different from one's own? It can be done, Gross argues, but only if sound scholarship is combined with empathy. Empathy involves temporarily "bracketing" one's own worldview, be it religious or not, and imaginatively "entering into the milieu of the phenomenon being studied." This empathetic practice, Gross quickly adds, does not imply that scholars should never evaluate what is being studied. The feminist critique of patriarchal beliefs and practices is appropriate even if traditional male-centered scholarship on religion thinks that such criticism compromises objectivity. Feminist scholarship on religion is bound to be more objective than androcentric scholarship because it is more inclusive. It pays serious attention to the way women's religion has been marginalized (see **Derrida**) and strives to develop a truly androgynous approach to world religions.

Three crucial questions must be faced. How are we to define feminism in this context, what is androcentric scholarship, and how does it differ from an androgynous model for the study of religion? The basic assumption of feminism is that women are as fully human as men. This implies an academic *method* that Gross prefers to call "women studies" and a *social vision* she calls feminism. Women studies are comparative and descriptive. However, the social vision entails a criticism of androcentrism and a shift to an androgynous model. Gross claims that methodology and social vision are independent in the sense that one can use the descriptive and comparative method without embracing the norms of the social vision.

Androcentric or male-centered studies of religion have three characteristics. First, they collapse the distinction between male and human being, second they appear unaware that male religiosity is only part of the story of religion, and third they do not uncover and examine the important roles that women have and do play in religious traditions. This results in distorted theories of religion that mask their androcentric biases. Gross calls for a "paradigm shift" in religious studies from a one-sexed, androcentric model to a two-sexed, androgynous model of humanity that regards the religious beliefs and practices of women to be as valuable as the beliefs and practices of men.

The use of an androgynous model results in the relativizing of patriarchy. Religions, especially monotheistic Western religions, justify male power over women by appealing to divine sanctions. Patriarchy becomes the "will of God" rather than a humanly created social arrangement of power that should be changed because it is unjust. But what would a post-patriarchal culture and religion look like?

There is much controversy about the nature of a post-patriarchal "ideal" androgynous social and religious order. One model is the equality model that tries to imagine a society in which the spiritual journeys of women are valued as much as those of men. However, Gross argues that equality is not enough. Rather she hopes for a new social order in which there is freedom for both men and women from culturally and religiously sanctioned gender roles. She recognizes this hope is radical and controversial but thinks that since both patriarchy and matriarchy depend on fixed gender roles, only freedom from gender roles will usher in a world in which one's sex is no longer a "relevant criterion for awarding roles or values" (Gross 1996: 26).

What difference for religious studies would a feminist approach make? Gross argues that it is not enough to supplement our present knowledge with a few women's voices. Rather the whole picture that androcentric studies of religion paint will have to be "thoroughly recast, not just supplemented." The opening quotation outlines some essential ingredients. Special attention would need to be paid to discontinuity between stereotypes and people's actual lives, as well as to the mechanisms women develop to deal with religiously constructed stereotypes.

As data is collected and described, new questions will arise, along with new answers. For example, how would the present ways of classifying religions need to change? Would the theories of the origin, development, and evolution of religion need to be revised? What new or revised comparative categories would be required? Gross acknowledges that none of this is undisputed territory and the necessary work is only in its infancy. There are, however, at least three approaches that have been and are being pursued. One is to consider each religion as relatively independent and provide accounts (historical, sociological, psychological, and so on) of women in each. So studies focused on women in religions like Christianity or Islam can provide valuable information.

Another approach is to discover the developmental patterns in women's religious involvement. For example, some scholars have argued that patriarchal religions are a late development. Evidence indicates that women had a higher status in foraging and horticultural societies and male dominance became more widespread and typical of religions with the introduction of agriculture and the creation of cities.

A third approach is to develop new comparative categories that arise from the actual religious lives of women rather than impose a predetermined set of categories. For example, relying on sacred texts and theological treatises for information about a religion often overlooks women's contributions because they were seldom represented in the textual tradition of the major patriarchal religions. However, in many cases women were more heavily involved in the daily "performance" of a religion. Thus categories relating to rituals, especially domestic ritual life, can be more useful for uncovering women's influence and power.

Gross recognizes that an androgynous theory of religion is still in the developmental stage. But critics have wondered whether her ideas are on the right track. Some have argued that her "androgynous" approach is as unbalanced as a male-centered approach because it amounts, in spite of its name, to a female-centered reading of religion. Others have pointed out that her "two-sexed" perspective does not construe the category of sex broadly enough. The variety of human sexuality cannot be adequately captured by the traditional categories of male and female. Still others maintain that she has blurred the line between a descriptive and normative approach, thereby blurring the line between advocacy and objectivity.

While such criticisms need to be taken seriously, there is little doubt that feminist-oriented studies of religion are transforming the academic study of religion as well as our understanding of religion. As a result, our understanding is richer, more contextualized, and more nuanced.

See also: **Foucault, Marx**

Major works

(1977) *Beyond Androcentrism: New Essays on Women and Religion*, Atlanta, GA: Scholars Press.

(1993) *Buddhism After Patriarchy: A Feminist History, Analysis, and Reconstruction of Buddhism*, Albany, NY: State University of New York Press.

(1996) *Feminism and Religion: An Introduction*, Boston, MA: Beacon Press.

(1998) *Soaring and Settling: Buddhist Perspectives on Contemporary Social and Religious Issues*, New York: Continuum.

(2000) ed. with Nancy Auer Falk, *Unspoken Worlds: Women's Religious Lives in Non-Western Cultures*, 3rd edition. Belmont, CA: Wadsworth Publishing.

(2001) with Rosemary Radford Ruether, *Religious Feminism and the Future of the Planet: A Christian-Buddhist Conversation*, New York: Continuum.

(2009) *A Garland of Feminist Reflections: Forty Years of Religious Exploration*, Berkeley, CA: University of California Press.

Further reading

Anderson, Pamela Sue. (1998) *A Feminist Philosophy of Religion: The Rationality and Myths of Religious Beliefs*, Oxford: Blackwell Publishers.

Young, Katherine K. (1999) "Having Your Cake and Eating it Too: Feminism and Religion," *Journal of the American Academy of Religion*, 67, 1: 167–84.

Young, Serinity ed. (1995) *An Anthology of Sacred Texts By and About Women*, New York: Crossroads.

http://plato.stanford.edu/entries/feminist-religion.

PASCAL BOYER (1957–)

That we fail to identify hidden hands and simple designs and instead discover a variety of underlying processes *that we know how to study* sometimes happens in scientific endeavors and is always for the better.

> The progress is not just that we understand religion better because we have better knowledge of cognitive processes. It is also, conversely, that we can highlight and better understand many fascinating features of our mental architecture by studying the human propensity toward religious thoughts. One does learn a lot about these complex biological machines by figuring out how they manage to give airy nothing a local habitation and a name.
>
> (Boyer 2001: 330)

With these words, Pascal Boyer, Luce Professor of Individual and Collective Memory at Washington University, St. Louis, closes his influential book *Religion Explained*. Boyer's explanation of religion derives from a relatively recent field of study called cognitive science. Its focus is on the "underlying processes," selected in the course of evolution, that give rise to thought (cognition). What are these processes, how do they work, are some unique to producing religious thoughts or are they the same processes that we use in other areas of thought?

Pascal Boyer received his doctorate in 1983 from the Universite de Paris in ethnology. Before accepting his present position at Washington University, he was senior research fellow at Kings College, Cambridge, a visiting fellow at the Center for Evolutionary Psychology at the University of California, Santa Barbara, and research director at the Centre National de la Recherche Scientifique in Lyon, France.

In two of his books, *The Naturalness of Religious Ideas* and *Religion Explained*, he argues that religious ideas are more likely to be noticed and recalled because they are "counter-intuitive" (see **Hume**). For example, agents that have superhuman powers, know everything, and are invisible grab our attention. Stories about their exploits are more likely to be recalled and passed on because they stand out from stories about normal human agents. According to Boyer, such seemingly bizarre ideas arise quite naturally and require no supernatural revelations. How does this happen?

The human mind is *not* a "blank slate" on which just anything can be inscribed as the "standard social science model" assumes. There are specific traits created by the long, twisting road of biological evolution as well as cultural constraints limiting the "material" with which mental processes can work. Boyer observed that certain types of religious representations (gods, spirits, ghosts, and so on) are both widely distributed in different cultures and remembered in oral and written traditions through many generations. Why is this so?

Boyer noticed that ideas about supernatural beings were similar to ideas about human agents but were "tweaked" in certain ways.

Humans, for example, die but supernatural agents, even though they have thoughts and feelings like humans, do not. We have a certain "intuitive ontology" that beings, which can think and feel, are agents. That such agents are immortal is "counter-intuitive." Because such concepts violate our normal expectations they grab our attention and are easy to remember. Trees that talk, for example, are the stuff of myth and legend.

Boyer argues that religious concepts are not popular because they are good for society or because humans have some sort of inherent need for them. The real cause of their popularity and pervasiveness is that they are more likely to be acquired *because they are counter-intuitive*. There is no "god gene" or "religious organ" but ordinary brain functions that produce religious concepts as a byproduct. This conception of religion opens the possibility of empirical experiments in cognitive neuroscience and puts the study of religion on a scientific footing. Hence Boyer's work has been heralded as a "new turn" in the academic study of religion.

Humans are genetically predetermined to perceive and think about certain entities in specific ways and hence to have certain expectations about entities in different "domains" (person, animal, plant, inanimate natural object, artifact). Humans are constantly searching for solutions to problems that arise in each of these domains and evolution has selected processes that are efficient and can contribute to the solution of those problems with a "minimum of cognitive fuss" (Boyer 2001: 201). For example, some animals are dangerous to humans and some are not. Knowing the difference and adjusting expectations quickly, efficiently, and accurately is a very useful ability in certain environments. When properties from different domains are mixed or expectations violated humans are faced with counter-intuitive ideas, which are the building blocks of religion.

Any religious concept is built on the following elements: (1) a particular domain, (2) a violation or breach of intuitive expectations, (3) a connection to the default or "normal" expectations, (4) a "slot" for elaboration by adding additional information, and (5) a lexical label (Jensen 2009: 141). For instance, a "god" has a "tag" (e.g. agent) that links it to the domain of person but it has counter-intuitive properties such as being in different places at the same time (ubiquity, in theological terms). Each of the five domains (see above) can be "tweaked" in a variety, but limited number, of ways. There can be physical, biological, and psychological breaches of expectation. For instance, the concept *tree* (belonging to the plant domain) can be "tweaked" by transferring psychological expectations from the human domain to the tree (e.g. talking trees). Once the concept of a talking tree becomes a part of the cognitive material with which the brain works, implications can be elaborated. Stories concerning what the trees talk about, how their views differ from human views, what they do, how they do it, their interactions with humans and animals, and the like, can be spun. A whole new way of thinking about trees is suddenly opened.

It should be noted that there are limits to religious inventiveness. Not any sort of counter-intuitive idea will stick. Invisible beings that are supernatural dishwashers that give birth to telephones are not likely to make it in the religious marketplace. Generally good supernatural concepts allow "all inferences not explicitly barred by the violation" (Boyer 2001: 87). You can attribute various properties to bleeding statues (miracles, answering prayers, and the like) but not the properties that contradict it being a statue (it's a Subaru) and bleeding (it's leaking oil).

It should also be noted that these processes are hidden from conscious view. We literally do not know from where our religious concepts come. They are very unusual, even strange, and thus beg for an unusual explanation. If they are about supernatural beings, then it is only reasonable to assume they come from supernatural beings.

Boyer uses his theory to address and explain a variety of elements typically found in religions. For example, religions seem to be preoccupied with death. Why is this so? Boyer hypothesizes that corpses trigger in the human mind conflicting and complex inferences. They look like humans, yet they do not act human. They no longer talk or walk, or act in any way at all. Their agency is gone. This challenges our normal expectations because if two things look similar we normally expect them to act in similar ways. But the dead are different. Perhaps they live someplace else or perhaps they will come back to life at some time in the future. These seem logical possibilities and once stories about ghosts, zombies, resurrected bodies, immortal souls and the like enter the human mind they can be elaborated in a variety of ways.

Ethnographic reports describe many examples of bizarre rituals, often involving scrupulous attention to detail. There are, Boyer notes along with **Freud**, striking similarities with patients suffering from OCD (obsessive-compulsive disorder). This provides a clue that rituals may be systems of taking "precaution against undetectable hazards" (Boyer 2001: 240). Rituals are also instrumental in forming coalitions and maintaining them in situations where loyalty is vitally important. Initiation rituals, be they secular or religious, help cement loyalty among those who go through the process (see **Turner**).

Boyer thinks his theory can also illuminate religious violence. Most religious violence, he notes, is directed at members of a religious group by other members of the same group. A person can leave "mainstream" religious groups without paying a horrible price. But "marginal" groups who fear defection and are rather loose coalitions of different people, whose loyalty may be in question, must make the price of defection high. Killing someone for defection is a very high price and will, if done publicly, serve to keep others in line.

Religion is dramatic and Boyer's theory is not at all dramatic. It tells us that religion is merely a side effect of the brains we have. It is like the smoke associated with fire. Fire is the main attraction, but the smoke comes with it as a byproduct. Is this too **reductionistic**?

Critics have answered yes. The historical study of religion, with all its rich and fascinating details, suddenly seems irrelevant. The cognitive science of religion is not really about religion, as the historian understands it, but about how human brains invent and deal with imagined agents. However, a complete and rich account of human cognition and symbol manipulation cannot be restricted to the brain. If it could be restricted then we would have to write off as irrelevant the historical, social, and cultural dimensions of religion.

Boyer is well aware that religion exists in a social context, but his primary concern has been with internal cognitive processes. That narrow focus has produced some remarkable insights and holds great promise for the future as cognitive scientists incorporate more analysis of the social and cultural dimensions. The cognitive genie is out of the bottle and there is no option but to go forward studying the relationship between the human brain and religion.

See also: **Burkert, Fuerbach, Girard, Hegel, Lévi-Strauss, Müller, Tylor**

Major works

(1990) *Tradition as Truth and Communication: A Cognitive Description of Traditional Discourse*, Cambridge: Cambridge University Press.

(1993) ed. *Cognitive Aspects of Religious Symbolism*, Cambridge: Cambridge University Press.

(1994) *The Naturalness of Religious Ideas: A Cognitive Theory of Religion*, Berkeley, CA: University of California Press.

(2001) *Religion Explained: The Evolutionary Origins of Religious Thought*, New York: Basic Books.

Further reading

Jensen, Jeppe Sinding. (2009) "Religion as the Unintended Product of Brain Functions in the 'Standard Cognitive Science of Religion Model,'" in *Contemporary Theories of Religion: A Critical Companion*, ed. Michael Stausberg, London: Routledge, 129–55.

Lawson, E. T. and R. N. McCauley. (1990) *Rethinking Religion: Connecting Cognition and Culture*, Cambridge: Cambridge University Press.

Pyysiäinen, I. (2003) *How Religion Works: Towards a New Cognitive Science of Religion*, London: Brill.

Sperber, D. (1996) *Explaining Culture: A Naturalistic Approach*, Oxford: Basil Blackwell.

http://www.guardian.co.uk/books/2002/feb/07/londonreviewofbooks/print.

GLOSSARY

Collective unconscious. A concept used by C. G. Jung and others to refer to an unconscious mind shared by all humans, which differs from the personal unconscious because it contains all the experiences of the species.

Deists. This term refers to a group of thinkers active primarily in the seventeenth and eighteenth centuries who rejected miracles, subscribed to determinism, and argued that God was like a clockmaker and the universe like a clock, set in motion and now running according to its own laws.

Empiricism. This label refers to the view that knowledge is based on sense experience. This epistemology (theory of knowledge) is usually contrasted with **rationalism**.

Enlightenment. This refers to a period of European intellectual history (roughly the eighteenth century) that rejected authority as the basis for determining truth and celebrated human reason as the best means for discovering truth.

Epicurean. The term derives from Epicurus (341–271 B.C.E.), the founder of a Hellenistic school of philosophy that developed an atomistic physical theory, an **empirical** theory of knowledge, and a hedonistic ethics based on the experience of pleasure and pain.

Existentialism. A philosophical movement that asserts the starting point of philosophical reflection is the existing individual in his/her concrete situation. To philosophize as a disinterested spectator thinking about abstract ideas is to miss the most important features of human existence such as subjectivity, anxiety in the face of death, and the freedom to decide one's identity and how one is to live.

Fideist. This term derives from the Latin *fides*, meaning faith. It refers to someone who subscribes to **fideism**, a position that holds that faith, not reason, is the primary basis of religious belief.

Hermeneutics. An intellectual discipline focused on the problems associated with interpreting meaning, primarily as expressed in written texts.

Immanence. In theology this refers to the presence of God in his creation. It is usually contrasted with God's **transcendence**.

Liminal. This term comes from the Latin for threshold and refers to a condition (**liminality**) of being between different social positions or roles.

Logical positivism. A theory that holds all genuine knowledge of the world is derived from **empirical** science, hence metaphysical statements, such as claims about God, are meaningless because they are incapable of **empirical** verification.

Moral attributes. This refers to moral predicates of the divine such as goodness, mercy, and justice as distinguished from the metaphysical attributes such as all-powerful and all-knowing.

Noumenal. **Kant** used this term to refer to things-in-themselves apart from how they appear to humans (opposite of **phenomenal**).

Pantheism. From the Greek "all god," this term as been used in a variety of ways but most commonly for the idea that God and nature are two ways of describing the same thing.

Phenomenal. This word derives from the Latin for "appearance" and is used by **Kant** to refer to what can be known by the senses (opposite of **noumenal**).

Phenomenology. With respect to the study of religion, this term refers to a comparative method that seeks to describe religion as a manifestation of the sacred, which is *sui generis* ("of its own kind"). It also seeks to uncover the meaning religious symbols have for the believer.

Rationalism. This refers to the view that knowledge derives from human reason. It is usually contrasted with **empiricism**.

Reductionism. Any theory of religion that explains religion with reference to non-religious factors. It denies that what people call the sacred is *sui generis* (see **phenomenology**).

Rites of passage. A name for rituals that mark important transitions in the human life cycle such as the rites associated with birth, marriage, and death.

Romantic. This refers to a movement in European arts and letters that developed between 1780 and 1830 that emphasized imagination, personal experience, emotional understanding, and a poetic relationship with nature in contrast to cold, analytical **rationalism**.

Structuralism. A term used for a theory and method that regards religion and language as sign systems whose elements (like words in a language) become meaningful in relation to the rules of the system (like grammar).

Theodicy. A technical term that means justifying the ways of God to humans and refers to proposed solutions to the problem of evil (why God allows evil and suffering in a world he created given the fact that he is all-loving and all-powerful).

Totem. An object, usually an animal or plant or its symbol, that a clan or tribe views as a sacred ancestor.

Transcendence. In theology this refers to the idea that God exists "beyond" or independent of the world. It is usually contrasted with God's **immanence**.

INDEX

Taylor & Francis

eBooks
FOR LIBRARIES

ORDER YOUR FREE 30 DAY INSTITUTIONAL TRIAL TODAY!

Over 23,000 eBook titles in the Humanities, Social Sciences, STM and Law from some of the world's leading imprints.

Choose from a range of subject packages or create your own!

Benefits for **you**
- ▶ Free MARC records
- ▶ COUNTER-compliant usage statistics
- ▶ Flexible purchase and pricing options

Benefits for your **user**
- ▶ Off-site, anytime access via Athens or referring URL
- ▶ Print or copy pages or chapters
- ▶ Full content search
- ▶ Bookmark, highlight and annotate text
- ▶ Access to thousands of pages of quality research at the click of a button

For more information, pricing enquiries or to order a free trial, contact your local online sales team.

UK and Rest of World: **online.sales@tandf.co.uk**

US, Canada and Latin America:
e-reference@taylorandfrancis.com

www.ebooksubscriptions.com

ALPSP Award for BEST eBOOK PUBLISHER 2009 Finalist
sponsored by

  Taylor & Francis eBooks
Taylor & Francis Group

A flexible and dynamic resource for teaching, learning and research.

www.routledge.com/religion

ROUTLEDGE

The Ideal Companion to
Fifty Key Thinkers on Religion

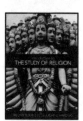

Introduction to the Study of Religion

By **Hillary Rodrigues** and **John S. Harding**, University of Lethbridge, Canada

The authors have crafted this book to familiarize novice students with key concepts and terminology in the study of religion. More advanced students will find a varied array of theoretical perspectives and methodological approaches to the field. Topics include:

- definitions of religion
- perspectives in the study and teaching of religion
- how religion began to be studied: traditional perspectives – philosophical and theological
- how people experience religion: perspectives in the study of religious consciousness and perception – phenomenological and psychological
- studying religion within communities: Social and cultural perspectives – anthropological, sociological, political and economic
- judging religion: critical perspectives –feminist approaches, the interaction of popular literature and religion
- contextual perspectives – historical and comparative

The book encourages students to think critically about the theories and methods presented. Students will find arguments for the strengths and limitations of these approaches, understand connections among religious studies and other intellectual movements, and develop their own ideas of how they might want to go about the study of religion. Summary boxes, a timeline, a glossary and other pedagogic aids help students grasp key concepts, along with a companion website.

Hb: 978-0-415-40888-2
Pb: 978-0-415-40889-9
eBook: 978-0-203-89172-8

For more information and to order a copy visit
www.routledge.com/9780415408899

Available from all good bookshops

www.routledge.com/religion

The Ideal Companion to
Fifty Key Thinkers on Religion

The Routledge Companion to the Study of Religion

Edited by **John Hinnells**, Liverpool Hope University, UK

The Routledge Companion to the Study of Religion is a major resource for courses in Religious Studies. It begins by explaining the most important methodological approaches to religion, including psychology, philosophy, anthropology and comparative study, before moving on to explore a wide variety of critical issues, such as gender, science, fundamentalism, ritual, and new religious movements. Written by renowned international specialists, this new edition:

- includes eight new chapters, including post-structuralism, religion and economics, religion and the environment, religion and popular culture, and sacred space
- surveys the history of religious studies and the key disciplinary approaches
- explains why the study of religion is relevant in today's world
- highlights contemporary issues such as globalization, diaspora and politics
- includes annotated reading lists, a glossary and summaries of key points to assist student learning.

Hb: 978-0-415-47327-9
Pb: 978-0-415-47328-6
eBook: 978-0-203-86876-8

For more information and to order a copy visit
www.routledge.com/9780415473286

Available from all good bookshops

www.routledge.com/religion

The Ideal Companion to
Fifty Key Thinkers on Religion

Religion: The Basics

By **Malory Nye**, Al-Maktoum Institute, Scotland

From the local to the global level, religion is – more than ever – an important and hotly debated part of modern life in the twenty-first century. From silver rings to ringtones and from clubs to headscarves, we often find the cultural role and discussion of religion in unexpected ways.

Now in its second edition, *Religion: The Basics* remains the best introduction to religion and contemporary culture available. The new edition has been fully revised and updated, and includes new discussions of:

- the study of religion and culture in the twenty-first century
- texts, films and rituals
- cognitive approaches to religion
- globalization and multiculturalism
- spirituality in the West
- popular religion.

With new case studies, linking cultural theory to real world religious experience and practice, and guides to further reading, *Religion: The Basics* is an essential buy for students wanting to get to grips with this hotly debated topic.

Hb: 978-0-415-44947-2
Pb: 978-0-415-44948-9
eBook: 978-0-203-92797-7

For more information and to order a copy visit
www.routledge.com/9780415449489

Available from all good bookshops

www.routledge.com/religion

The Ideal Companion to
Fifty Key Thinkers on Religion

Religious Studies: The Key Concepts

By **Carl Olson**, Allegheny College, USA

Religious Studies: The Key Concepts is an accessible, A-Z resource, defining and explaining key terms and ideas central to the study of religion. Exploring broad and recurring themes which are applicable in both eastern and western religions, cross-cultural examples are provided for each term to give a comprehensive overview of the subject.

Subjects covered include:

- Afterlife
- Comparative religion
- Festivals
- Ethics
- Gender
- Monotheism
- World religions
- Modernity
- Pilgrimage
- Sacred
- Theism
- Secularization

With cross referencing and further reading provided throughout, this book provides an inclusive map of the discipline, and is an essential reference for all students, academics and researchers.

Hb: 978-0-415-48721-4
Pb: 978-0-415-48722-1
eBook: 978-0-203-84191-4

For more information and to order a copy visit
www.routledge.com/9780415487221

Available from all good bookshops